Administrative Transformation in Central and Eastern Europe

Towards Public Sector Reform in Post-Communist Societies

Edited by
Joachim Jens Hesse

Blackwell Publishers

ISBN 0-631-19056-2

First published 1993

Blackwell Publishers
108 Cowley Road, Oxford, OX4 1JF, UK
and
238 Main Street, Cambridge, MA 02142, USA.

British Library Cataloging–in–Publication Data. A catalogue record for this book is available from The British Library.

Library of Congress Cataloging in Publication Data applied for

Typeset by Techset, Salisbury
Printed and bound in Great Britain by Page Brothers, Norwich.

CONTENTS

III COMPARATIVE OBSERVATIONS

I INTRODUCTION

JOACHIM JENS HESSE

The countries of Central and Eastern Europe are currently undergoing fundamental, if not revolutionary changes affecting the very foundations of their
political, social and economic life. Although both the extent of the transformation
processes that have thus far taken place and the pace differ considerably from
country to country, it is undoubtedly possible to detect a number of shared
characteristics which suggest a common pattern of political and societal change.
The distinguishing features include:

— the transition from what were effectively, if not in name, systems of one-party
  rule, in which the leading role of the Communist Party in all sectors of society
  was firmly entrenched, to pluralist, multi-party parliamentary systems with
  democratically elected and accountable governments;
— the abandoning of the principle of 'democratic centralism' in favour of a
  far-reaching deconcentration and decentralization of political power to be
  exercised under the rule of law;
— the rejection of the principle of unity between politics and economy which
  involves the emergence of distinct spheres of political and economic life; and
— far-reaching economic reforms whose principal aims are the strengthening of
  private enterprise, the denationalization (or rather privatization) of a large
  share of the previously state-controlled productive capital and a substantial
  deregulation and liberalization of the national economy.

The underlying ideas spurring the ambitious reform attempts at replacing a
nationalized, centralized and planned economic system with a market economy
are, in principle, also being applied to the task of reorganizing or perhaps re-
founding public administration. Thus, there are moves to strengthen democratic controls over state administration and to increase its accountability to
democratically elected bodies; efforts are underway which aim at the deconcentration and decentralization of the bureaucratic apparatus; the need to bring
public administration strictly under the rule of law and to guarantee the legality
of administrative acts is stressed; and it is universally accepted that administrative
efficiency, effectiveness and flexibility must be increased. All this implies that
the organization of governance is subject to the same pressures for change which
have already led to radical political reforms, which show signs of transforming
the economy and, partly by extension, revolutionizing the fabric of society.
    The task of modernizing public administration, or as it were the public

Joachim Jens Hesse is Ford-Monnet Professor of European Institutions and Comparative Government in the
University of Oxford and Director of the Centre for European Studies at Nuffield College, Oxford.

sector at large, goes much beyond subjecting it to the basic legal norms of conduct which govern the execution of public responsibilities in the majority of the industrialized countries of the western hemisphere. The challenge with which public administration is faced in Central and Eastern Europe, is to redefine even its role in society or, more concretely, its relations with politics, the economy and the civil community. It is, therefore, worthwhile to recall that the dynamics of administrative transformation are intimately linked to changes in the political, legal, social and economic environment in which public institutions operate and on whose material and immaterial inputs they crucially depend. Legitimacy, authority, legality, acceptance and finance are amongst the most important resources required for effective administrative activity, and they cannot be generated by public administration itself. Accordingly, the outcome of policies aimed at public sector reform is decisively shaped, albeit pre-determined, by political, legal, social and economic developments. Although public administration is both the object of reform and, almost invariably, its chief agent, the reform process is an interactive one. It follows from this that the study of administrative transformation requires a perspective which takes account of the interdependence and interrelatedness between public administration and its environment. Such a 'contextual' or 'ecological' view promises to yield significant insights both into the main driving forces behind reform efforts and into restrictive or even obstructive factors.

Given this background, it is certainly a surprising and regrettable experience that the task of transforming public administration has been significantly underestimated during the early stages of the reform process in Central and Eastern Europe. It is only recently that national governments, western donors and international organizations have realized that without a solid institutional and administrative underpinning the reform processes in Eastern Europe are bound to fail. The inadequacy of a number of economic assistance programmes, the growing disenchantment of large parts of the population with ongoing reform attempts and a still significant political and social instability testify to that.

It seems to be high time, therefore, to take stock of the present state of transforming public administration in Eastern Europe. This should, of course, not be done in a patronising way, by teaching legislators and administrators in Central and Eastern Europe how to reform their administrative systems, but – above all – by an attempt to provide basic information, to analyse the available evidence, and to comment on major shortcomings and reform options. This publication tries to do so by concentrating predominantly on the experience of three countries: Poland, the former Czechoslovakia and Hungary. For comparative purposes, a briefer look at the transformation processes in Russia and the former German Democratic Republic is added. Contrary to publications on other aspects of the transformation process, in which western observers try to analyse the situation, academics and practitioners of the mentioned countries themselves have been asked to comment upon administrative reforms. This includes articles by leading officials such as Michal Kulesza, Imre Verebélyi and Olga Vidláková; suffice it to say that they do not write in their official capacity.

This selection of articles concludes with three explicit attempts at comparative analysis. Whereas Theo Toonen examines the use of analytical approaches developed for public sector reforms in western industrialized countries, and Jon Elster takes stock of the various attempts at constitution-making, the editor summarizes his findings while observing ongoing transformation processes in Poland, in what used to be Czechoslovakia, and Hungary. Based on longer stays and extensive empirical field-work in these countries, the policy-oriented conclusions might be of interest to both practitioners and scholars of public administration.

What emerges is a differentiated picture. Whereas one should obviously refrain from exporting solutions as blueprints, western expertise is certainly still needed. This refers to findings of how to induce and stabilize institutional change, to secure an ongoing process of organizational development, to sustain the political will to engage in administrative policies, and to implement reform programmes. A narrow managerial attitude will definitely not help under these circumstances, it needs a thorough initial analysis of the given context structures. On the basis of the information compiled concerning the legal, political, economic and social environments, one could then examine different options for change and for implementing them. Since the countries of Central and Eastern Europe are entering the second stage of the reform process, here described as moving on from transformation to modernization, empirically based, but analytically minded Western expertise could be of interest.

It should not be forgotten, though, that administrative policies still take place within a turbulent political environment. Party systems are not always fully developed or have already degenerated by pursuing rather selfish interests; parliamentary routines have often not yet been established to an extent that they truly stabilize the situation and help in creating identity and trust within the population; there is still an ongoing and partly unsolved (or even unsolvable) conflict between representatives of the old and the new élites; and, last but not least, some observers even draw attention to the fact that presidential regimes might turn authoritarian. In that still turbulent political environment, at least two consequences are to be noted: first, whatever institutional solutions are sought or recommended, one ought to be aware of their political implications and prerequisites; and secondly, due to the political and economic instability, public administration gains potentially in weight, a further and much needed justification to pursue institutional change and administrative policies, policies that are otherwise often misunderstood, underestimated or — worse — discredited due to the previous regimes. It comes as a relief, therefore, that there is undoubtedly a growing awareness that democratization and marketization in Central and Eastern Europe will not work without a stable institutional and administrative environment. To promote institutional stability and to induce administrative change are, therefore, not at all peripheral tasks but policies at the heart of the transformation process that is still characterized by political and economic uncertainties, significant implementation problems, a demoralized and to some extent ill-prepared personnel and occasionally misguided foreign assistance.

Special thanks in compiling this collection of papers are due to my collaborators in Central and Eastern Europe. They did not only engage in the task of writing their manuscripts under difficult conditions, but were kind enough to join us in three conferences in Copenhagen, Prague and Brussels to discuss the given situation and policy options at hand. Jens Bastian, Klaus H. Goetz and Brian Wilkinson helped in editing the individual contributions, as did Jean Frostick – with unlimited enthusiasm.

II ADMINISTRATIVE TRANSFORMATION IN CENTRAL AND EASTERN EUROPE

POLISH PUBLIC ADMINISTRATION BETWEEN CRISIS AND RENEWAL

JANUSZ LETOWSKI

I INTRODUCTION

In his first speech to the Polish Parliament as Prime Minister, Jan Olszewski said in September 1991: 'Our state is threatened by paralysis caused by disorder in public administration and its inability to carry out its basic tasks.' A few sentences later on, he added that the patience of society had changed into hopelessness. Although Olszewski has since been replaced as Prime Minister and a new government has taken office, few would question that Olszewski's remarks still apply. There is no shortage of explanations for the current problems, but, in themselves, these explanations are of little use in trying to change matters for the better. The rulers of today tend to blame their predecessors – the Communists and the governments which followed them – for their present difficulties. Whilst they have certainly inherited a difficult legacy, this cannot serve as a convenient excuse for all present ills and shortcomings.

One of the key explanations for current problems in political, economic and administrative reform is the lack of any broad political agreement on its basic direction, let alone the details of reform measures. In the parliamentary elections of October 1991, no party emerged as a clear winner. In fact, the elections resulted in a legislature that is characterized by extreme fragmentation, with the largest party, the Democratic Union, gaining a mere 12.31 per cent of the votes for the *Sejm*, giving it just 62 out of 460 seats. In total, almost thirty parties and political groupings gained representation in the *Sejm*, with the majority winning five seats or less. The results of the elections have meant that the formation of a stable government, enjoying parliamentary support, has proved extremely difficult. Since then, there have been three Prime Ministers (Olszewski, Waldemar Pawlak, and Hanna Suchocka), with little continuity in government personnel and a rapid succession of ministers in key

Janusz Letowski is a Member of the Polish Supreme Court and Professor in the Institute of Legal Studies of the Polish Academy of Sciences, Warsaw.

portfolios. This instability in government and executive leadership personnel has been accompanied by a lack of clear policy orientation. Even where relatively clear-cut policies have had time to emerge, support in Parliament is often difficult to obtain. As the ruling coalition does not command a solid majority, the withholding of parliamentary approval for key government proposals is not unfamiliar.

The election results and political instability to which they have given rise have underlined that there is no dependable political agreement which could secure the Polish reform process; they have also highlighted the increasing general mistrust and dislike of political élites. Some argue that the political élites have, in fact, already lost most of their control over the direction of reform, whilst becoming more and more absorbed by political infighting. According to this argument, political parties are more concerned with filling government and public administration with their followers than with guiding the reform pro-gramme. Perhaps more worryingly, social consensus is said to be rapidly disintegrating. Fundamental principles of legality, justice, and equality of oppor-tunity are no longer beyond questioning: the 'Christian values' offered in their place are too general and too abstract to be able to inform political life. In this situation, it is not surprising that successive governments, although professing their allegiance to Catholic ideas, have been unable to count on sufficient societal support, and have seen their political and professional legitimacy questioned. (Mr. Marek Jurek, one of the leaders of the Catholic faction in the Polish Parliament, has recently written that 'the idea of human rights is an attempt to destroy Christian civilization and its institutions'.)

Insufficient popular legitimacy is compounded by a lack of coherence in government, which reflects uneasy and unstable coalitions. Thus, it has been said of the Olszewski government, that

> this cabinet strikes one as a group of rather accidental persons who seem to have little idea of how to tackle the mounting social and economic problems .... Apart from expressing an understanding of the reasons for social frustration and appealing for patience, the Prime Minister was able to propose very little .... Since the time of the accession to power of the Solidarity camp, this is our third cabinet, and once again we have new people who are even less prepared to govern. Once more they are replacing even less important officials in the ministry, governors, heads of department of various state institutions. Changes are most often based on political criteria; the personnel merry-go-round continues, and there is ever less place in it for stability and professionalism (*Glob*, 20 January 1992).

Under such conditions, internal co-ordination even in basic tasks seems almost impossible. If this is, in fact, the case, then the crisis facing Polish public administration goes far deeper than it might appear at first glance. It is then not just a matter of structures, procedures and personnel, but a crisis of ideology and psychology.

The deep-seatedness of the crisis has been increasingly recognized in official pronouncements. Thus, the last report of the outgoing Polish Commissioner for

Civil Rights Protection contains many highly critical assessments of Polish public administration (Annual Report 1991). The main criticism is that there is a growing tendency to avoid administrative problem solutions. There is an atmosphere of uncertainty, a tendency to wait and to postpone, and to find ever new excuses to avoid taking action. This style of administration raises particular problems in situations which cannot be resolved merely through regulations, authorizations or prohibitions. Helplessness in situations which require imagination and decisive action can be found at all tiers of public administration, from the level of ministers down to the offices of local authorities. 'Decision-making opportunism', i.e. the tendency to postpone action on difficult matters, can take different forms, including, for example, a failure to respond to requests, 'passing the buck', or procrastination. The virtual paralysis of public administration before elections or an imminent change in government is particularly problematic in this respect: virtually all activity comes to a halt, matters are not taken care of and there is no response to pressure. Similarly, anticipated changes in legal regulations can lead to an unofficial suspension of administrative activity. These problems are compounded by the inability to achieve effective inter-administrative co-ordination, even in cases where it is absolutely crucial. Structures and procedures for horizontal co-ordination and co-operation are underdeveloped at all levels of public administration, and intergovernmental relations suffer from an acute lack of co-ordinating capacities.

Some of the shortcomings mentioned can be found in every system of public administration; some, however, are specific to the Polish case. Of the latter, some might be called 'objective', and they can only be addressed through basic changes in the system. Others are of a 'subjective' nature, and are open to more easily available remedies. Finally, some are likely to prove resistant to any reform attempt, because, ultimately, they are an expression of the fallibility of human nature.

It should be clear from the preceding discussion that the starting point for attempts to modernize Polish public administration is not auspicious. Under such conditions, it can be politically risky even to begin such action, as failure is a distinct possibility. However, the risk has to be taken. To make it manageable, all proposals need to be evaluated from different points of view, as there are no reforms that benefit everybody. Like in every reform, some will win and some will lose, and this needs to be openly acknowledged.

II   THE DIRECTION OF REFORM

Although many current administrative shortcomings could be resolved by decisive government action, there can be no doubt that the present administration is largely paying the price for mistakes made by previous generations of rulers. Like other countries, Poland, over the last thirty years, experienced periods of administrative euphoria, only to conclude later on that promises were difficult, if not impossible, to keep. Current administrative slogans might be different from those it propagated thirty years ago, but they are often listened to with exaggerated hopes. Thus, there are demands for 'less law' and more deregulation, which would create increasing scope for free initiative by the people and greater legal flexibility (Chenot 1988). A radical flattening of the systems and structures of public administration, decentralization and self-government are advocated, with more matters left to regulation by social organizations and individual citizens. Finally, and perhaps most importantly, privatization in the broad sense of a gradual withdrawal of the state from certain areas of social life is propagated as a way forward. Of course, not all of these demands will become reality, but some are likely to have long-term consequences. However, it is important to remain cautious and calm if faced with demands of 'radical de-étatisation' or 'general self-government' or 'drastic administrative simplification', even if one is inclined to agree with the general direction of such calls.

Today, the programming, planning and implementation of administrative reforms has developed into a specialized branch of academic study, with an extensive professional literature and its own well-developed theories. The current emphasis is on the necessity for continuous change in the administrative system; since the world is continually changing, the argument runs, public administration must change with it. But it is a long way from recognizing the need for change to defining what precisely has to change and how. Here, the Polish situation is still characterized by a somewhat naïve belief in the ability of 'people of good will' to find 'right' solutions, if only they are given enough reliable information on the basis of which they are able to determine the 'correct' course of action in a given situation. This thinking is ultimately based on the conviction that a 'good government' will always be able to at least improve the situation, if not actually solve the problems at hand. This is why one of the constantly reiterated slogans of administrative reformers is to improve personnel policy, to recruit new people in an attempt to strengthen democratic procedures and decision making (Letowski 1990).

Obviously, the matter is not that simple. Contemporary public administration is, at heart, about conflicts and their resolution. These conflicts are becoming ever more 'objective'; in other words, in contemporary public administration, there are ever fewer solutions that are universally beneficial. It is, therefore, impossible to find solutions which would satisfy everybody. What appears as a good and proper solution to some, might be called lawlessness, injustice and favouritism by others. The times of an authoritative administration are gone for good, and it is important to keep this in mind in all discussions on administrative reforms (Ploszajski 1990).

Another pitfall in the administrative reform discussion should be mentioned at this stage: the tendency to concentrate almost exclusively on the anticipated positive outcome of administrative reform, and to down-play, ignore or even hide their negative effects. Unjustified expectations are raised, and, as a result, later disappointment and political embarrassment are almost inevitable. Such set-backs could however be at least partly avoided. For this, it would be wise to include in all reform proposals substantial information about their potential risks, limitations and drawbacks. More generally, in commissioning future research and consultancy on administrative modernization, emphasis should be placed on what might be called a 'lathology' (from the Greek word *lathos*, meaning error), which would focus on the typical errors, gaps and deficiencies in the political, social, economic, legal, and personnel aspects of public administration. At present, the virtual absence of such studies in Poland is painfully felt.

III EXPECTATIONS OF PUBLIC ADMINISTRATION

The basic social and political task of government and public administration in contemporary Poland is to provide citizens with a feeling of security. If they fail to fulfil this duty, or discharge it poorly, they face the prospect of being removed. This feeling of security must be understood in a most fundamental sense. It means guaranteeing a secure present and future for citizens, including employment, housing, education, health-care, recreation, culture and the provision of essential goods and services. For decades, Polish society was used to the idea that these are things that can be taken more or less for granted. Provision might have been at a relatively low level, but it seemed at least secure. Despite efforts by the post-Communist governments to reduce popular expectations, not much has really been achieved. Attitudes have proved enduring, and after more than four decades of a 'People's Poland', no government is likely to be able to quickly change this situation. The consequences of this are more far-reaching than one might imagine at first glance. Under today's conditions, politics and public administration are absolutely inseparable, and without the feeling of security on the part of the citizens, there is, ultimately, no contemporary state or any contemporary public administration.

Many signs of a fundamental lack of confidence in the state and its ability to provide security can be observed in contemporary Poland. In its extreme form, the lack of confidence manifests itself in more or less open calls for breaking up the state, for dividing it and replacing it with a network of self-governing organizations including local government, social associations and enterprises. Undoubtedly, the beliefs which inform such suggestions are to a large extent based on illusions. In general, self-government tends to be promoted and supported by central authorities when they seek to shed responsibility for problems with which they cannot cope themselves. Self-government, in whatever form, is not an easier or more pleasant form of governance. On the contrary, it is, in many respects, a much more complex, difficult and also troublesome way to govern. In particular, there is a natural tendency for self-governmental bodies to behave like pressure groups, the chief *raison d'être* of which is to extract more benefits from the government for their clientele, to gain a greater share in the 'riches' that are at the disposal of the centre, and to fight competing organizations. As a consequence, an emphasis on political and societal self-government is likely to be in itself a new source of conflict, as its natural result is inequality.

The concept of self-government also raises the question of the rights of the individual. Much of today's discussion in Poland centres on the protection of the individual from the abuse of state power (Norwegian Academy of Science and Letters 1991, ch. II). However, it should be remembered that individuals should be offered the same degree of protection from abuses on the part of fellow citizens, especially when the latter are organized. This is especially crucial in a situation where even small groups can become 'self-governing and independent'. In such cases, it is their decision which determines the participation of the individual and the benefits on which his existence might depend. In this connection, it is worth remembering the remark that no central tyrant will limit the right of the individual with as much enthusiasm as his neighbours, co-workers or people belonging to the same organization. Evidently, then, the development of self-government needs to be accompanied by moves to ensure adequate legal protection for the individual citizen.

The above comments should not be interpreted as general arguments against decentralization and the development of self-government. To advocate centralization would both be without sense and unrealistic. These arguments merely serve to underline that there is not, and cannot be, an ideal division of tasks and powers amongst institutions of state government and administration, on the one hand, and self-government, on the other. Every system has its advantages and disadvantages, none will be welcomed by everybody, every one of them will be a source of conflict, and after some time they will all become outdated and impede progress. Under modern conditions, there is no 'perfect' system of government and public administration; each has its weaknesses and drawbacks. Consequently, the problem of choosing tends to boil down to the question which sickness we agree to suffer in order to avoid a more serious and painful one.

The recent discussion on local government in Poland may help to illustrate this point. The following verdict by a Polish journalist on the outcome of local government reform is not untypical:

> What bad laws mean we see from the example of Warsaw. This city is dying before our eyes. It is not only the victim of the general collapse of the country, but also of the labyrinthine division of the city into independent communes. Above the communes is a mayor who is virtually powerless .... If anything threatens us now, it is certainly not dictatorship or authoritarianism, but anarchy in the machinery of government. Let us look at the fate of Warsaw. Is the entire country to sink in the same way?

At present, a further reform of local government and administration is now much talked about, and, at the beginning of 1992, the government announced its intention to launch a programme for a structural reform of the local level. This included plans for developing new concepts of administering metropolitan agglomerations and for a new territorial division of the country. The latter aimed at the restoration of administrative districts and a form of regionalization through the creation of large provinces. Some of the proponents of such plans intend to create large self-governing territorial units modelled on the German *Länder*. Such proposals look quite appealing, but they would have to be implemented under conditions characterized by an enormous budget deficit and very little enthusiasm for still more reforms. Indeed, if such plans were to be carried out, they would amount to the seventh or eighth fundamental reform of Polish subcentral administration since World War II. It is unlikely that any public administration could withstand a basic reorganization every five years or so without suffering serious damage. It is scarcely conducive to stabilization if every new government that comes into power announces the need for far-reaching, fundamental structural and functional reforms. More often than not, reforms of this kind are primarily a political manifestation of good-will. In practice, they tend to resemble a 'shooting in the dark', based on the assumption that major flaws can be ironed out as the project moves on. Evidently, this is an expensive and wasteful system of reform, but there is some hope that a more systemic approach to reforming the public sector might be adopted in the future.

IV   INSTITUTIONAL TRANSFORMATION AND CHANGES IN MENTALITY

Despite the formidable obstacles to successful administrative reform, it is becoming ever more obvious that further reform efforts in the Polish system of public administration are vital. They will have to give particular attention to operating procedures of government; redefine the relations between citizens and public administration; and effect fundamental changes in conflict resolution. More specifically, reform will have to be broadened to concentrate not just on the institutional framework, but on administrative processes and the substance of administrative action. Above all, it needs to tackle an area that is perhaps most resistant to change, i.e. the way people think. Legal regulations can make a difference here, but their effects can only be of a long-term nature and cannot be as unambiguous as in the case of formal and institutional change. The law works slowly and with recalcitrance; nonetheless, once changes have been made, they are gradually assimilated by people and finally function almost automatically.

One important step in this connection is the acceptance of the principle of mutual confidence as a cardinal rule in relations between the citizenry and public authorities. In its general form, this principle can be understood in two ways. Firstly, it demands a social situation in which a legal amendment or an administrative decision do not come out of the blue, as something which no rational person could have expected. In other words, administration needs to be reliable and predictable. Secondly, the principle implies that citizens who are prepared to act with confidence in government and public administration must not, for this reason, be disadvantaged. If this could be ensured, the principle of confidence would have an extremely important educative role.

Confidence needs to be complemented by increased openness in government and administration. Openness is understood as the obligation on the part of the administration to supply the public with better and more complete information about the rationale, goals and methods of administrative action. Obviously, openness and information cannot be ends in themselves. They are means which allow the public a more effective control over public administration and, by implication, reduce the power of the administrators. Fundamentally, the aim here is to encourage participation, consultation, agreement and cooperation. This implies, *inter alia*, the obligation on the part of public administration to present its goals and intentions in an understandable manner. Measured against this yardstick, the practice of Polish public administration is often scarcely tolerable. Occasionally, one cannot help the suspicion that the woolliness and impenetrability of administrative plans presented are used as conscious weapons against future attempts to control administrative actions and hold administrators accountable. Unfortunately, examples of this can be found at all levels of public administration.

Two comments suggest themselves at this stage. First, it is often argued that Polish public administration was for many years used to operating in conditions of complete freedom, i.e. freedom from the law and from popular control. Its overriding concern was to ensure and to maintain the smooth co-operation with the centres of political decision-making. Today, however, when it is being subjected to increasingly vigorous controls, when decisions have to be adequately justified, and when representative bodies have to be taken more and more into account, public administration is often helpless. Ultimately, there is little chance of changing such ingrained administrative behaviour overnight. But there is reason to expect that what many older administrators perceived as external interference and a waste of time, will seem routine behaviour to those who will succeed them.

A second comment concerns the general crisis in the methods of forecasting and planning which we are witnessing in present-day Polish government. Circumstances are changing so rapidly that even the most carefully prepared prognoses and plans can very quickly lose their value. One of the key requirements for public administration will, therefore, be to explain to the public honestly and as fully as possible that forecasts do contain elements of risk and uncertainty and that they are, to a certain extent, influenced by unpredictable and uncontrollable factors. Accordingly, it needs to be made clear that there can be no guarantees for the attainment of certain goals and objectives (IIAS 1988).

Perhaps one of the most fundamental changes in Polish public administration is the emergence of a new conception of the rights of citizens *vis-à-vis* the state and public administration. This does not just refer to the protection of the individual rights of the citizen. It also extends to questions asked by citizens regarding their 'participatory' rights and entitlements. Whilst it might be possible to put such questions off for a while, this merely opens the door to political set-backs. In short, the notion of civil rights has changed. Classical civil rights were largely restricted to protecting the citizens against lawlessness; but this boundary line has long been crossed, and public administration needs to respond to this fact.

Such an extended definition of civil rights has important implications for administrative law. Since the state lacks sufficient resources to satisfy all claims and expectations, there is great pressure for improved procedural norms through which entitlements can be allocated. One of the basic principles of classical administrative law is the assumption that administrative agencies ought to remain neutral towards the cases brought before them; their behaviour is expected to be guided strictly and exclusively by the law. In reality, however, this 'principle of legalistic neutrality' has never been fully realized in practice, and today the objective appears more elusive than ever. There is a clear political element present in public administration and, perhaps even more importantly, administration is staffed by people and not machines. However much they might wish to be neutral, individuals are inevitably biased. No form of legalistic control, including control by the courts, will be able fully to make up for this. Partly, we see this reflected in the contemporary direction in which the control of public administration is progressing, which increasingly stresses not just the control of institutional actions, i.e. chiefly decisions, but the control of the behaviour of officials too.

V THE ROLE OF ADMINISTRATIVE PERSONNEL

One cannot talk about the future of Polish public administration without looking at administrative personnel. The public, with the willing assistance of the mass media, is often led to believe that administrative staff constitutes the main impediment to positive change in public administration. The common dislike of administrators extends to the government, and only very recently efforts have been made to partially change this perception. There is no doubt that it becomes increasingly difficult for administrators to simply rely on their authority, to hide behind their institution or instructions 'from above' to justify their decisions. Consequently, the personal trustworthiness and prestige of public officials become ever more important. In this respect, it is necessary to re-emphasize traditional ethical and moral values, such as personal honesty or the rejection of the privileges regarded as unjustified by society. Another important element is professionalism, as is the capacity to manage public resources prudently. Finally, and perhaps most importantly, administrators need to have the capacity for open, convincing and effective co-operation with the public.

In this respect, administrative law has an important part to play. Changes in administrative law can stimulate different behaviour both amongst administrators and the administered, not only by direct prohibitions and commands, but also by creating a certain style of thinking about administration and its social tasks. Obviously, these problems cannot be solved through a single regulation; nor, indeed, are they problems which can be effectively addressed without sacrificing something else in exchange. It is, in fact, hard to imagine a professional civil servant confident of his knowledge and position who would gladly yield to demands for closer co-operation with, and control by, the public, especially to such an aggressive and demanding public as we find in Poland today. However, it is a problem which needs to be addressed, and the choices available are relatively clear: either to accept that officials cannot be better than the society they live in, or by explicitly acknowledging the educative responsibility of officials as representatives of the state.

In the education of public officials, there have been a number of interesting developments in recent years. Perhaps the most stimulating has been the establishment of a National School for Public Administration, which admitted its first students in 1991. The foundation of this institution undoubtedly represents a step in the right direction. Perhaps understandably, the School models itself on the French Ecole Nationale d'Administration (ENA); the image of the exemplary French administrators – competent, multilingual, cosmopolitan – is attractive for many. But it is open to debate whether such a type of official is what is really needed in contemporary Poland. Perhaps, the model of the official/technocrat, as it is, for example, found in the German School of Public Administration in Speyer, might be better suited to Polish realities. However, it needs to be stressed that even if not all high hopes can be fulfilled, the idea of a special training for an administrative élite should not be abandoned.

It has long been common to discuss the issue of public personnel in Poland in categories such as insufficient training, education and inadequate pay. However, it would seem that the problem is more complex than that. For example, recent studies show that in view of the increasingly difficult job market, local governments are not complaining as loudly as they once did about shortages of trained administrative professionals (although a shortage of professional lawyers is still painfully felt). Instead, new problems have been emerging. Thus, top local administrators are complaining about the lack of job security as they are appointed by local councils and can easily be dismissed. It is not unusual that a local council, in an atmosphere of conflict, simply fires an official, without giving sufficient reasons.

VI CONCLUSION

By way of a conclusion, the following recommendations might be of interest:

— Plans for the next fundamental transformation in public administration ought to be approached with great caution. In the present situation, structural 'earthquakes' are not desirable. Corrections should be made prudently and without haste.
— Attention must be paid to the procedures for effecting changes. The positive and the negative effects of change ought to be set out as clearly as possible and the risk inherent in change should be explicitly acknowledged.
— Greater scope for self-government is indispensable, but this should not be presented as a magic remedy for all ills affecting government and public administration. Like every other system, self-government has weak points, especially in a poor country.

— We have inherited a relatively well-functioning and complete system of institutions to control the legality of the actions of public administration. In the near future, particular attention needs to be paid to financial and economic controls.

— The relationships between public administration and the citizenry have to be based on a legally formulated principle of confidence. This principle will also have to include the basic code of administrative conduct.

— As regards administrative law, a reduction in the number of regulations, their standardization, their simplification and the working out of stable, clear general rules of administrative procedure need to be emphasized.

— Basic rules of the procedures in all relations of public administration with the citizens are of special significance. In particular, this includes a clear definition of powers; attempts to secure the greatest possible openness for the interested party; an honest and fair justification of administrative decisions; and full judicial control.

— Personnel policy must be directed towards increasing professionalism, trustworthiness and personal prestige.

Some of these principles ought to be marked out by being included in Poland's new constitution. Amongst these are the rights of the individual *vis-à-vis* the state; the openness of administrative actions; the principle of confidence; the principle of public compensation; the universality and completeness of judicial control; the principle of the substantive and legal justification of all decisions. Of course, this list could easily be extended, but, for the moment, it would represent a major advance, if these principles could actually be given constitutional status.

REFERENCES

Chenot, B. (ed.). 1988. *Les déréglementations*. Paris: Economica.
International Institute of Administrative Sciences. 1988. 'Administration without bureaucratization', *Proceedings of the Round Table of IIAS in Budapest*. Brussels: IIAS.
Jurek, M. 1992. 'Prawa chlowieka czy troska o naród i ludzi', *Sprawa Polska* 12.
Letowski, J. 1990. *Au carrefour de l'administration contemporaine*. Warsaw: Ossolineum.
Ploszajski, P. (ed.). 1990. *Philosophy of social choice*. Warsaw: Institute of Philosophy and Sociology of the Polish Academy of Sciences.
Polish Commissioner for Civil Rights Protection. 1991. *Annual report on citizens' rights*. Warsaw: Commissioner's Office.
Norwegian Academy of Science and Letters. 1991. *The role of the constitution in the changing society*. Oslo: Norwegian Academy of Science and Letters.

CHANGES IN POLISH PUBLIC ADMINISTRATION 1989–1992

WOJCIECH TARAS

I INTRODUCTION

Reforms in government and public administration are the subject of continuous interest for the legal sciences. In fact, it can be argued that at least the foundations for a science of reforming public administration have by now been established. Although there is, then, a relatively mature international literature on administrative reform, first attempts to achieve conceptual-theoretical advances for the academic observers writing about administrative reform can pose empirical and intellectual difficulties; and writing about reforms in Poland certainly meets with some particular obstacles. Before turning to the actual administrative developments over the past three years or so, it might make sense, therefore, to hint at some of the problems which an analysis of the Polish reform process has to confront.

Perhaps the most basic question is whether one can really talk of reform in Polish public administration rather than simply change and reorganization. If one takes the view that the ultimate objective of administrative reform is to create a citizen-oriented attitude amongst officials and, conversely, a generally positive attitude on the part of the citizens towards public administration, then what we have been witnessing over the last three years scarcely qualifies as administrative reform, at least not a successful one. Nonetheless, change there has been, and we will use the notion of 'reform' in the following, bearing in mind that change does not necessarily imply progress.

Another problem concerns the identification of a convenient cut-off point for a longitudinal analysis. In many relevant areas – local institutions, territorial governance, personnel regulations, or public service training and education – Poland has experienced continuous change for decades, with some parts of the public sector undergoing major reforms every couple of years. This unfortunate state of affairs has been the result of frequent shifts in the ruling élite, and a

Dr Wojciech Taras is Reader in the Faculty of Law and Administration at the University of Marie Curie-Sklodowska, Lublin.

tendency by new governments to reverse the initiatives of their predecessors in the vain hope of winning popular support. Hence, the following discussion of major administrative developments during the last three years or so often has to refer to earlier reform attempts during the Communist era.

Finally, the question marks over Poland's further constitutional and political development make predictions about the future course of administrative reform difficult. The elections of October 1991 have resulted in a Parliament which – for the first time in more than half a century – reflects the political divisions in Polish society. The seats in the *Sejm* are divided amongst a large number of political parties, a fact which has necessitated the formation of fragile multi-party coalition governments. Governmental instability has helped to prevent the emergence of a clear vision for administrative development. Moreover, it is difficult to start considering the details of the governmental system and public administration as they are likely to be determined by the new constitution. Such a new constitution has yet to be adopted, but it is unclear when this will be the case. Undoubtedly, however, the course of future reforms will to a large degree depend on the stabilization of the centre of political power. Recent years have seen intense institutional rivalries between Parliament, the President, and the government. In view of the fragmentation of Parliament, it is likely that it will be the President and the government which will constitute the main centres of future reforms. The outcome of the current power struggle will have a decisive impact on the shape of public administration. At present, then, there is no comprehensive administrative reform programme nor an accepted model of public administration. It is, however, possible to comment at least on some aspects of the reforms which have already been undertaken and one may try a first tentative appraisal, although such an assessment can only be of a fragmentary character.

II PROBLEMS OF LEGISLATION

The quality of legislation for administrative reform during recent years has not differed significantly from legislative standards in earlier periods. The quality of Polish legislation is generally considered unsatisfactory, and thus far there are few signs of any real improvements (Letowski 1990). In a series of articles in the government newspaper *Rzeczpospolita* (1990) a number of key problems in the system of law and legislative technique have been identified. Thus, Z. Radwanski, former Chairman of the Legislative Council attached to the Prime Minister's Office, has noted that the government often fails to seek expert advice in preparing legislation, and if it does call on experts, there is usually little time for any detailed consideration of their opinions. D. Frey, a prominent journalist, has argued that the main assumptions and objectives behind legal acts are not sufficiently discussed in the legislative organs. Instead, Parliament only becomes involved in the discussion once draft versions have already been prepared by lawyers; it is, then, these drafts on which the discussion concentrates. Moreover, when putting draft legislation before Parliament, the government does not, as a rule, also produce the suggested implementing regulations. Finally, R. Malinowski, a prominent expert in administrative and economic law, has criticized the fact that old regulations are often still in force but are no longer applied by state organs. At the same time, many essential issues, for example the transfer of state property, are not addressed by legal regulations, or only in a superficial manner. To make matters worse, regulations concerning economic activity tend to be incoherent and are sometimes contradictory.

Evidently, none of these problems have arisen only during the period of radical reforms in the governmental system; rather they have hampered the Polish legislative process for a long time. The reforms of recent years have only brought to light their full extent, as legislative change is much faster and more extensive than before. Suffice it to mention just one example, the introduction of new customs and tariff regulations in 1991. The new legal act comprises approximately 400 densely printed pages, and, obviously, the problems connected with customs and tariffs are fairly complex. However, it was almost impossible to obtain a copy of the text before the new tariffs actually came into force, and even customs offices had barely a day and a half to acquaint themselves with this complicated act. The new text was prepared in great haste, which is one of the main reasons why many of its detailed regulations are generally deemed insufficient (Rymuszko 1991). Unfortunately, this is by no means an exceptional case. Legislation concerning the fundamental economic reforms of late 1989 was introduced in a very similar manner. The great speed of legal change is, then, one of the distinguishing features of the Polish reform process. Evidently, the conflict between desirable stability in law – 'only old law is good law' – and the necessity of legal adjustment to changing political, economic, and social conditions cannot be solved in a way that will satisfy everybody. Essentially, the difficulties involved are the price to be paid for establishing a democratic state and a market oriented economy based on the rule of law.

Some of the legal and legislative difficulties associated with the transition from a Socialist state to a democratic polity are discussed in the 1990 Report of the Polish Commissioner for Civil Rights Protection (Biuletyn RPO 1990, pp. 77–82). The Commissioner's report identifies the following central shortcomings. First, the legal situation of citizens is often regulated through acts of a wrong status. For example, instructions are being issued where the law would require statutory regulations. Legal acts are promulgated which exceed the authority of the legislative organ concerned. Sometimes, new acts are not published, and the distribution of the official law gazette announcing new legislation is frequently delayed. Moreover, there is a lack of control over the issuing of ministerial instructions and regulations. Intertemporal law is often abused, and, in this way, it undermines the citizens' confidence in the state. Legislators interfere with the contents of civil law contracts, the legislative procedure itself is inadequate, laws are often vague, and are, therefore, open to conflicting interpretations. The Commissioner's criticisms are directly concerned with the protection of citizens' rights; indirectly, however, they refer to the system of law and legislation as a whole.

Arguably the most substantial problem in Polish legislation is still the so-called 'ministerial law'. It includes, firstly, legal acts promulgated by ministers as implementing provisions to statutes and government regulations, and, secondly, ministerial legal regulations adopted without specific authorization ('autonomous ministerial law'). For the most part, such ministerial regulations remain unpublished; they have different names which often do not reflect their content, and they do not only contain legal norms, but also recommendations and information. Frequently, they also repeat regulations from acts of a higher rank, and, at the same time, interpret them. Critically, the drafting and adoption of such ministerial laws are neither subject to regular interministerial co-ordination procedures nor are they controlled by the Cabinet Office. Often, ministerial law contradicts statutory law, and, as far as 'autonomous' ministerial regulations are concerned, the courts do not recognize them as legal acts. For many years, ministerial law has played the role of a 'prosthesis' for parliamentary and governmental legislation which often failed to keep pace with developments (Rot 1980, pp. 80–117; Jablonska–Bonca 1987; and Hoff 1987).

One of the characteristic features of ministerial law is a periodic review carried out in individual ministries on the basis of government resolutions. After such a review, the individual ministries are expected to publish lists of ministerial acts which are still in force. All acts not included in these lists automatically lose their binding force. During the 1988 review, some 7,730 acts in 28 government ministries were examined; of these, little more than half, 3709, were recognized as being still binding. The example of the Ministry of National Education might illustrate the review procedure and its results (Mazur 1989, pp. 41–3). Here, the minister asked about 500 organizational units for suggestions and appointed an external expert team to conduct the review. After the appraisal was completed, the minister promulgated a list of 443 legal acts which continued to be in force; this means that 149 acts had been repealed, in particular those of a supervisory character. Nonetheless, the results of the review were judged unsatisfactory. Although they had not been published, 29 acts remained in force; several acts came into force which were to be applied retroactively; and many reservations were expressed about editorial and linguistic errors in the acts.

An example of decentralizing trends in legislation can be found in the changes concerning the government's rights for promulgating legal acts which were introduced in 1989. This reform was based on the assumption that the government should take responsibility for the main lines of the state's development, including defence and citizens' rights, whereas legislative competences in other matters should be handed over to the individual ministers. Since a parliamentary act is necessary to establish responsibility for the promulgation of implementation regulations, the government prepared a draft law concerning the transfer of part of its law-making competences to the individual ministers. Following an analysis of nearly 1,300 provisions authorizing the Council of

Ministers to promulgate legal acts, the government decided that about 220 of these should be transferred to the ministers. Under the new arrangements, law-making powers are distributed between the Council of Ministers and the individual ministers in accordance with the following principle: the government promulgates legal acts in cases where an explicit authorization to do so is contained in the constitution, where matters of defence, public security, religion, or foreign affairs are concerned, and where ministerial law specifies obligations imposed on the citizens by the legislators. In the economic sphere, the government has responsibility for promulgating legal acts concerning, *inter alia*, the construction of motorways, the location of infrastructural projects, the definition of fishing zones, and long-term planning. The Council of Ministers also retains the competence for acts on the supervision of ministers and lower level administrative organs and their competences. The new arrangement envisages that, in principle, all matters specifically concerning a ministry's sphere of responsibility are to be regulated by the minister in charge, or, in cases where the law-making competence is, for some reason or the other, entrusted to the government or to another minister, in agreement with the responsible minister. The main goal of this solution is to relieve the government of technical problems and to increase the ministers' responsibility for the state of law. The hope is that this will result in greater legal consistency (Mazur 1988).

Originally, it was hoped that these principles should be adopted as part of a more comprehensive statute regulating legislative procedures. Calls for such a statute date back as far as the early 1970s, but it was only in 1987 that a draft bill on legislative procedures was prepared. During the discussion of the bill, its supporters argued that the bill would help to standardize and simplify legislative procedures. Specifically, the new statute should regulate the general principles for the creation of law; the principles governing the formulation of legal acts, the system of legal acts and the relations between legal acts, the binding character of legislation and the principles of its promulgation; and legislative procedures (Wronkowska and Wroblewski 1987). However, the draft bill was not adopted. Since some of the questions to be addressed in the proposed statute raise constitutional issues, a majority argued that work on this bill should only be continued after the adoption of a new constitution.

The speed with which legal change is currently effected requires a good legal background amongst those deciding on the adoption of draft legislation. However, the shortage of people with law-making experience in Parliament is one of the most crucial problems in the legislative process. If one further considers that most statutes receive their final shape through precarious compromises between the competing political groups in Parliament, the oft-raised calls for a partial transfer of Parliament's legislative rights to the government are scarcely surprising. Of course, the division of legislative powers between Parliament and government is not for the first time a contentious issue in Poland. After 1926, the President of the Polish Republic had the right to promulgate acts with the force of statutes, and after the Second World War, the same power was first accorded to the government (until 1952) and then to the Council of State (1952–89). More recently, some emergency legislative powers, which, however, excluded the right to promulgate acts with the force of statutes, were granted by Parliament to the Rakowski government in February 1989 for the period until the end of 1990. By contrast, the government of Tadeusz Mazowiecki refused powers to promulgate decrees. The successor government of Jan Krzysztof Bielecki introduced a bill in Parliament, which would have given wide-ranging emergency powers to the Council of Ministers, immediately after a motion to dismiss the government had failed. The stated aim of this bill was to make sure that economic reform would not be bogged down in endless parliamentary quarrels. In other words, the government should be given the means to push through the economic reform process without having to work out complex compromises in lengthy discussions with Parliament. One observer wrote at the time that 'The government resembled a man condemned to death, who was waiting for the axe to fall, was pardoned in the last second, then eagerly jumped from the scaffold and before brushing the dirt off his knees, began calling for a crown and sceptre' (Majman 1991). Under the draft bill, the government would have been allowed to issue legislative decrees to regulate all matters of state, excluding only questions of the highest importance and matters concerned with the legal rights and responsibilities of citizens. Under the proposed provisions, the government would not have been authorized to change the constitution, the Constitutional Tribunal, the Tribunal of State, the Supreme Chamber of Control, the Courts and the Public Prosecutor's Office. Also, the government would not have been permitted to amend legislative codes other than the Commercial Code, or limit the rights of organizations, political parties and trade unions. Nor would it have been allowed to set new taxes for citizens or determine the 1992 budget (Goszczynski 1991).

There are, indeed, valid arguments for giving the government the power to promulgate legal acts with the force of statutes in order to ensure the continuation of economic reform. The main reasons were mentioned above: the long-winded legislative procedure in Parliament, the inconsistency and incoherence of Polish law, and the lack of effective control over ministerial law. However, the form in which the Bielecki government demanded emergency powers raised many objections, and the timing of its request, only a few weeks before the parliamentary elections, was very unfortunate. Many members of Parliament and many citizens considered the government's proposal an ill-disguised attempt to restrict unduly the scope of action of the future Parliament. At the time, it was difficult to avoid the impression that the aim of the government and the President, who supported the government, was not so much to ensure the success of economic reform, but to humiliate Parliament, which was still dominated by former Communists and their allies. The idea seems to have been to force Parliament to pass a statute which would have deprived it of a considerable part of its law-making power, or, alternatively, to take advantage of the refusal of Parliament by arguing that the former Communists were trying to impede the democratic reforms of the Solidarity government. To be sure, there is a strong case for granting the government the right to promulgate decrees concerning economic matters, but in trying to achieve this aim the principles of political culture should not be thrown overboard. At the time, some argued that 'the government seeks to change the political system in a way reminiscent of the imposition of martial law' (Goszczynski 1991). Unfortunately, the government's tactical manoeuvring in trying to obtain emergency powers provided ample ammunition to the opponents of the very idea, and turned part of popular opinion against the granting of such powers to the government as a matter of principle.

As regards the law-making capacities of other organs, the reform of local government in 1990 only partially affected the powers of the intermediate and lower levels for creating local legal regulations. The *voivods*, as representatives of state administration, took over most of the law-making powers of the former provincial People's Councils; this, undoubtedly, strengthened the *voivods'* position. By contrast, the position of local government is more complicated. The Polish Constitution lays down that local governments fulfil public tasks according to the principles defined by the relevant statutes. It follows that the provisions contained in these statutes should be sufficiently general and abstract to leave to the municipalities (rural communes, towns and 'town-communes') substantial scope for discretion; in other words, the statutes should indeed be limited to establishing the principles of fulfilling public tasks, but not define precisely how the municipalities' tasks should be realized. However, at present, local government legislation tends to be highly detailed. As a result, the municipalities resemble executive organs which merely implement statutory provisions in their own area. Under such circumstances, the independence of local governments in fulfilling their own tasks is narrowly circumscribed (Taras and Wrobel 1991).

III   INSTITUTIONAL CHANGE AT THE CENTRAL LEVEL

In an analysis of Polish administrative structures, one can usefully distinguish three spheres: central administration, territorial state administration, and the institutions of local government. Looking first at the central level, it enjoys the greatest degree of independence, or even autonomy. Unlike local government, central administration has not yet undergone a process of reconstruction, and it is still awaiting comprehensive reform. The latter will probably only be possible once the political situation has stabilized. The problem of decentralization is still very much associated with the central level. Every new government since 1956 has raised the issue of decentralization, but little has been achieved. Consequently, the centre still concentrates far too much authority to be able to exercise it in an effective manner. The time of real, as opposed to rhetorical, decentralization of ministerial powers has not yet arrived. As was pointed out above, the government transferred part of its law-making competences to the individual ministers in 1989 to allow government to focus on those problems which require decisions of a political nature (Graniecki). Nonetheless, ministers still deal with far too many detailed issues, and this centralization of responsibilities is directly connected with ministerial structures and the failure to effect a fundamental reorganization of the ministerial administration.

Since 1944, change in the number of ministries and the delimitation of their competences has been commonplace in Poland. The first post-war government was composed of 13 ministers, but after two years this number had increased to 20. In 1949, the post of the Minister of Industry and Commerce was abolished and, in its place, six new ministries were established. At the same time, the Presidium of the Cabinet was created – an institution not envisaged by the constitution – which played an important role as an intermediate body between the government and the ministers. Also in 1949, the Commission for Economic Planning was established, which assumed the character of a ministry. In the years between 1950 and 1953, another eight ministries were created. The first period of substantial decentralization were the years 1956/57, when Gomulka assumed power. In the place of ten of the old ministries, five new ones were established, and some of their powers were transferred to the intermediate level of state administration. During the 1960s, the situation stabilized, but some centralist tendencies led to the establishment of a new ministry in 1967 and to the restoration of the Presidium of the Cabinet. When Gierek came to power, further steps were taken to decentralize power from the central to the intermediate level; at the same time, the number of cabinet ministers was decreased by putting four in charge of several portfolios. The failure of Gierek's economic policy resulted in still further changes in the central organs: two ministries were abolished and five new ones were established. After August 1980, decentralizing pressures were mainly connected with calls for increased autonomy for state enterprises. In 1981, four ministries were created in place of nine that had existed previously, and in 1982, the post of Minister of Prices was added.

W. Goralczyk Jr., after analysing the post-war changes in the Polish ministerial structure, arrived at two important conclusions. Firstly, the concentration of power in central organs always resulted in an increase in the number of ministries, as the existing organs proved unable to exploit their new powers. Secondly, there is a certain pattern in the changes of ministries and the political crises of 1956, 1970 and 1980. It is characterized by centralization, followed by a drop in the effectiveness of the ministries' work, and, subsequently, political crisis, which in turn leads to decentralization, stabilization, and, eventually, recentralization (Goralczyk 1986 pp. 123–7).

The changes in the system of ministerial administration which took place during the second half of the 1980s and at the beginning of the 1990s already followed a different rationale. They can primarily be interpreted as attempts to find a solution to the problem of how to run a country in a deep and long-lasting economic crisis, with widespread social disaffection and a lack of trust in public authorities. There were no plans for the eventual shape of the state structure, and changes in government and economic policy were frequent. As a result, modifications in ministerial organization occurred almost every year. In 1985, six ministries and six central offices were abolished, and in their place four new ministries and one central office established. Also, the powers of the Cabinet Office were considerably extended. In 1987, the government's powers were reduced or decentralized, and, at the same time, the scope of activity of five ministries was changed. In addition, the post of the Minister of Industry was established replacing four previously existing economic ministries. In the following year, the Commission for Economic Planning was replaced by the Central Planning Office and the system of the government's advisory committees was comprehensively reorganized. The next year, 1989, brought further change. When Mazowiecki's government came to power, each of the four deputy premiers was put in charge of a ministry, and four ministers without portfolio were appointed. At the end of 1989, the new post of Minister of Communications was created, and in 1990 a Ministry for Ownership Transformation (Privatization) was established. In 1991, the Ministries of Industry and Commerce were merged (Jelowicki 1989; Jarosz 1989 and 1990). In the same year, Parliament rejected a bill, which, if adopted, would have created the post of a Minister of Public Administration and have led to major changes in the activities of the Cabinet Office and the Ministry of the Interior. The reasons for voting down these proposals were the same as those put forward when Parliament rejected the bill on the government's emergency powers.

At present, it is difficult to predict the future shape of the ministerial structure (Sokolewicz 1990). Suffice it to make two remarks. First, the frequency and extensive modifications in the ministerial structure partly result from the unfounded assumption that by establishing a new structure or a new institution this will by itself solve a given problem. That is why the legal regulations concerning the structures of state organs are very comprehensive, whilst regulations on horizontal co-ordination are, at best, fragmentary. Second, there is clearly a need to continue work on a revised statute on the Council of Ministers and to pass such an act quickly.

As far as the internal structures of central ministries are concerned, they are defined by legal acts of different rank. With the exception of the Ministries of Justice and of Defence, all ministries have been established through individual statutes. As regards the Ministry of Justice, its competences are defined in a statute on court proceedings, while the competences of the Minister of Defence are laid down in the statutes on compulsory military service. In the 1960s and 1970s, the statutes on the establishment of ministries tended to outline merely the main organizational pattern and left detailed regulations to the government. Since 1980, the statutes contain more detailed definitions of the ministerial structures and activities (Mazur 1990). On the basis of these statutes, the Council of Ministers then promulgates regulations defining the detailed scope of activity of a given ministry. However, such more detailed regulations are not always adopted. For example, no such detailed regulations existed for the Ministry of Industry between 1987–1991.

A ministry typically consists of the minister's personal staff, departments and offices; but there is no uniform structure, and some ministries are built upon a section structure. The individual departments are run by directors with the help of one or two deputy directors. The tasks of each organizational unit are defined through special organizational regulations. For this reason alone, it is very difficult to assess reforms within the ministries, as every new minister may make changes in the internal organization simply by promulgating an enactment, which is a legal act of a low rank, and, as such, not normally published (Jarosz 1989, pp. 6–7).

IV   TERRITORIAL GOVERNANCE

Modifications in the structures of administrative organs at the intermediate and lower levels of public administration are directly connected with changes in the territorial division of the country (Szyplinski 1989). Between 1944 and 1950, the regulations introduced before the Second World War were still in force. They provided for a three-tier territorial division of the country and an internal state and local government organization which corresponded to this division. These regulations envisaged a uniform internal structure of territorial government: there was a small number of administrative levels in municipal and district administrations, whilst at the highest level of territorial governance, in the provincial (*voivodship*) offices, a larger number of administrative tiers existed. The more complex structure of the provincial offices reflected the fact that they were often responsible for administering large areas. In 1950, territorial self-government was formally abolished, and elements of centralization were introduced into the structures of the territorial offices of state administration. At the district level, the organizational characteristics became vertically more differentiated, whereas the municipal offices retained a flat structure. In 1954, further centralization took place when the administrative structures were expanded on all three levels – province, district, municipality – without, however, providing opportunities for differentiation. Instead, a common organizational pattern was imposed by the centre.

In 1958, and again in 1963, the internal structures of the provincial offices were expanded, so that they began to resemble those found in the central ministries. The expansion of the provincial offices beyond a size which allowed their effective management was accompanied by increasing specialization of the individual organizational units and progressive professionalization on the part of officials. The same development could be observed at district level. However, as far as the municipal level was concerned, office structures remained more or less unchanged, as the municipal authorities were very much seen as mere auxiliary units for the district administration. One characteristic feature of this system was its organizational uniformity: although the offices had to function under very different economic conditions in different parts of the country, organizational structures followed a standard pattern.

The years between 1972 and 1975 saw a major reorganization in the territorial governance of the country. The district level was abolished, leaving just the levels of the provinces and the municipalities. The abolition of the district level was accompanied by an increase in the number of provinces. Instead of 17 provinces, 49 much smaller ones were created. This resulted not only in the breaking up of strong historic bonds between the provinces and their territory, which had existed in Poland for about five centuries, but also led to a rapid increase in special territorial administrative divisions. Despite its formal abolition, the district level retained an important role for internal administrative organization in many branches of deconcentrated state administration (Chróścielewski 1987). As part of the reform, the municipal level, too, underwent change. The apparent aim was to give local authorities greater freedom to shape their own structures, for example, by allowing the establishment of joint People's Councils and joint administrative organs. The new statutes also allowed local administration to hand over certain tasks to other administrations in the same area, provided that these tasks belonged to their original competences.

The new statute on the People's Councils of 1983 did not introduce significant changes in the organization of local organs. In mid-1989, the Cabinet Office undertook what turned out to be the last examination of the organization and efficiency of territorial institutions before the local government reform of 1990. On the basis of this examination, a number of conclusions were formulated. Amongst other things, the Office criticized the expansion of the internal structures of territorial authorities and the excessive number of posts for deputy directors. Following the report, the number of departments in the *voivodship* offices decreased from 251 to 201, i.e. by 19.9 per cent, but these were more or less incidental changes and did not lead to a general flattening of the structures of provincial offices or to a significant decrease in employment (which fell by merely 7.2 per cent). In larger local authorities, too, change was small-scale (in one town office the number of deputy directors increased to eight with the same number of organizational units), and the changes which did occur did not follow any systematic pattern. If one finally looks at the communal offices, there is, indeed, evidence of simplification and a stream lining of administrative structures. On the other hand, however, no use was made at the communal level of the possibility of entrusting other organs with the management of administrative tasks (Skweres 1989).

The Acts of 1990, which restored a sphere of independent local government, leave the organs of state administration and of local government considerable scope in shaping the internal organization of their offices. The government lost its powers to issue regulations on the administrative structures of provincial offices, which had played a large role in ensuring organizational uniformity across the whole country. Thus, at present, the structure of general state administrative offices is largely defined by the *voivod*. In the municipalities, organizational structures are defined through regulations adopted by the municipal councils on the suggestion of the council's presidium.

V   LOCAL GOVERNMENT REFORM

It is not easy to classify the changes in the structures and procedures of Polish public administration on the basis of their importance. However, there can be little disagreement that the restoration of a sphere of local self-government in the spring of 1990 must be counted among the most significant. The main institutional features of this reform have already been described elsewhere (Niewiadomski 1990; Gorzelak and Mularczyk 1990). Therefore, the present discussion concentrates on an analysis of some of the major difficulties which have arisen in reforming the local level. Undoubtedly, local government reform has encountered greater problems than most observers initially predicted. For one thing, local councillors, local government employees, judges, and many academic observers have complained that local government legislation is formulated too imprecisely (*Wspolnota* 1990, 1991; Piekara 1990; Kowalewski 1991). The legislator has used different terms to refer to the same object and important issues, such as, for example the openness of council meetings, have not been addressed at all. Moreover, some regulations are contradictory, for example, as regards the powers of the *voivod* and the municipalities. Insufficient clarity and incoherence can partly be explained by the hurry in which the reforms were prepared and the lack of technical expertise in drafting the bills. Partly, they also reflect the fact that no genuine local self-government had existed in Poland during the last five decades. Moreover, the original draft legislation was amended substantially during the legislative process. As a result, a considerable part of the local government acts of 1990 are unintelligible not only for ordinary citizens, but also for professional staff.

One of the most common misconceptions about local government is that it implies full independence for the municipalities. From a legal perspective this is mistaken, since municipalities cannot be treated as institutions that are fully separated from the state (Letowski 1986). The independence of municipalities is limited by three basic factors: the powers that are granted to them by law, financial resources, and hierarchical control, exercised by state administrative organs. Concerning the first issue, the 1990 local government reform failed to provide the municipalities with the full range of powers needed to respond effectively to local needs. In fact, the municipalities were first of all put in charge of those matters which require them to execute central acts. Thus, the municipal organs are, to some extent, treated as agencies of state administration, while a significant part of the powers required to address local matters satisfactorily remain the prerogative of the state (Kulesza 1991). In fact, some have argued that – compared to the old People's Councils – local government has lost a large part of its competences to the state (Zawadzka 1990). Moreover, according to current regulations, municipal organs do not possess the right to adopt local legal regulations on the basis of a general authorization to perform their own duties. Modest powers and insufficient legal means to secure their effective realization imply a considerable restriction of municipal independence.

Turning to the financial basis of local government, it is clear that the municipalities' financial situation cannot be considered in isolation from the budgetary problems of the state. In a situation of economic crisis and very tight fiscal resources, most municipalities find it extremely difficult to perform their mandatory tasks. This applies particularly to policy areas involving major public expenditure, such as environmental protection, public safety or education. Examples of the difficulties posed by inadequate resources abound. Thus, many municipalities have been forced to close down local kindergartens or charge fees equalling almost one third of the parents' monthly earnings (*Trybuna*[4] 1991). Some local authorities have resorted to cutting teachers' pay, in extreme cases halving their salaries (*Trybuna*[6] 1991). In such a situation, many municipal councils have started to look for additional sources of revenue. One option has been the establishment of profit-oriented municipal enterprises (*Trybuna*[5] 1991), which is permitted under current local government regulations. Budgetary difficulties have meant that many municipalities adopt a short-sighted financial policy geared towards raising revenue at almost any cost. This can, for example, involve excessive increases in rents on local properties, which impede economic activity, or the selling-off of municipal property at very low prices.

Limited local powers and insufficient financial resources do not imply that municipal councils and their administrations suffer from a lack of work. However, it is often difficult to escape the impression that local activities are more about symbolic gestures, aiming at popular emotions, than about adequate local service provision (*Trybuna*[1] 1991). For example, a great deal of time and effort has been devoted to the issue of renaming streets and public buildings and discussions on the removal of monuments from the Communist past.

The third factor limiting the independence of local government is the control exercised by state organs, though this factor limits local activities not nearly as much as legal and financial constraints (Leonski 1990; Podgorski 1991; Niewiadomski and Szreniaswki 1991, pp. 74–88; Zawadzka 1990, p. 23). Municipalities cannot be completely independent of the state, and existing regulations contain fairly precise definitions of the cases in which state administration may exercise control over municipal activities. There is no evidence of any systematic abuse of the state's rights to control local government activities, and the courts have consistently confirmed that local governments may seek legal protection if they feel that the state is exceeding its control powers. However, it should be mentioned that central government, in extreme cases, has the right to dissolve a municipality through merging it with another local authority. Since this is not considered a means of control, but a way of achieving changes in the territorial organization of the country, such a decision by the state is not subject to court control.

The municipal councils are supposed to act as the representatives of the local community. Whilst there can be no doubt that the local government elections of May 1990 satisfied democratic criteria, it is less clear to what extent the new municipal councils are truly representative of the popular will. Election turnout was low at 42.1 per cent. Civic committees supported by Solidarity won 41.47 per cent of all local mandates; significantly, however, non-aligned candidates scored almost as many votes and won 39.52 per cent of municipal council seats. With the exception of the Polish Peasants' Party, which won 5.76 per cent of the mandates, no political party gained more than 1 per cent of the seats in the local council. The by-elections for municipal councils held in May 1991 produced even more worrying results. In villages, turnout nowhere exceeded 45 per cent, and in some towns it fell as low as 2 per cent. In a few localities, by-elections could not be held, because nobody wanted to contest free seats. Non-aligned candidates won the majority of mandates.

Against this background, the representativeness of municipal councils is open to question. Quite obviously, society at large took little interest in the elections. This lack of interest can partly be explained by the narrow competences enjoyed by local government; this confirms a strong popular view that societal problems can only be solved by state institutions. On the other hand, the increase in the number of municipal councils in which none of the 84 political parties registered in June 1991 is represented might be viewed as a positive sign. The electorate would seem to give priority to individual personalities rather than general programmes of particular political groups.

Contrary to the stated intentions of local government reform, the municipal councils have not become the central players in the local government system. Depending on local conditions, the decisive role in the municipalities might be played by the *voivod*, groups linked to the Solidarity movement, local civic committees, or authorities of the Catholic Church. Relations between the *voivod* as a representative of the state and local government institutions are of a supervisory nature. By contrast, the relationship between local government and groups connected with Solidarity often resemble those found in a classical party system. As regards the ties between local government and the Catholic Church, it is important not to over-generalize. Certainly, however, one finds many instances of far-reaching local compliance with the demands and expectations of the Catholic clergy. In view of these facts, there is much to be said for the following assessment:

> In the old system there always existed some external authority which solved all conflicts. The solutions did not necessarily have to be accepted – but they were provided and had to be obeyed. Now the conflicts will have to be solved by the localities themselves on the grounds of democratic institutions and procedures. Will the losers – present in any dispute – accept the verdict of the democratically elected body? Will the local communities invent their own procedures for resolving conflicts or will they follow the experience already existing elsewhere? If not, the new system could become partly unmanageable and the scope of the local autonomy would have to be limited by calling upon the decisions of the external judges (Gorzelak 1990).

There is, however, a further dimension to the representativeness of municipal councils. Attempts to solve complex social problems through strikes, demonstrations and other forms of direct action have long been a characteristic feature of Polish social life. This tendency to seek to resolve contentious issues outside the established channels for problem-solving is also evident at the local level. A lack of local government tradition, the weakness of the present system and, at best, tenuous social support for its actions are among the chief reasons why political and social disputes tend to be settled outside the municipal council by stronger bodies. The problem is aggravated by a widespread misunderstanding on the part of local councillors of their proper role in the community. Instead of relying on the legal and political means at their disposal, councillors often tend to take direct action which merely serves to highlight the weaknesses of the local government system. In the town of Sejny, for example, a quarrel between the councillors representing the town and their colleagues from surrounding villages over real estate taxes led to a boycott of the council sessions and, ultimately, resulted in the appointment of a government commissioner to manage the town's affairs (*Trybuna²* 1991). In Lublin, a local councillor staged a two-week hunger strike in the town hall to protest against the lack of resources for the struggle against alcoholism, and in Poznan, local councillors, instead of deciding on the closure of a market threatening the outbreak of an epidemic, started tidying it up themselves (*Trybuna³* 1991).

Looking, finally, at the future of local government, predictions are difficult. The legal foundation for local self-government are in place, and many councils and officials try hard to tackle local problems. However, the citizens still look primarily towards central government for the solution of everyday problems.

VI   CO-ORDINATION IN PUBLIC ADMINISTRATION

Insufficient inter-administrative co-ordination is one of the decisive weaknesses in Polish public administration and helps to explain many performance deficits. To the extent that inter-administrative relations are at all taken into account in establishing or reforming administrative structures, it is vertical ties that tend to receive most attention, whereas horizontal linkages are scarcely acknowledged and very poorly developed. At the ministerial level, for example, individual departments and administrative units work largely autonomously, since proper procedures for co-ordination and information exchange rarely exist. This results in incoherent and often contradictory decisions adopted by particular ministries, and, more generally, in a slowing down of all administrative policy making which requires inter-ministerial co-operation.

One of the main impediments to improved horizontal co-ordination is the ministerial division of tasks in administrative organs. This applies particularly to the intermediate level of state administration. Here, different departments in the provincial offices fall under the supervision of different ministers. Moreover, the proliferation of deconcentrated units of state administration existing outside the *voivodship* offices further impedes horizontal co-ordination. As far as inter-provincial co-ordination is concerned, *voivods* are, in principle, obliged to co-operate, but legal regulations in this sphere are only fragmentary (Wrzosek 1989). Research conducted in 1989 suggests that co-operation between *voivods* is more extensive where the character of the task very clearly requires it. This seems to be particularly the case in the spheres of environmental protection, leisure (for example, the exchange of children for holidays), public health, transport, and the development of higher education. Typically, such co-operation takes the form of meetings between *voivods* or between working groups. However, mutual contacts have up to now been hindered by the lack of established co-operation programmes and co-operative patterns. For this reason, any decentralization of central competences must be accompanied by a strengthening of co-operative ties between the *voivods* and also increased rights to transborder co-operation (think, for example, of the need for cross-border co-operation between Poland and Czechoslovakia in environmental protection (Biegunski 1989).

Inter-administrative co-operation at the intermediate level is directly connected with the problem of regionalization, an issue which has received wide attention in the academic literature (Elzanowski, Maciolek and Przybysz 1990). Thus far, however, there is little agreement on regionalization, beyond the fact that it should be addressed in the new constitution. In particular, the question remains unresolved whether the newly created regions should be centres of state administration or constitute a higher level of self-government. Obviously, this fundamental question needs to be settled before more detailed issues can be resolved. The latter include decisions on the number of regions to be established (current proposals suggest between 10 and 15); the boundaries of these new regions; the competences of other administrative organs at the regional level; and, finally, more wide-ranging changes in the territorial division of the country. It is crucial that a decision on the establishment of regions is not postponed indefinitely, but is made as soon as possible after the political situation has stabilized and Parliament has resumed work on the constitution.

VII ISSUES IN PERSONNEL POLICY

The proposition that 'a good administration begins with good personnel' is certainly a truism, but it is no less accurate for that. It also provides a useful starting point for a consideration of the state of the Polish public service. Throughout the period of Communist rule, public administration and its employees tended to be treated as necessary evils which would only vanish once the state was transformed into a Communist self-government. Of all the groups for whom the state acted as an employer, i.e. for about 73 per cent of the total labour force during the 1980s, those working in public administration enjoyed the least protection, and they were generally held in low popular esteem. After the Second World War, pre-war public service personnel could not play a significant role in shaping the standards of public officials, as a large proportion of them had died during the war or emigrated, and the remaining ones were only exceptionally admitted to higher positions for political reasons. The new personnel of the Socialist state was selected, appointed and promoted largely with ideological considerations in mind, but lacked professional experience and a relevant education.

Examining the quantitative challenges confronted by the Polish public service, it is first worth emphasizing that by no means all branches of public administration were over-staffed during the Communist era. In fact, the problem of excessive staffing levels only concerned the administration of the state enterprises and the industrial ministries. By contrast, other branches and levels of public administration, most notably the municipal tier, often suffered from staff shortages. Despite the evident difficulties involved in cross-country comparisons of public service employment, it still seems worth quoting at least some figures (Muszalski 1990; Gajdzinski 1991). In 1980, about 137,000 staff were employed in public administration. This figure had risen substantially to 177,000 by 1985, but fell to 168,000 in 1988, and further declined to 158,000 by the first half of 1992. Of these total figures, about 42,000 were employed in central government institutions in 1988; their number rose to 53,000 in 1991, of whom around 10,000 worked in the central ministries. Amongst the ministries, the Cabinet Office consisted of around 600 employees.

Regarding personnel policy, it is almost universally recognized that until now a rational approach has not evolved. The most frequently cited obstacles to the development of a coherent personnel policy include, *inter alia*, low pay, inadequate training, and politicization at all levels of the public service. As regards the first of these obstacles, low pay, it should be noted that the remuneration of public employees has for decades been lower than in other branches of the national economy; this is especially true of employees at the lower levels of public administration. In 1980, average pay in local offices reached 76.7 per cent of the pay in the sphere of material production; the equivalent figures for 1987 and 1988 were 85.4 per cent and 79.9 per cent respectively. In 1989, the government decided to raise this proportion to 112 per cent by 1992, but because of the budget deficit, it has been impossible to achieve this target (Stawowiak 1989).

Turning to education and training, the foundations of a comprehensive training system have yet to be laid. Thus far, attempts at creating a system for preparing personnel for public administration in the form of secondary administrative schools and university level education with a specialization in public administration have not produced significant results. By contrast, in-service training, in the form of public service apprenticeships, and post-graduate studies appear to produce rather better outcomes. In this connection, the establishment of the National School of Public Administration in May 1990, which is modelled, as mentioned, on the French Ecole Nationale d'Administration and is directly subordinated to the Office of the Cabinet, augers well for the future (Bartyzel 1991).

The politicization of the public service refers to the fact that there are still not enough qualified officials who can be trusted to perform their duties reliably regardless of political changes. There can be no doubt that administrative personnel under Communist rule were to a large extent politically indoctrinated (Kasten 1990). The formation of the first post-Communist government and the first free local government elections started a process of replacing public personnel on all levels of public administration. This procedure was necessary and fully justified, but did little to stabilize the public service, especially since many employees left the service at their own request, despite a positive assessment. The vacant posts were then often filled by employees who lacked experience, but enjoyed the political confidence of the governing parties. Frequent changes of government at the national level have meant a high turnover of staff in positions of administrative leadership. To some extent, this resembles the situation at the beginning of the Polish People's Republic in the 1940s (Radzikowska 1991). By contrast, the propagation of religious views by public employees exercising public functions is a new phenomenon. In this respect, it is worth noting that more than 90 per cent of the Polish population declare their allegiance to the Catholic Church, but, at the same time, about 80 per cent oppose the clergy's active participation in political life (Uznanski 1991).

The lack of a rational personnel policy has a number of negative consequences. First and foremost, it is responsible for the instability in the public service, where annual turnover of staff reaches up to 20 per cent in some provinces (Nadolski 1989). Second, there are signs of an excessively high share of female employment in public administration. Thus, in central offices, around 50 per cent of all employees are female; in provincial offices this figure reaches about 60 per cent, and in municipal offices around 77 per cent (Muszalski 1989). Third, personnel with university degrees are territorially very unevenly distributed. At the lowest level of public administration, only about 3,000 people, or 12 per cent of all local employees, possess a university degree. In the municipal offices in the Lublin region, 201 university-trained people were employed, but in the offices at the same level in the Jelenia Gora region, only 23 possessed such a qualification. University graduates in public administration are mainly concentrated in large urban areas, centres of academic life, and the developed industrial centres. By contrast, they are a rarity in rural areas. In the Biala Podlaska province (with 32 municipalities), only a single lawyer was employed at the municipal level. By contrast, in the Gdansk province, with a total of 37 municipal offices, 40 lawyers were to be found at this level (Nadolski 1989). Finally, as regards the prestige of public servants, research conducted in 1984 concluded that 'In Polish society lack of confidence in public servants must be evaluated as critically high' (Sarapata 1988). If similar research were to be conducted today, the assessment would, in all likelihood, scarcely be more positive.

REFERENCES

Bartyzel, D. 1991. 'Schools in for civil servants', *The Warsaw Voice*, 35, p. 9.
Biegunski, L. 1989. 'Wspolpraca miedzywojewodzka', *Gospodarka — Administracja Panstwowa* 16–17.
Biuletyn RPO — Materialy. 1990. No. 9, pp. 77–82.
Chróścielewski, W. 1987. *Podzialy terytorialne specjalne*. Warsaw: Państwowe Wydawnictwo Naukowe.
Elzanowski, M., M. Maciolek and P. Przybysz. 1990. 'Region jako instytucja prawnoustrojowa', *Panstwo i Prawo 8*.

Gajdzinski, P. 1991. 'Przywiazani do biurka', *Wprost* 35.

Goralczyk, Jr., W. 1986. *Zasada kompetencyjnosci w prawie administracyjnym*. Warsaw.

Gorzelak, G. 1990. 'Apocalypse now'. Local government reform in Poland', *The Warsaw Voice* 18, p. 11.

Gorzelak, G. and K. Mularczyk. 1990. *Polish local government reform*. Warsaw/The Hague.

Goszczynski, A. 1991. 'To rule by decree', *The Warsaw Voice* 37, p. 6.

Graniecki, M. 'Government of the Republic of Poland – its position within the system of government and organization of work' (unpublished manuscript).

Hoff, W. 1987. *Wytyczne w prawie administracyjnym*. Warsaw: Państwowe Wydawnictwo Naukowe.

Jablonska-Bonca, J. 1987. 'Prawo powielaczowe', *Studium z teorii panstwa i prawa*. Gdansk: Wydawnictwo Uniwersytetu Gdańskiego.

Jarosz, A. 1989. 'Minister przemyslu w systemie centralnej administracji panstwowej', *Organizacja – Metody – Technika* 10.

——. 1990. 'Zmiany w organizacji i zakresie wlasciwosci niektorych naczelnych organow administracji panstwowej', *Organizacja – Metody – Technika* 5 and *Rzeczpospolita* 120.

Jelowicki, M. 1989. 'Nowe organy w centralnym aparacie administracji panstwowej', *Organizacja – Metody – Technika* 6.

Kasten, M. 1990. 'Kryterium lojalnosci jako kryterium doboru kadr kierowniczych administracji panstwowej', *Organizacja – Metody – Technika* 4.

Kowalewski, A. T. 1991. 'Trudne poczatki samorzadu terytorialnego', *Samorzad Terytorialny* 1–2, p. 95.

Kulesza, M. 1991. 'Zagrozenia reformy – w sprawie zadan i kompetencji samorzadu terytorialnego', *Samorzad Terytorialny* 1–2, p. 89.

Leonski, Z. 1990. 'Nadzor nad samorzadem terytorialnym w swietle ustawy z 8 marca 1990 r.', *Panstwo i Prawo* 12.

Letowski, J. 1986. 'The commentary on the Supreme Court decision of January 29, 1986/IV CR 488/85', *Panstwo i Prawo* 11.

——. 1990. 'Prawodawstwo w czasach konfliktow', *Panstwo i Prawo* 5.

Majman, S. 1991. 'Kryuchkov's long hand', *The Warsaw Voice* 37, p. 8.

Mazur, J. 1988. 'Podzial kompetencji do stanowienia aktow wykonawczych miedzy rzad a ministrow', *Panstwo i Prawo* 8.

——. 1989. 'Porzadkowanie prawa resortowego na przykladzie resortu edukacji narodowej', *Gospodarka – Administracja Panstwowa* 8, pp. 41–3.

——. 1990. 'Prawo dla rzadu', *Rzeczpospolita* 5.

Muszalski, J. 1989. 'Pozycja spoleczno-prawna kadr administracji panstwowej-elementy wybrane', *Organizacja – Metody – Technika* 7, pp. 12–13.

Muszalski, W. 1990. 'Stan zatrudnienie polskiej administracji panstwowej w porownaniu z innymi krajami', *Organizacja – Metody – Technika* 5.

Nadolski, J. 1989. 'Polityka kadrowa w administracji w latach 1987–1989', *Organizacja – Metody – Technika* 2, p. 7.

Niewiadomski, Z. 1990. 'Die Wiedereinführung der kommunalen Selbstverwaltung in Polen durch das Gesetz über die territoriale Selbstverwaltung', vom 8, Mäyrz, *Archiv für Kommunalwissenschaften II*. Halbjahresband.

Niewiadomski, Z. and J. Szreniawski. 1991. *Zarys ustroju administracji lokalnej Rzeczypospolitej Polskiej*. Lublin.

Piekara, A. 1990. 'Wartosci i funkcje spoleczne samorzadu terytorialnego', *Panstwo i Prawo* 8, p. 13.

Podgorski, K. 1991. 'Nadzor nad samorzadem gminnym', *Samorzad Terytorialny* 1–2.

Radzikowska, B. 1991. 'Zjawisko dyskryminacji na tle politycznym w dzialalnosci Rzecznika Praw Obywatelskich', *Biuletyn RPO – Materialy* 10.

Rot, H. 1980. *Akty prawotworcze w PRL. Koncepcje i typy*. Wroclaw: Wydawnictwo Uniwersytetu Wroclawskiego.

Rymuszko, M. 1991. 'Celne-niecelne', *Prawo i Zycie* 34.

Rzeczpospolita. 1990. Nos. 20, 37 and 76.

Sarapata, A. 1988. 'Zaufanie spoleczenstwa do pracownikow administracji panstwowej', *Organizacja – Metody – Technika* 11–12.

Skweres, J. 1989. 'Urzedy w nowych strukturach', *Gospodarka – Administracja Panstwowa* 21.

Sokolewicz, W. 1990. 'Rzad w przyszlej konstytucji', *Panstwo i Prawo* 7.

Stawowiak, Z. 1989. 'Ustawa o ksztaltowaniu srodkow na wynagrodzenia w sferze budzetowej', *Gospodarka – Administracja Panstwowa* 5.

——. 1989. 'Nowa sytuacja placowa pracownikow administracji panstwowej', *Gospodarka – Administracja Panstwowa* 6.

Szyplinski, M. 1989. 'Wplyw podzialu terytorialnego na rozmieszczenie organow administracji oraz ksztalt ich struktur w latach 1944–1988', *Organizacja – Metody – Technika* 11.

Taras, W. and A. Wrobel. 1991. 'Samodzielnosc prawotworcza samorzadu terytorialnego,' in: *Samorzad Terytorialny* 7–8.

Trybuna[1]. 1991, nos. 95, 110, 126, 127, 129, 130.

——[2]. 1991, no. 100.

——[3]. 1991, nos. 106 and 126.

——[4]. 1991, nos. 126 and 128.

——[5]. 1991, no. 127.

——[6]. 1991, no. 129.

Uznanski, A. 1991. 'Priest and Politician', *The Warsaw Voice*, 37, p. 8.

Wronkowska, S. and J. Wroblewski. 1987. 'Projekt ustawy o tworzeniu prawa', *Panstwo i Prawo* 6.

Wrzosek, S. 1989. 'Z problematyki dzialnosci wydzialow urzedow wojewodzkich', *Organizacja – - Metody – Technika* 1, pp. 24–5.

Wspolnota. 1990. 'Mienie gminne, czy gminy?' *Wspolnota* 28, p. 10.

——. 1991. 'Zmieniamy prawo. Propozycje nowelizacji', *Wspolnota* 4 (supplement).

Zawadzka, B. 1990. 'Samorzad terytorialny w swietle regulacji ustawowych', *Panstwo i Prawo* 8, p. 22.

OPTIONS FOR ADMINISTRATIVE REFORM IN POLAND

MICHAL KULESZA

I INTRODUCTION

In the Republic of Poland the transformation of the political system and the gradual reorientation of the economy have been accompanied by only slight changes in the functioning of public administration. The mechanisms of administrative activity are determined by the old regulations still in force, and also by surviving habits and administrative routines. They do not change automatically, either under market pressure or as a result of changes in the state structure. Consequently, the organization and the functioning of Polish public administration are basically still those that prevailed under the previous regime when it served an alien state, other political goals and a different economic system. With these conditions having changed, it has now become clear that a fundamental reform of public administration is an absolute necessity. This has emerged as the main and most urgent task of government. Its success constitutes a *sine qua non* condition for further societal and economic change. Public administration is without doubt the very cornerstone of all states. In contemporary Poland, however, the administrative structure has become dysfunctional. As a system, it has reached the limits of controllability, beyond which there would only be inertia and chaos.

Work on the reform of government and public administration has been carried on during the past three years with varying intensity. Since 1989, we have witnessed a gradual reconstruction of Polish statehood based on democracy, the rule of law, respect of individual rights, private ownership and market mechanisms. The so-called 'Little Constitution', voted by Parliament on 17 October 1992, clearly proclaims its support for a political system with a three-tier division of power (art. 1). This Constitutional Act also sets the directions of change needed to design efficient and clear mechanisms for the functioning of executive powers, *i.e.* government in connection with the Presidency of the Republic and public administration.

Professor Michal Kulesza is Government Plenipotentiary for Public Administration Reform in the Republic of Poland. He would like to express his gratitude to Oliver Freeman who translated this paper.

The successive governments that have been in office since the elections of 1989 have not shown coherence in all areas of policy making. There has however been a consistent effort to transform the state into a rational structure, *i.e.* well organized and civically oriented, and to rebuild a competent and effective administration. On the initiative of the Polish Senate, territorial self-government was returned to the local councils in August 1989 by the Government of Tadeusz Mazowiecki. This was a fundamental and very successful move towards state reform, and also the first step in the construction of a civil society. The government of Jan Krzysztof Bielecki contributed to this development by carrying out various analyses, appraisals and other projects. Many of these were prepared by the Committee in charge of Conceptualizing Changes in the Territorial Organization of the State and by the Committee for Public Administration Reform. The conclusions drawn by the latter were spelt out in a report entitled 'Preparatory Proposals for the Reform of Public Administration', the principles of which were accepted by the government of Jan Olszewski. The report underlines, among other things, the fact that any fundamental and extensive changes in the mechanisms of administrative activity can only prove successful if a special governmental body is created to implement the reform and to co-ordinate the work undertaken by the different state organs and institutions. This postulate was accomplished on 13 October 1992, when an Act of the Council of Ministers established the post of the Government Plenipotentiary in charge of Public Administration Reform. Since taking office, the government of Hanna Suchocka has declared clearly and unambiguously its political will to proceed with the reform, primarily in three areas: (1) the functioning of central and decentralized state administration; (2) the local government system. The priority here is to rationalize administrative divisions of the state and to complete the decentralization initiated in 1990 by the introduction of a second-tier of local self-government, the *powiats* (districts); (3) the civil service.

Independently of the conceptual progress made by the successive governments since 1989, many concrete reform measures of a legal and organizational nature have already been, or are in the process of being, implemented. But by following mainly departmental requirements, they are dispersed, and unfortunately often lack cohesion. Some of the projected or already introduced changes do not always fit into a clear overall vision of the administrative structure. This is particularly the case when they do not produce spectacular and qualitative changes for the administration. It must be added that, apart from the action taken by the government (and also those taken by Parliament, such as the creation of regional financial audit offices), non-governmental initiatives are playing an important and increasing role.

The aim of this overview is to outline the main tenets and orientations of public administration reform in Poland. It is important to emphasize that these changes must not be viewed (and even less carried out) as one uninterrupted and concentrated process capable of bringing clear and global results within a very short span of time. On the contrary, contemporary states are trying as much as possible to avoid important structural change, and if they do, it is only after long and extensive preparations. Instead they keep monitoring the structures and functional mechanisms of the administration, and intervene, if necessary, only through small adjustments. In the Polish context however, certain transformations, chiefly territorial reform, do require fundamental structural reorganization. It is therefore all the more important to try and avoid making simultaneously such wide-ranging alterations in other areas. The main challenge is to introduce new mechanisms without destabilizing the state as such. In other words, this means that change must be introduced with caution.

Public administration reform is not a once-and-for-all act of reorganization, but involves a whole series of decisions and undertakings following the same direction and objective, but varying in nature, scope and timing. Sometimes it will include preparing future organizational and legislative measures by good coordination during the preparatory phase. This should be done, for example, when considering the future districts, or designing new rules and mechanisms for the public service. In other cases, it will mean taking separate decisions quite independently from other activities and time constraints (like for example the introduction of regulations on public procurements). As already mentioned, the extent and scope of the indispensable changes can only be measured by the present crisis of Polish public administration. Therefore the role of the Plenipotentiary in charge of Public Administration Reform is mainly to propose measures capable of producing the widest effects while at the same time incurring minimal costs in terms of resources needed and potential threats the reform may generate. The regulation of public procurements belongs precisely to this category. If it is supported by a wide educational programme, it might induce a completely new approach to public expenditure, paving the way not only for an important increase in spending efficiency, but also for a change in administrative ethics.

In certain sectors, as well as in some circles of society, the hopes, but also the fears, associated with change are particularly visible. This is one of the reasons why the implementation of reform is of such a political character. Proposed change must therefore be examined from the technical (organizational, functional, etc.) point of view, but also in terms of its social implications. Not only the electorate, but also the users of and suppliers to public administration, as well as the civil servants and private sector managers must be satisfied. This requirement should be given special attention because it is in fact the key to the success of future change. Even the most scrupulous preparation of important administrative reform measures, like for example the introduction of local self-government in 1990, or the proposed creation of the districts (*powiats*), means nothing more than establishing the legal and organizational frameworks for effective change. Their operational capacity depends first and foremost on the positive and active attitudes of the social and administrative élites.

A natural feature of all administrations is, and always has been, strong conservatism associated with inertia and reluctance to change. It is not surprising therefore that administrative structures are very strongly opposed to reform, and even more so if they are fundamental. Such a situation can be overcome only if the dynamics of change are stronger than those of the system it will affect. In other words, the success of reformatory measures requires a favourable social climate as well as the agreement of the main political forces not only on their implementation, but above all on the basic framework proposed by government. Divergence and discussions may (and should) arise concerning specific issues, but general agreement is an absolute condition before any essential and concrete decisions can be taken. In countries like Poland, where Parliament is politically fragmented, consensus on reform can only be reached on a minimal platform. All important political forces should be prepared to endorse it above their own particular interests and in a feeling of responsibility for the essential well-being of the country. If not, the state as such will be in jeopardy. This article aims at presenting the minimal or essential changes that are indispensable, first of all to stop any further degradation of the state apparatus (especially of its executive function), and secondly to assign some elementary and indisputable goals to the transformation of the Polish political system.

Below are listed the main goals and values which ought to inspire the reform process, and those sectors it should concern in priority.

II   A RATIONAL, MANAGEABLE AND COMPETENT GOVERNMENT

The administrative system which is presently operating in Poland makes it impossible for the government to manage efficiently public affairs. This situation is the consequence of taking over the state structures that existed under the former regime without introducing any substantial changes. Before 1989, the Council of Ministers did not actually 'govern', but acted more as a co-ordinating committee subject to the political power of the centre, which was in fact the real government. State policy making, decision-making mechanisms, information flows, staff selection, etc. were all determined by this reality. The current situation calls therefore for a new definition and organization of the functions previously fulfilled under the provisions of the leading role of the Communist Party and through the use of the party-state structure. As far as the organization of public administration is concerned, it will also be necessary to eliminate the negative effects of the local government reform introduced in 1975. This caused considerable overlapping owing to the multiplication of specialized (departmental), deconcentrated government agencies. This trend has developed even further over the last few years.

The issues to be raised in order of priority are:

— the organization of governance, the principles guiding the services provided to the government and to the Prime Minister, the position of ministers as members of government (politically endowed executive power) as well as the main representatives of state administration (heads of a department);
— the role and organization of the ministries, especially within the context of a necessary distinction between political functions (the minister and his

cabinet as a changing element of the executive power system) and administrative functions (administrative units of a professional, stable, loyal and politically neutral character);

— the place and the role of central administrations and other organs (agencies, boards, etc.) at the same level, placed under the authority of the government or of a particular minister, with different levels of autonomy in decision making and recruitment policies, and fulfilling different basic functions like administrative control, legal regulation, organization and delivery of basic public services, administration of state property, ownership transformation, promotional activities, statistics, information, etc.;

— the organization of the territorial structure of the state as a whole and of the administrative structure existing within it. Special attention ought to be given to the position of the *voivod* as the representative of (central) government and as the co-ordinator of state administration at the *voivodship* level. This is essential in the face of the uncontrolled increase of tasks and specialized administrative bodies;

— the definition of the *voivod's* responsibility in implementing and co-ordinating the social and economic policies of the state in the *voivodship*, and, related to this, the determination of a new formula for the *voivods'* budget;

— the development of a model of public service defining the principles of personnel policy and the training requisites of administrative officers, together with the formulation of the principles governing the public service, like advancement procedures and administrative ethics;

— the introduction of new techniques of administrative work, the improvement of information flows, the amelioration of the mechanisms and procedures to be followed in the preparation and execution of government decisions, as well as the definition of methods to attain agreement, co-ordination and mediation;

— the development of information and computing facilities;

— the creation of a separate Ministry (or Agency) of Public Administration responsible for the organization and functioning of state administration, the public service, administrative training schemes, the computerization of state offices, the supervision of local government, and permanent monitoring of the changes occurring in the system of state administration.

III A CIVIL STATE

In 1990 Poland saw the reintroduction of the classical dualist system of public administration in the form of a distinction between state administration and local self-government. The introduction of local government was the first step towards the creation of a civic state and the construction of new political élites from the 'bottom-up'. But at the same time, the mechanisms of the bureaucratic state and of the provincial authorities were reinforced through the multiplication of specialized agencies in charge of important public responsibilities without the slightest external control. Today Poland is faced with a dilemma, the solution to which will determine its administrative system for years to come. It can develop either into a civil state or into a bureaucratic state. The answer to this does not seem to raise any difficulties. But practically this means:

— proceeding with the decentralization of public administration by completing the transfer of public tasks and administrative powers of local character to the larger urban communities, and otherwise introducing into rural areas the second tier of local government (rural *powiats*). This concerns all tasks, administrative competences, as well as those organs, services, institutions and the like, responsible for supplying collective needs at the local level and/or which should be the object of scrutiny by the local authorities (rural *powiat*/district councils and town councils independent of the *powiats*);
— the simultaneous creation of the essential intervening mechanisms designed to protect the interest of the state in affairs under its responsibility but implemented by local authorities;
— preparing the conditions for a third-tier of territorial government at the *voivodship*/regional level which may eventually be introduced at later stages of the reform as the result of further functional decentralization.

IV   AN ECONOMICAL AND EFFICIENT STATE

Systemic changes induced by the abandonment of centrally planned economics and the adoption of market mechanisms based on competition, have important consequences for public administration, especially on public finances. Administrations will be able to select from an open market of goods and services. But this requires a different management of public resources, as well as new methods of control. Therefore the reorganization of the state apparatus should take account of the fundamental division between administration and economics by distinguishing the administrative functions of the state from the tasks of the economic system. In this regard, it is particularly important:

— to set out completely new criteria for public procurements, redesigned organizational forms for these activities, as well as new legal norms and a professional code of ethics;
— to continue work on the institutions and legal status of the State Treasury. Special care should be given when it comes to deciding on the principles and legal–organizational forms of the administrative body responsible for state ownership (with its various components, depending on their nature, function, assignment, etc...), as well as on the criteria according to which its tasks will be fulfilled with respect to the organization and competences of central, regional and local administration;

— to consider the problem of the central and local government budgets, especially when introducing the new budgetary mechanisms. The latter will have to reckon with a further decentralization of public tasks and the important changes which will inevitably occur in the system of public finance.

V   A FAIR, ACCOUNTABLE AND IMPARTIAL STATE

The state, the economy, but also the civil servants, their attitudes and behaviour, are undergoing radical change. Such a process requires extreme caution because of the different kinds of dangers that may appear due to the uneven, and sometimes even dysfunctional, course of legislative and institutional change. This could destabilize the administrative mechanisms that have survived until now without yet being replaced by new ones, and could provoke the relaxation of organizational discipline, personal efficiency, etc. In this regard, the most important questions to be dealt with are:

— the provision of legal guarantees for administrative procedure and executive accountability. The legal institutions in charge of this will have to adapt to the new systemic conditions of dualistic public administration;
— the reinforcement of the legal protection of individual and collective interests in the realms of public law. This requires the further development of administrative courts and the drafting of a complete procedure of administrative law;
— the stimulation of further professional legal expertise in administrative matters;
— the establishment of local systems of protection against the abuses of public authority and collective security enforcement (also in social and ecological matters). This should be based on the relationship existing between the interests of the local community and the public assessment of the efficiency of the protection supplied, and should take into consideration the conditions of the state as a whole;
— the introduction of measures against corruption and other administrative pathologies and the creation of appropriate mechanisms to enforce law in this respect.

The government will not take any global decisions on the issues listed above. The matters for reform are far too extensive, complex and internally differentiated. Above that, they cannot be considered in isolation from other tasks and areas for which the state is responsible (see, for example, some of the priority tasks recently identified by the Polish government). In this situation we should expect and hope that not only the government, but also the political forces in Parliament approach these problems as a systematic, and not a speculative, attempt to sort out and rebuild public administration. Suffice to say that this describes a long-term task.

It is up to the Government Plenipotentiary for Public Administration Reform to ensure the most important part of the groundwork by inspiring and co-ordinating the activities of the various authorities and circles involved in the reform process, by undertaking analyses and preparing projects, by elaborating plans and setting schedules for the reform process in its various aspects (the calculation of costs, *inter alia*), by making sure that the partial changes introduced in the meantime do not collide with the overall objectives of public sector reform, by securing and co-ordinating foreign assistance, and finally by designing adequate information and educational policies.

It should be added that in most areas, the reform requires not only the preparation of a new legal framework, but also, and above all, the creation of new institutions, new attitudes, habits, techniques, administrative routines, methods of collaboration within the administration and with external partners. In some areas change must be preceded by preparations of an analytical and practical nature (i.e. facts and not only programmes or resolutions). These tasks will only be fulfilled with competence and efficiency through the intensive co-operation and active participation of all central and decentralized state and local government organs, and all the other circles, associations or organizations concerned with reform. Last and not least, the whole process will succeed only if all the main political actors in Poland express clear and unambiguous support for the general framework.

One of the main challenges (and at the same time a condition for the implementation of reform at all levels) of the process of public administration reform is to promulgate within society the habit of thinking in categories of the public interest, to create a positive feeling towards the values which inspire action for the common good, and finally to reinforce the idea that public administration is above all a service to the community.

TRANSFORMING CZECHOSLOVAKIAN PUBLIC ADMINISTRATION: TRADITIONS AND NEW CHALLENGES

DUŠAN HENDRYCH

I INTRODUCTION

The traditions of public administration in (the former) Czechoslovakia reach deeply back in history, and they are closely connected with administrative developments in other European countries, particularly her Central European neighbours and France. The most important elements of this tradition include the establishment of an effective administrative state structure on the one hand; and the development of an independent sphere of local and territorial self-government on the other, connected, particularly in Bohemia and Moravia, with the historical rights of the Bohemian crown and the requirements of independence (Bauer 1991; Maly 1986).

In economic terms, Czechoslovakia was, at the turn of the century, a state with a highly developed industry and with a remarkably productive agricultural sector. After 1918, Czechoslovakia ranked amongst the most industrialized countries in the world, with a developed market economy and a comparatively high standard of living for the majority of the population, especially in Bohemia and Moravia. In the Slovak part of the country, however, economic conditions were much less favourable, with a scarcely developed industrial base and a decidedly weaker agricultural sector.

II PUBLIC ADMINISTRATION, 1918–39: AN OVERVIEW

During the interwar period, public administration in Czechoslovakia still exhibited many of the traits inherited from the Austro-Hungarian Empire. However, unlike in many other European states during that time, public administration retained a consistently democratic and legal character. Judicial control of public

Dušan Hendrych is Professor of Public Law in the Law Faculty of Charles University, Prague.

administration; a significant degree of self-government at all lower levels, including the lands; qualified officials; and a developed administrative culture – all these factors offered hope for further cautious reforms, particularly towards progressive democratization and the solution of national and ethnic problems. In organizational terms, public administration was founded on the traditional Central European model of a duality of state administration and local self-government; in legal terms, the central basis was provided by the Constitution of the Czechoslovak Republic of 1920, which defined the new state as a parliamentary republic.

The organization of public administration in Czechoslovakia was not uniform. There were differences in administrative organization between the so-called 'historical countries' (or 'the countries of the Bohemian Crown'), i.e. Bohemia, Moravia, Silesia on the one hand, and Slovakia and Subcarpathian Ruthenia on the other. They reflected the distinct historical development of the two parts of the new unitary state. Efforts to unify these different administrative systems were only partly successful; some progress towards harmonization was achieved in organizational structures, but the diverse legal bases, grounded in historical differences between Austrian and Hungarian law, remained largely unchanged.

During the interwar years, the main administrative institutions included:

— the organs of the state, i.e. central government and the ministries, other state authorities at the level of the lands and the districts, and professional state authorities;
— organs of territorial self-government, including the lands, representative districts, and localities;
— self-governing corporations in the professional, economic and social spheres, based on the principle of mutuality; and
— private subjects in cases specified by law or by a public law agreement.

In this differentiated structure, one particular problem concerned the definition of an intermediate level of state administration. The Province Act of 1920 envisaged the creation of 20 regions (or provinces); however, in the face of strong political resistance, the Act was only partly implemented. Opposition to the Act came from two sides, both nationalist in character: centralists, who insisted on a strictly unitary state without any autonomous structures, and autonomist and separatist forces, the more extreme of which clamoured for the break-up of the new state. Thus, in 1927, a new Act on the Organization of State Administration was adopted, which represented a far-reaching revision of the Province Act. The new law sought to reduce the tensions between centralists and autonomists by the re-introduction of the historical land organization. Under this legislation, four lands were established – Bohemia, Moravia with Silesia, Slovakia and Subcarpathian Ruthenia – which formed administrative units, with their own juridical identity. The lands themselves were subdivided into districts, which represented administrative units of the lower tier, with state or communal district authorities (Bianchi 1978; Lipscher 1979).

The 1927 Act strengthened state administration vis-à-vis the higher levels of self-government. Representative bodies at the land and district level were empowered to deal with economic and social issues, but were precluded from addressing explicitly political questions. Such representative bodies included boards (with two-thirds of elected members and one-third of appointed professionals), committees and commissions.

The introduction of the land organization was largely justified by reference to historical traditions. In spite of this, however, it did not provide a satisfactory solution to the complex nationality problems. In the broader European context, the period of 1918–39 saw these problems gradually develop into separatist movements inimical to the state.

The war and the Communist era stopped the development towards a more decentralized state power. The further development of public administration in Czechoslovakia took an entirely different course, based on values which were fundamentally at odds with those that had previously informed administrative development.

III   THE IMMEDIATE POST-WAR CHANGES, 1945–49

Already towards the end of World War II, the administrative changes required in the post-war years began to be discussed. Unsurprisingly, opinion differed regarding the necessary degree of continuity or discontinuity with the pre-war administrative structures, with the future status of local government being particularly contentious. The Communists and their allies amongst left-wing social democrats rejected the principle of duality in public administration and argued vigorously for the establishment of national committees as the organs of the sovereign power of the people. The Presidential Decree on National Committees and the Provisional National Assembly of 1944 largely followed their views.

As a result, Soviet-type National Committees replaced the previous system of distinct spheres of state administration and self-government, although the veil of duality was maintained in the beginning. The intention of the pro-Communist forces was evident, however: to destroy the 'bourgeois' state organization and to create a monolithic, hierarchically structured system for the exercise of state power, which would be vertically and horizontally intermeshed with the apparatus of the Communist Party. The possibility of a diversified public administration was effectively eliminated; in its stead, the foundations for a uniform state administration, comprising all levels of public administration, were laid. Until 1949, there existed a three-tier structure of national committees at the land, district and local levels. Their administrative competence was generally universal, i.e. they were the only organs to exercise public administration in their territories.

Administrative change in the immediate post-war period was not restricted to the territorial organization of state administration. Changes also took place at the central level, primarily in response to the perceived requirements of post-war reconstruction and the promotion of a planned economy. As early as 1945, new types of central authorities began to be created. They included, *inter alia*, the Economic Council as the central organ for formulating and co-ordinating economic policy, and the State Planning Authority. Formally, these two new authorities had no decision-making powers; informally, however, their power was considerable. Gradually, authorities of this type developed into the cornerstones of an extensive economic state administration, embodying centralism and administrative control over the economy.

IV   PUBLIC ADMINISTRATION, 1949–68

The Communist take-over of February 1948 represented the most important milestone for the further development of public administration in Czechoslovakia, though it did not result in any immediate changes in state administration. To be sure, increasing political pressure was brought to bear on public employees at all levels of the administration, but structural changes along the lines of the Soviet model were only made in the course of 1949 on the basis of the new constitution of May 1948. These changes need to be seen in the context of the resolution of the congress of the Communist Party on the general guide-lines for the establishment of socialism in Czechoslovakia, according to which one of the chief tasks was the 'consolidation of the people's democratic state power'. The principle promoter of the process of socialization was the central government, which almost immediately began restructuring public administration.

The legal basis for the subsequent structural transformation in central administration was provided by a Constitutional Act of 1950 No. 47/1950 COL on the changes in the organization of public administration. For decades, this Act provided the legal foundation which allowed the government to create, merge or abolish central administrative institutions and to decide on their competences by means of a simple governmental order subject only to the consent of the President. The 1950 Act also brought about substantial changes to the 1948 Constitution, which up to this point had not, at least in formal terms, been entirely at variance with European constitutionalism and, more specifically, Czechoslovak constitutional traditions, although it already displayed many of the traits of the Soviet constitutional conception.

The principal motivating force behind the changes in central and territorial state administration was the desire to copy the Soviet model of economic controls by means of central planning and to ensure the effective implementation of economic policies. This dirigism resulted in the establishment of a new type of state authority, the so-called economic ministries. These ministries controlled directly and comprehensively all production enterprises in certain sectors (for example, engineering industry, power generation or agriculture). As was already briefly mentioned above, additional central economic authorities were established, which were primarily concerned with tasks such as planning, capital construction, or technical development at both central and lower levels.

Throughout the period under consideration, administrative development in

Czechoslovakia was intimately linked with political developments in the Soviet Union. As a result, political changes in the Soviet Union during the first half of the 1950s and a certain improvement in the political climate were also reflected in Czechoslovakian public administration. In 1956, some measures were adopted which were designed to restrict excessive centralization of decision making by the economic ministries. This was followed by more significant changes in 1958. The individual departments in the economic ministries (the so-called main administrations controlling the individual industrial branches subordinated to the ministry) were abolished, and operative management was transferred to newly formed 'production units'. They concentrated the enterprises of the same production branch in an integral unit which separated from the ministerial structure.

Turning to territorial administration, a number of important changes, in particular regarding the national committees, need to be mentioned. In the first place, the 1948 Constitution recognized the national committees as part of the uniform system of representative bodies, as the representatives of state power in communities, districts, and new regions, and as the sole organ of public administration in all respects, except in the cases explicitly provided for by the law. Secondly, the new constitution brought about significant changes in the territorial organization of state power. The lands were abolished and replaced by regions as the intermediate tier of public administration. The chief purpose of this change was not to decentralize administration but, on the contrary, to ensure effective control over lower level administrative units. That was also the reason why the control of national committees was entrusted to the central government.

In 1960, a new, 'socialist' constitution was adopted. In the field of local administration, it resulted in yet another change to the territorial division of the state. The number of regions and districts was reduced, in the hope of strengthening their economic and political position. However, this did not have any practical consequences, as the planning monopoly of the central authorities was not reduced and the power monopoly of the Communist Party remained unquestioned. The enlarged districts faced the difficulty of having to control effectively the activities of the larger number of communes in their territories. At that time, the neuralgic points of territorial organization were already apparent: the internal administrative organization of communities, the need to reduce their number, and, perhaps most importantly, the separation of local administration from central administration and a concomitant increase of local financial and administrative powers (Sojka and Tomsová 1969).

V   PUBLIC ADMINISTRATION, 1968–89

The year 1968 saw an attempt to achieve a fundamental political and economic reform of the Stalinist type of socialism and a constitutional change in the organization of the Czechoslovak state. However, 1968 also marked the beginning of the period of 'normalization', i.e. the conservation of political, administrative and social structures. It is ironic that the proclamation of the rights of national self-determination seemed to be exchanged for restrictions in human rights and basic freedoms.

The Constitutional Act on the Czechoslovak Federation in 1968 was intended to satisfy the Slovaks' desire for national identity and state sovereignty. With this Act, the previously unitary state was transformed into a federal state with two constituent members. The new state was initially conceived as a relatively loose association of the two national economies with complete state authorities at the level of the two member Republics; in constitutional terms, the constituent Republics enjoyed broad competences compared to the federal authorities, particularly in the field of executive power.

As regards administrative organization, federalization brought about the following main changes:

— the formation of two separate spheres of state administration, federal and republican, the relations of which were not those of subordination but co-operation;
— the competences of the previously unitary state were divided between the Federation and its constituent Republics. The legislative and executive powers of the federal authorities were enumerated in the constitutional act (in exceptional cases also in subsequent ordinary acts);
— local administration was generally within the jurisdiction of the Republics, and the republican governments managed and controlled the activities of the national committees. The federal government and its organs could perform activities on the territory of the Republics only on the basis of explicit legal authorization;
— both the Federation and its member states established their own legislative, executive and judicial authority and exercised their powers within the limits of their competences (Hendrych 1972; Jicinsky 1991).

In 1970, the initial federal concept was partly modified at the cost of the member states, in conformity with the process of normalization. The increase in the powers of the central federal authorities corresponded with the political and economic ideas of dirigism, which aimed at the conservation of the old order. This step resulted in the gradual deterioration in the relations between the two Republics, which, however, could manifest itself openly only after the changes of November 1989.

Whilst reform attempts in central administration aimed more or less at improvements through rationalization, at the level of local administration there was an attempt to give the impression of increasing self-government and democracy. Preparations for more far-ranging changes in local government date from the beginning of the 1970s. The main changes, which were carried out gradually and with numerous restrictions imposed by the highest political authorities, consisted mainly of the following measures:

— a reduction in the number of local administrations through the amalgamation of localities and the establishment of joint authorities, combined with the building up of 'settlement-centres' as the natural focus of social and economic life in their surrounding territories;

— decentralization of powers and competences, particularly to settlement-centres and towns, accompanied by increased economic and financial independence;

— the categorization of towns and cities into three groups and the subsequent differentiation of their status within the system of national committees;

— the redefinition of the task of lower-tier national committees in the comprehensive social and economic development of territorial units.

In spite of these partial measures and the growing activities of various reform groups, particularly in the economic sphere, the Czechoslovak regime after 1968 showed an almost complete inability to transform and adapt. Political changes were ruled out, economic changes were kept to an absolute minimum and the Communist hierarchy was to be preserved at almost any price.

VI   PRINCIPAL TRENDS OF THE CURRENT REFORM PROCESSES

Since 1989 Czechoslovakia has faced a number of economic, political, and administrative challenges. They include the need to achieve further progress in economic reform, whilst paying attention to its implications for social stability and employment; the need to reconsider the territorial organization of the Czechoslovak state, eventually resulting in the break-up of the Federation; and the demands for a territorial re-organization of the Czech Republic. These challenges still tend to dominate the administrative reform agenda, in particular the discussion on its future tasks and structures.

Amongst the changes in the administrative environment which have a direct effect on public administration, it is first of all necessary to take account of the transformation in the system of government, i.e. the transition from the state governed centrally and by dirigist methods to a democratic state based on the rule of law. This implies, for example, the need to create an effective constitutional and administrative judiciary, a system for the control of the use of state funds which is independent from executive power (independent auditing), and proper administrative supervision of the operation of lower level public authorities. One important attribute of a democratic state and an open society consists in the performance of certain administrative tasks by self-governmental units; their status and competences need to be derived from the constitution or from law, which awards them certain institutional guarantees and ensures the necessary stability.

Turning to economic change, it is clear that the organization of the economy in the former socialist countries had the most profound impact on the tasks and organization of public administration. Czechoslovakia was the most 'socialized' country in Central and Eastern Europe; its industry, agriculture and virtually the whole tertiary sector were owned either by the state or by co-operatives (in the Marxist conception). The private sector was practically non-existent, and private property was all but liquidated. The centralist and highly detailed system of controls over the economy required extensive administrative staff, whose professional and political profile rarely conformed with current ideas of a civic society and public administration.

If Czech and Slovak public administration is to play a constructive role in the political, social and economic reform process, it is imperative to

— reassess its tasks, with a view to bringing them in line with the standards of other European democracies based on market-type economies;
— re-define the responsibilities of the different levels and branches of public administration; this includes the development of effective judicial controls over administrative authorities and competent supervision by higher administrative authorities over the operation of lower level units;
— create an administrative culture which is informed by the virtues of economy, efficiency, effectiveness, professionalism and an orientation towards citizens' needs.

Obviously, all this requires adequate technical equipment and a satisfactory information basis for administrative decision-making. Most importantly, however, it calls for investment in human capital through improved training and re-training. At the moment, a number of new initiatives in this respect are under consideration, but a clear line has not yet developed (Hesse 1991).

Until now, the discussion on the reform of the administrative systems has focused largely on the following issues:

1   Decentralization

It will be necessary to determine the division of competences between central and decentralized administrations both with regard to those traditional tasks of the public sector which remain more or less unaffected by the political and economic changes and the new tasks of public administration in a democratic, market-oriented system. This applies to the vertical distribution of competences in state administration as well as to the allocation of powers and responsibilities between state institutions, on the one hand, and organs of local self-government, on the other. At the same time, the issue of whether certain administrative tasks can be handed over to semi-public or private institutions needs to be considered. In this context, it must be remembered that in the socialist system state administration was almost invariably performed by the state through its authorities; only in very exceptional cases were non-state institutions entrusted with carrying out administrative activities on behalf of the state.

2   Deregulation

The socialist management and control system created a need for permanent regulation, the setting of specific rules of behaviour for citizens and institutions and a detailed regulation for sanctioning individual and institutional conduct. These regulations pervaded all levels of public administration as well as economic and social life. The high degree of centralization and the great number of ministries and other central authorities which were the hallmark of the socialist administrative system can be interpreted as direct results of the systemic requirement for detailed control. The restriction of legal reglementation and excessive regulation, in particular through secondary legal acts issued by the government and the ministries, has to be one of the prime aims of administrative and constitutional reform, and it needs to be accompanied by corresponding adjustments in administrative structures.

3 Administrative personnel

The creation of a new civil service ranks among the principal tasks of administrative reform, as improvements in administrative performance depend, to a large extent, on the abilities and skills of administrative personnel at all levels of the public sector. So far, however, progress in this respect has at best been partial and has tended to be more or less accidental. Apart from improved in-service training, which includes systematic retraining of most of the present staff, it is crucial to develop a modern system of high-level, university education for public administrators, both generalists and specialists. First steps in this direction have been taken in the form of lectures on administrative sciences in the faculties of law, the establishment of special faculties for public administration and local economy at a number of universities, and the incorporation of public administration into the curriculum of the economic universities. It is clear, however, that these can only be first steps and that the problem requires more sustained attention and action than it has received so far.

4 Legislation

The Czechoslovak legal system has been based on the principle of continuity, i.e. step-by-step, gradual processes of normative adaptation. The exceptional legislative activity during the last years resembles the dynamic periods of 1918–23 and 1945–50 during which the normative corpus was fundamentally changed within five to six years. The main aims of the recent reconstruction of the legal system include the achievement of internationally recognized standards of civil rights and basic freedoms and the creation of legal guarantees for their observation and effective protection; and the creation of the necessary legal framework for economic restructuring. The latter includes, *inter alia*, the privatization of national property and the development of private enterprise as well as legal guarantees for foreign investors.

The speed of economic and political reform legislation is not as high as many would wish, though, since the task facing legislators is an extremely difficult one. Foreign models and experience are valuable and inspiring, but they can only exceptionally be incorporated into the given legal system without substantial modifications. This is perhaps the principal obstacle to a more speedy process in the preparation of reform legislation, and it also explains many

TABLE 1   Legislation passed by federal, Slovak and Czech authorities 1990/91

Acts passed by federal authorities:	1990	1991	Total
laws	50	44	94
amendments to laws	62	27	89
by-laws, directives, etc.	194	128	322
Acts passed by Czech authorities:			
laws	32	36	68
amendments to laws	15	26	41
by-laws, directives, etc.	92	132	224
Acts passed by Slovak authorities:			
laws	44	32	76
amendments to laws	11	22	33
by-laws, directives, etc.	80	111	191

of the errors which have been made. It is also inevitable that reform legislation is the subject of party political controversy. Here it has not just been the differences between left-wing and right-wing parties which need to be mentioned, but also, and perhaps more importantly, the conflicts between the parties representing the Czech part of the country and those representing Slovakia. At the federal level, these conflicts between representatives from the two republics resulted in a slowing down of the decision-making process on constitutional and economic issues.

Table 1 helps to illustrate the exceptional legislative activity during 1990 and 1991. Amongst the most important legislative measures at the federal level the following deserve a particular mention:

— The revision of the constitution which aimed at eliminating its 'socialist' principles (for example, the leading role of the Communist Party in state and society) and laid the legal foundations for the transition to an open society and the establishment of democratic institutions (for example, the establishment of a sphere of local self-government). Another important change in the constitution guaranteed all types of property the same status and the same protection (Constitutional Amendment on Property Rights). For the structure of public administration, the provisions of the constitution on the division of powers between the Federation and the Republics were of particular importance. However, the constitutional changes of 1990 did obviously not represent a satisfactory solution; therefore the problem of the division of competences has become a neuralgic point in the relations between the

Federation and the Republics. Other important pieces of constitutional reform legislation concerned the establishment of a Constitutional Court and the law on the referendum.

— The Constitutional Act introducing the Bill of Basic Rights and Freedoms (No. 23/1991 COL). This Act also contained provisions that were of immediate relevance to the legal system as a whole. Thus,

  (i) all constitutional Acts, laws and further legal rules, their interpretation and their application must conform to the Bill of Basic Rights and Freedoms. All laws and other legal rules had to be harmonized with the Bill of Basic Rights and Freedoms by 31 December, 1991. On that day, all provisions not conforming to the Bill of Basic Rights and Freedoms ceased to be effective. Basic rights and freedoms came under the protection of the Constitutional Court;

  (ii) international treaties on human rights and basic freedoms, ratified and promulgated by the Czech and Slovak Federal Republic, are generally obligatory in its territory and take precedence over Czechoslovak law.

— Amongst further laws concerning civil rights, mention should be made of the laws on petition rights, on the right of assembly, on the right of association, on political parties and movements, on elections, on the acquisition and loss of citizenship, on judicial rehabilitation, and on extra-judicial rehabilitation as well as the new versions of the Civil Code, the Code of Civil Judicial Procedure (including the provisions on administrative panels in general courts) and, finally, the Penal Code.

— Amongst the laws that created the prerequisites for the transformation of the Czechoslovak economy, at least the following should be mentioned: the new Commercial Code, the laws on 'small' and 'big' privatization, the law on joint-stock companies, the foreign exchange law, the customs law, the law on cheques and bills, the bankruptcy law, and the laws introducing a new system of taxation.

As regards the legal framework of public administration, it is necessarily of a transitional nature. Some laws, however, are likely to have a long-term impact and they should briefly be mentioned. The new division of competences between the Federation and the Republics undoubtedly strengthened the latters' executive power, particularly through the transfer of much of what remains of economic administration to the republican governments and ministries. On this basis, the republican Parliaments have adopted several laws concerning, *inter alia*, the structure of the central republican administrations and the competences of individual authorities. Of even greater significance however, are the republican laws on local government and the laws on district authorities as the territorial organs of general state administration. Finally, mention should be made of a number of other laws which provided the basis for some special administrative authorities, e.g. tax offices, labour offices, or trade authorities.

5   Changes in the structure of central and subcentral administrative authority

Until the end of 1992 the central administrations at both the federal and republican levels followed a common structure: government – ministry (or another central authority at the same level) – lower state administrative authorities. However, differences existed in the scope of their competences, and they manifested themselves also in the relations between central and local administrations. Both (state) local administration and territorial self-government were, although to different degrees, within the competence of the republican legislative and executive authorities. This applies also to specific public authorities and their institutions. Federal authorities were allowed to act in the territory of the Republics only as professional organs, unless their activities were not explicitly within the competence of the federal executive authorities, such as customs or army administration.

The most serious change in the structure of public administration has certainly been the reform of local government. Its purpose is to separate state administration from territorial self-administration. The previous system of National Committees as organs of state executive power has been abolished and self-government has been introduced in towns and localities. These units have become independent legal subjects and have obtained the authority to exercise public administration. In 1991, there were 5,745 towns and localities in the Czech Republic and 2,830 in the Slovak Republic. However, the reform of local administration has not yet been completed. General political authorities have been established only at the level of the districts of which there are 75 in the Czech Republic and 38 in the Slovak Republic. These territorial units are not, however, large enough to be able to carry out an effective regional policy and integrated local administration. Different solutions to these problems are prepared in both Republics. The situation is more complicated in the Czech Republic (Illner 1991), which is larger than the Slovak Republic and where there is, moreover, a certain pressure to recreate the former land administrations. This would mean the creation of two or three lands in the framework of the Czech Republic; the lands themselves would be subdivided into districts and communities. Another possible alternative, which is close to Slovak ideas, is the transformation of the existing districts into major regions; according to current proposals, their number would be somewhere between 15 and 30 in the whole of the Czech Republic. At the moment, the questions of upper-tier units of self-government, particularly at the land level, and their potential competences remain open. Since they touch upon constitutional questions, problems can only be resolved within the framework of a new constitution for the Czech Republic.

The prevailing view so far has been that land organizations should indeed be restored in the Czech Republic. For this purpose, a bill on land self-government has been put before the Czech National Council; according to this bill the lands should represent a second tier of territorial self-government. The draft bill proposes the establishment of three lands: Bohemia, Moravia and Silesia. Such a solution would be chiefly based on political reasons and on the traditions of land administration, dating back to the time of the Austro-Hungarian Empire (Bauer 1991) and pre-war Czechoslovakia (Lipscher 1979).

In this respect it is interesting to consider public opinion in the Czech Republic as it is documented in a survey organized by the Institute of Sociology at the Czechoslovak Academy of Sciences. From this opinion survey, it is evident that the population agrees only partly with the solution just described. The relations between Bohemia, Moravia and Silesia are considered important, but popular opinion in the Czech Republic does not rank them as amongst the most urgent and most serious problems to be solved at present. Amongst 13 selected items, including the transition to a market economy, social security or environmental protection, territorial organization ranked only tenth in importance. Territorial organization was considered a serious and urgent problem by 31 per cent of the population in the Czech Republic. There were, however, important differences between the three major territories comprising the Czech Republic. Thus, in Moravia, the problem of territorial organization was considered serious and urgent by 40 per cent of the population, whilst the corresponding figures for Bohemia and Silesia were 27 per cent and 28 per cent respectively. Here, as in many other issues, the similarity of opinions in the population of Bohemia and Silesia is clearly evident.

As regards the preferred type of territorial organization, no clear preferences have emerged. In Bohemia and Silesia, the regional organization, which assumes the creation of between 15 and 30 administrative regions without a land tier, commands the highest support (37 per cent). The second most widely supported type is the land variant in various modifications (28 per cent). Only 23 per cent of those polled in Bohemia and Silesia supported the replacement of the present Czech Republic with a Bohemian Republic and a Moravia-Silesian Republic. As regards the second tier of territorial self-government, a majority of the population in the Czech Republic supported the establishment of representative district boards, with their own budget and property. The current distribution of political forces makes changes in territorial administrative organization and local government very likely; but it is still too early to discuss potential solutions and their possible variants.

REFERENCES

Bauer, H. 1991. 'Reviving local government in Austria', in J. J. Hesse (ed.) *Local government and urban affairs in international perspective*. Baden-Baden: Nomos.

Bianchi, L. 1978. 'Weiterbestand der munizipalen Gauverwaltung auf dem Gebiete der Slowakei in den Jahren 1918–1928', in K. Kovács (ed.) *Entwicklung der städtischen und regionalen Verwaltung in den letzten 100 Jahren in Mittel- und Osteuropa*. Budapest: Universität Eotvos Loránd.

Hendrych, D. 1972. 'Central organs of state administration in the Czechoslovak Socialist Republic', *Bulletin of Czechoslovak Law* 1–2, 5–17.

Hesse, J. J. 1991. 'Administrative modernisation in Central and Eastern European Countries', in *Staatswissenschaften und Staatspraxis* 2, 197–217.

Illner, M. 1991. 'Problems of local government in the Czech Republic', in G. Petéri (ed.) *Events and changes*. Budapest: LDI Foundation.

Jicinsky, Z. 1991. 'Grundlegende Entwicklungsprobleme der tschechoslowakischen Föderation', in J. J. Hesse and W. Renzsch (eds.) *Föderalstaatliche Entwicklung in Europa*. Baden-Baden: Nomos.

Lipscher, L. 1979. *Verfassung und politische Verwaltung in der Tschechoslowakei 1918–1939*. Munich-Vienna.

Maly, K. 1986. 'Zur Entwicklung der Selbstverwaltung in den böhmischen Ländern in den Jahren 1848 bis 1915', *Die Verwaltung* 19.

Sojka, A. and J. Tomsová. 1969. 'Die Entwicklung der Staatsverwaltung nach 1945 in der CSSR', *Die Verwaltung* 2.

ADMINISTRATIVE MODERNIZATION IN CZECHOSLOVAKIA BETWEEN CONSTITUTIONAL AND ECONOMIC REFORM

RICHARD POMAHAČ

I CONSTITUTION AND ECONOMY IN TRANSITION

The starting point of the present discussion is the year 1988, when the now defunct Czechoslovak Communist Party launched a project of constitutional reconstruction aiming at the genuine federalization of the Czechoslovak state. It was also in 1988 that the new federal government, headed by Prime Minister Adamec, for the first time openly acknowledged the need for fundamental economic reform, attacking excessive centralization and a lack of self-management in the economy. Both projects, constitutional and economic reform, however, ran into the opposition of the old ruling élite, which refused to contemplate change of any kind. As a result, efforts to reform the political and economic system from within were unsuccessful. There was, though, a political opposition that was prepared for exactly such a task, and in the end, the Communist regime collapsed almost overnight.

Until mid-November 1989, all positions of state power were under the control of the Communist Party. Yet, only a week after the police assault on student demonstrators on 17 November 1989 in Prague, which sparked off protests and strikes throughout Czechoslovakia, the entire leadership of the Czechoslovak Communist Party had resigned. Four days later, on 28 November, the Civic Forum, which had emerged as the main Czech opposition movement, was legalized. The next day, the Federal Assembly resolved that the leading role of the Communist Party and Marxism-Leninism as the guiding principles of education and teaching should be deleted from the constitution. The termination of the Communist Party's constitutional monopoly of power was quickly followed by the progressive relinquishing of the leading offices of state. On 7 December 1989, Prime Minister Adamec resigned, having failed to form a

Dr Richard Pomahač is Senior Lecturer in Public Administration in the Law Faculty of Charles University, Prague.

government in which the opposition forces were offered the status of a junior partner. In his place Marian Calfa, a member of the Communist Party (he resigned from the Party in January 1990), was appointed Prime Minister. On 10 December 1989, a new federal government was formed, with a majority of non-Communist ministers. President Husak resigned on the same day. At the level of the two Republics, governments with non-Communist majorities were formed under the Czech Prime Minister Pithart and his Slovak counterpart Cic on 5 and 12 December 1989 respectively. The change in the leadership of the country was completed after the elections to the bicameral Federal Assembly and the Czech and Slovak National Councils, held on 8/9 June 1990, which produced clear mandates for the former opposition movement.

From the very beginning of the transition process, two problems dominated the agenda: federalism versus unitarity in political reform, and gradualism versus radicalism in economic reform. As regards the former, the first draft of a new federal constitution was published by the Civic Forum immediately after the takeover of power in December 1989. However, it became evident very soon that this draft did not enjoy the support of a broad majority amongst the reformist forces, primarily because its conception of a federal state order resembled too closely that which had been adopted in the 1968 constitution, but partly also because it provided a wider scope for social and economic rights than the socially and economically more conservative elements in the former opposition movement were prepared to contemplate.

The course of constitutional and economic reform took a new direction in April 1990. As regards economic reform, the first major reshuffle in Calfa's Cabinet signalled a move towards more radical economic solutions than those that had thus far been proposed. At the same time, the two republican governments began to meet to discuss the Federation's further constitutional future without the presence of the federal government. This should be the beginning of the process in which the initiative moved increasingly towards the republican level, making it more and more difficult for the federal government to influence the fate of the Federation. It should, however, be realized that in 1990 economic reform still overshadowed the constitutional issues surrounding the reform of the Federation. In fact, many argued that the constitutional reform of the Federation should be postponed until the most immediate economic problems had been tackled.

The main tasks of the federal government in the economic sphere were set out in very strict terms by the then Federal Minister of Finance, Vaclav Klaus (1991, pp. 12–13):

> The new Czechoslovak government of national understanding declared that the only feasible solution to the economic problem is to accept the market as a basic dominating principle of our future economic system. The Czechoslovak economists, therefore, stress the difference between the so-called instrumental concept of the market, on the one hand, and the genuine market, on the other, and with this difference in mind they warn against an irresponsible use of the word market in the Eastern European

reform rhetoric. Our long and extremely negative experience with the Czechoslovak 'Road to serfdom' makes us radical and impatient. We hope that we are now 'free to choose' and we have, therefore, decided that our choice is a market economy without any complicating or obfuscating adjectives added to the word market. So far such a radical economic ideology has not provoked any negative reaction of the Czechoslovak public and it must be a permanent task of the new government to explain it and to defend it against its critics.

It soon became clear, however, that the constitutional issue could not be postponed until economic reforms had been pushed through, and it also became transparent that the economic reform process would be much more prolonged and controversial than many had initially assumed. As a result, the original timetable for economic reform and a revision of federal arrangements soon became obsolete. Thus, it had initially been expected that by the end of 1991 at the latest, the Federal Assembly and the Czech and Slovak National Councils should have adopted three new constitutions for the Federation and the two Republics, as a logical triangle providing a stable and lasting foundation for a new legal system. In the economic sphere, the process of voucher privatization and the restitution of property should have gone hand-in-hand with other forms of privatization. Also, parallel to the steps in economic reform, clear strategic concepts should have emerged in the social sphere and concerning industrial and environmental restructuring. As regards the former, the idea had been to create a system of legislative and administrative guarantees in close collaboration with trade unions to cushion the effects of economic reform on the individual. Concerning restructuring, there was a clear understanding that industrial and, in particular, environmental reconstruction could not be left to the market alone, but would require decisive government action.

All this, obviously, placed huge demands on public administration, but an insufficient legal framework, an acute shortage of experienced personnel, and discredited institutions made it very difficult to adjust to the new demands, and in particular to the need to mediate interest conflicts (Matula 1991). This raises the question of what kind of legal and institutional changes are required in order to promote the transition from a dirigist administration to the structures and methods typically associated with a democratic government under the rule of law. Evidently, there can be no simple answer to this question, not least because the transitional period itself calls for a different role for public administration than that which is eventually to be achieved.

Returning to the issues of federalization and economic reform, first steps were taken in 1990 to create a real 'dual' federation through the adoption of a constitutional law which redistributed executive powers between the two Republics and the Federation. Perhaps not surprisingly, the practical implications of this law were disputed from the start. At the same time, in the economic sphere, reform legislation gained in momentum throughout 1990, resulting in major legislation towards the end of 1990 and in the first half of 1991.

This included:

— the first and second Restitution Law and the first and second Privatization Law (October 1990–February 1991),
— the Anti-Monopoly Law (January 1991),
— the Land Privatization Law (May 1991), and
— the amendment of the Civil Code and a new Commercial Code (November 1991).

All these acts were adopted under conditions of political fragmentation in the Federal Assembly. Increasingly, the old antagonism between ex-Communists and the former opposition forces was replaced by political conflict over the speed and direction of economic reform between conservative forces and advocates of a more 'social-liberal' approach. Those identified with the conservative tendency stressed the need to achieve a market economy without any complications or obfuscating adjectives, and they ruled out any discussion on the basic strategy of the economic reform. In their view, the transition should be simple, speedy and fundamental. On the other side, advocates of a more social-liberal approach argued in favour of a reform strategy that would be flexible and open to discussion of alternatives; in their view, there was no need for unnecessarily hurrying the decision-making process. In the event, reform legislation was adopted very quickly, but it often left the most controversial or complicated issues unaddressed. Thus, parliamentary fragmentation was reflected in fragmented laws. The first political casualty of the new political constellation was the Slovak Prime Minister Meciar, who was dismissed from office by a narrow majority of votes in the Slovak Parliament in April 1991.

II   PRIVATIZATION AND DECENTRALIZATION

Privatization and decentralization tend to be studied as two separate problems. However, in the case of Czechoslovakia, there are good reasons for looking at the two problems together. As was indicated above, the reform proposals of 1988 were presented as decentralization without privatization. Since then, of course, privatization has moved to the centre of the economic reform agenda. Both decentralization and privatization have involved different types of innovations – radical, reformist, destructive, restorative, marginal, and in some cases even reversive. A radical type of innovation is certainly the replacement of the concept of polysectoral structural change, which would have aimed at some kind of balance between the public, semi-public and the private sectors, with an approach favouring radical privatization. Considering that until the end of the 1980s the Czechoslovak economy was almost entirely in public ownership, the rate of change has been remarkable. Thus, by the end of 1991, the private sector already accounted for 17.7 per cent of the labour force, and this figure has continued to rise rapidly since.

From the point of view of public administration, it is important to realize that privatization and property restitution as radically managed processes have taken up much of the administrative capacities of the central authorities.

The examination of property restitution claims is a complex, time-consuming and highly controversial task. Privatization, on the other hand, equally requires both administrative expertise and takes up a significant part of central administrative personnel. In so far as it is possible to pass judgement at this stage, the administration appears to have handled both processes rather well. The first wave of privatization based on the voucher model will come to an end in the winter of 1992/3, and it is likely that this procedure will be repeated with the rest of state-owned property in 1993/4. This is not to say, of course, that privatization has not been the subject of a broad and critical debate which has concerned both the methods for privatizing as well as the handling of individual privatization projects. On the whole, public opinion in the Czech lands is much more favourably disposed towards privatization than in Slovakia. Czechs tend to emphasize the potential benefits of privatization, such as increased competition and an improved supply of goods and services, whilst Slovak respondents often fear that privatization leads to profiteering and the selling out to foreigners.

In connection with this discussion, mention should be made of the unprecedented law suit filed against the government in connection with the privatization of the Karlovy Vary porcelain works. Here, the firm's management argued that the government did not act in the best interest of the firm when it decided to divide up the enterprise for the purpose of privatization. The government had argued that the issue was outside the jurisdiction of the court, since privatization disputes were at the discretion of the owner of the company, which, in this case, was the state. However, the Czech Supreme Court did not follow this line of argument, and fined both the Czech government and the Czech Ministry of Privatization for contempt of court. Until a final verdict is reached, the relevant privatization prospects approved by the government have been halted. The problems surrounding the privatization of Karlovy Vary have already led to revisions in the privatization procedures, affecting both the direct selling of state property and larger privatization. The essential aim of the privatization project has, however, remained the same – decentralization of property.

Turning from economic conditions to constitutional reform, the dominant development has certainly been institutional decentralization. Here the original strategy of reform was one of restoration rather than radical change, but as events over the last year or so have shown, the process has become increasingly radicalized. Part of the explanation of the move towards a break-up of the Federation can certainly be found in the characteristics of the Czechoslovak Federation itself. First, it needs to be remembered that Czechoslovakia originated as a unitary state which was only federalized in 1968, after fifty years of its existence. Second, the fundamental principle of the Federation was the national question, that is the relations between the Czech and Slovak nations. Finally, the Federation always represented a unique bipartite system, the coherence of which was dependent on many political variables.

In analytical terms, one can distinguish between five possible outcomes of the crisis. The break-up of the existing state into two fully independent states; a confederation; a bipartite federation; a federation built on historical regional principles; or a unitary state. Although only the first of these implied full disintegration, there can be little doubt that any confederative solution would merely have been a transitory arrangement on the road to full mutual independence. Similarly, a bipartite federation would have contained the seeds of disintegration, since it would have been permanently threatened with the possibility of secession by one of the two constituent Republics.

In 1991, all efforts by the then President, Vaclav Havel, and the federal government to work out a compromise on future federal arrangements that would be acceptable to both Czechs and Slovaks ended in frustration. The decline of the centrist parties in the elections has undermined the bases for durable political, economic and constitutional compromises. Shortly after the elections, on 23 July 1992, the new republican leaders, Klaus, for the Czech side, and Meciar, for the Slovak side, agreed on what has been described as a 'blueprint for the dissolution of Czechoslovakia'. Although the details of the 'velvet divorce' were still to be worked out, it was obvious that this agreement would, in the end, eventuate in the emergence of two separate states in a comparatively orderly, negotiated fashion.

III   THE RE-EMERGENCE OF PUBLIC MANAGEMENT AND THE PRESTIGE OF THE CIVIL SERVICE

The first significant attempts at organizational innovations in public administration and improvements in administrative human resources can be traced back to the second half of the 1980s, which marked the beginning of a purifying process in the state apparatus and, at a more modest rate, in the economic sphere. New patterns of personnel policy began to evolve, and there was at least some attempt to experiment with forms of entrepreneurial activity exploited in mixed economies. Partly due to the half-hearted nature of the reform attempts, and partly due to the strong resistance which even these modest attempts met on the part of many Communist hard-liners, these efforts brought about only marginal changes. Nevertheless, they can be interpreted as the beginning of a process which has accelerated dramatically since 1990. In the opinion of one of the architects of economic reform in Czechoslovakia, Vaclav Klaus (1991), there are many serious technical issues which must be solved; but the most pressing obstacle to economic reform which he identifies is the ideological prejudice against the market and its side-effects, the dreams of the possibility of muddling through, based on minor improvements of the existing system, and, lastly, fears of overstretching the tolerance of the population or of some powerful organizations with their well-defined vested interests.

These arguments also have implications for administrative reform. The advocates of radical anti-bureaucratism did not criticize the system of central planning as such, but rather particular representatives. Thus, an officially sanctioned criticism of the white-collar class, which expanded a specifically Czech behavioural pattern, was, on more than one occasion in the past, a popular as well as populist instrument. Such an unproductive approach blocks any far-reaching social change, especially in a situation in which very vocal and self-confident technocrats stress the superiority of technical knowledge, fail to understand the systemic explanation of social events and believe in social engineering and rationalistic constructivism. As a result of a technocrat faith in the inevitable power of progress, many bureaucrats seem to be surprised when this progress is not actually happening in their own country.

What the Czechoslovak bureaucratic environment really suffers from is a lack of a value-preserving mentality and, at the same time, an over-supply of retrograde conservatism which is listless and defenceless against the external pressures of 'progress' unleashed by politicians. It is then not surprising that public bureaucratic culture shares values such as the consciousness of being indispensable for the so-called economy of shortages and an emphasis on corporate solidarity, as a logical consequence of an over-extended state.

It cannot be simply assumed that a national style, or culture, necessarily shapes the course of administrative reform. In other words, the question is whether an understanding of distinctive national characteristics is really a prerequisite for making sense of the institutional structure. It is worth keeping in mind that Czechoslovakia – like other countries in the European periphery – profited less from welfare than from 'workfare'. It is not merely by chance that the relative per capita indebtedness of countries such as Poland, Hungary and Czechoslovakia in the 1920s and 1930s was almost the same as it is now. In other words, not all the Contemporary problems can be blamed solely on the past forty years of the communist experiment. Viewed from another angle, the proportion of non-manual workers is in the long perspective higher than justified by the level of economic development. All signs indicate that it is these unjustifiably high numbers working at the lower levels of administration that have caused the increase in the proportion of non-manual workers and not the number of professionals, who do generally intellectual work.

Against this background, it is not surprising that the percentage of active earners employed in administrative and managerial occupations was almost the same in the 1920s as it was in the 1980s, i.e. about 13 per cent. Perhaps an even more significant phenomenon is the relatively small increase in the number of non-administrative and non-managerial intellectual occupations by only 8 per cent from 1921 to 1989. On the other hand, the power of professionals to affect social life is not, of course, accidental. Much of it is based on the explicit delegation of public authority and rule making or, in some cases, the persistence of common practices which have evolved over the centuries. As a rule, professions and even nascent professions use public authority to externalize risks and costs of those individuals who are or will be members of the professional group. Ultimately the citizens bear the cost of these displacements either as consumers or as tax payers.

TABLE 1   The sectoral distribution of public employees in 1992

General administration	52,700
Administration of foreign affairs	1,700
Financial administration	18,000
Economic and trade administration	16,200
Service for agriculture and for environmental protection	28,100
Health care	293,100
Social care	45,200
Education and science	381,700
Security and justice	87,800

In order to get a better understanding of the structure of the public non-profit sector, it is perhaps useful to look at the sectoral distribution of public employees. The numbers for 1992 appear in table 1. Clearly, the challenge which faces personnel policy is not just a quantitative one, relating to the size of the public service and to the need to re-adjust personnel capacities in the individual branches of public administration. Perhaps a more important challenge is of a qualitative nature, relating to the qualification and motivation of public personnel. For example, one of the key problems in this respect has been the move of many of the most competent officials to the emerging private sector, which is almost invariably able to offer much higher material rewards than the public service.

It is interesting to note that about 90 per cent of the normative acts that have been adopted since the beginning of 1990 have been aimed primarily at public administration, its rights, duties, and organizational structures. As regards personnel, the most widely and controversially discussed piece of legislation has certainly been the screening law (see Jicinsky 1992 and Mikule 1992). Under this law, former Communist officials, people who collaborated with the Communist secret service, and other groups of citizens with close relations to the old regime are banned from political, administrative and economic offices in the public sector until 1996. The number of public posts falling under these provisions is estimated at around 250,000, and the number of people working in the public service who might be banned from public offices on the basis of these provisions is estimated at around 50,000. The law has been heavily criticized not only by the left parties and President Havel, but also by international organizations, such as the International Labour Organization. By contrast, its most ardent supporters are to be found amongst the strongly anti-Communist parties and amongst those supporters of the new regime who have benefited particularly from developments over the last two to three years. Whilst critics of the law do not deny the need for a legal procedure by which the country's political and administrative institutions can be rid of compromised individuals, opponents of the screening law argue that this in violation of existing Czechoslovak and in particular international labour legislation and human rights guarantees. Besides legal arguments, critics also point to the fact that the law creates an atmosphere of fear amongst those who live an honest life. Nobody can be sure whether or not they are registered in the files of the former secret service, and the decisive criterion is not whether somebody violated the law under the old regime or persecuted other citizens, but simply whether his or her name is registered in the secret police's files. In this situation members of the Federal Assembly and the Czech National Council have sent a request to the Constitutional Court asking for the screening law to be tested for its constitutionality. This has put the Court in a very delicate position, because five of twelve judges of the Court voted on the law as former MPs, including the current Chief Justice, who played a particularly active role in promoting the law, and has stated repeatedly in the past that he has no doubts about its constitutionality.

It should, however, be realized that this screening law represents an essentially retrospective measure. By contrast, the qualitative challenges in personnel recruitment, utilization, motivation, representation and training are only beginning to be realized to their full extent and the political discussion on how to best address them is only just getting under way. It is questions of this kind which are likely to be amongst the chief priorities of Czech and Slovak administrative reformers for the rest of the decade.

REFERENCES

Belohradsky, V. 1985. 'Bürokratie und Kultur in der modernen Gesellschaft', *Leviathan-Sonderhefte* 6, 126–35.

The Economist 332, 21–4. 1992. 'Eastern Europe's past: the complexities of justice'.

Gerloch, A. 1991. 'Nad variantami noveho statopravniho usporadani ceskoslovenskeho statu', *Pravnik* 130, 499–510.

Hesse, J. J. 1991. 'Administrative modernisation in Central and Eastern European countries', *Staatswissenschaften und Staatspraxis* 2, 197–217.

Illner, M. 1991. 'Problems of local government in the Czech Republic', in G. Peteri (ed.), *Events and changes*. Budapest: Local Democracy and Innovation Foundation.

Jicinsky, Z. and V. Mikule. 1992. 'Nektere ustavnepravni otazky tzv. lustracniho zakona', *Pravnik* 131, 227–33.

Klaus, V. 1991. *A road to market economy*. Praha: Top Agency.

Kostečka, J. 'Reforma státní služby a její ústavní zakotvení', *Pravnik* 131, 661–76.

Matula, M. 1991. 'Statni sprava a spravni pravo pred listopadem a po listopadu 1989', *Pravnik* 130, 626–38.

Peska, P. 1992. 'Devatero omylu', *Lidove noviny* 190, 10.

Sládeček, V. 'Legislativní činnost Federálního shromáždění po listopadu 1989', *Pravnik* 131, 761–78.

OPTIONS FOR ADMINISTRATIVE REFORM IN THE CZECH REPUBLIC

OLGA VIDLÁKOVÁ

I INTRODUCTION

Since the elections for a new Czech Parliament, the National Council, in June 1992 and the subsequent formation of a new republican government under Prime Minister Vaclav Klaus, the need for a comprehensive reform of Czech public administration has been discussed with growing urgency. Increasingly, it has been recognized amongst political decision-makers that a re-examination of administrative tasks, structures, procedures and personnel has to include both state administration and the institutions of local government. In this context, state administration is understood to encompass both the government departments and all other executive state institutions at the republican or subcentral levels, whereas local government comprises the municipalities and their offices with their elected officials and appointed staff. Together, state and local government form the sphere of public administration.

Such an approach, which takes account of the complex interconnections between the different levels of public administration, is still by no means the norm; in fact, after the political changes of 1989, the reform discussion focused almost exclusively on state administration. However, given the manifold ties between central and deconcentrated state administration and local government, a broader perspective, which reflects the functional, organizational and territorial differentiations as well as interlinkages in public administration, is essential. On the basis of such a more comprehensive approach, the reform process over the coming years needs to concentrate on

— the horizontally and vertically differentiated state administration;
— local government;
— the territorial organization of public administration; and
— personnel policy and personnel management.

Professor Olga Vidláková is Director of the Department of Public Administration in the Office for Legislation and Public Administration of the Czech Republic, Prague.

II   ADMINISTRATIVE REFORM SINCE 1989: A BRIEF REVIEW

It is frequently argued that as a consequence of the dissolution of the Czech and Slovak Federation, administrative reform in the Czech Republic must, inevitably, return to its starting point; put casually, Czech reformers are said to have to 'start from scratch'. In other words, the modest achievements in administrative reform over the last two to three years are thought to have been more or less undone by the federal state's demise, with the Republic's public administration facing a fundamentally altered constitutional and political environment. There can, indeed, be no doubt that the final split between the two Republics and the resulting transfer of federal competences to the republican level will have a profound impact on the structure of Czech public administration. It is also clear that this transfer process needs to be accompanied by far-reaching changes in the Czech legal system; this, in turn, necessarily involves a partial re-definition of the tasks of Czech public administration. It is, then, clear that the demise of the federal state affects the republican administration in more than marginal ways. However, it must also be recognized that the past few years have already seen some very substantial modifications in Czech administration, not least in response to the progressive hand-over of federal competences and responsibilities, and these adjustments are not invalidated by the final dissolution of the Federation. The 'velvet divorce' was a prolonged process, and the divorcees had already begun to adapt to the end of the marriage before the separation was finally announced.

The most immediate impact of the end of the Federation is felt at the level of the central republican administration. The Federal Constitutional Act No. 493/1992 COL provided for the abolition of several federal ministries, including the Ministries of Foreign Trade, Labour and Social Affairs, Transport, Communications, and Strategic Planning. This left only a core federal departmental structure, consisting of the Ministries of Finance, Foreign Affairs, Interior, the Economy, Control and Defence. At the same time, a number of central administrative agencies, such as the Federal Committee for the Environment or the Federal Office for Economic Competition, were abolished. Obviously, this winding up of federal authorities and the transfer of administrative competences from the federal to the state level has meant that the republican ministries face substantially altered tasks. In policy areas where both the Federation and the Republics had substantial competences, the republican ministries find themselves with considerably enlarged responsibilities; where the Federation had prime executive responsibility, the Republics need to build up relevant administrative capacities.

As regards local government, the impact of the Federation's demise is much less evident. Local government reform required an amendment to the Federal Constitution of 1960, which provided for a unified system of National Committees as the representatives of state power and administration in the municipalities, districts and regions. The role of these National Committees had been spelled out in more detail through a Federal Act of 1967. According to this Act, national committees were state bodies of a self-governing nature, designed 'to meet the general social needs and the needs of their territorial units, in the first place the needs of municipal development, and to harmonise the interests of society as a whole with local, group, and individual interests'. Of course, in reality, national committees were never institutions of genuine local government. They were, above all, state authorities representing the state's unified power, and, in practice, they were subject to the operational control by the local units of the Communist Party. Up to November 1989, around 32,000 staff worked in these national committees.

The municipal, district and regional national committees survived up to the local elections of 24 November 1990 when the Federal Constitutional Act No. 294/1990 COL, amending the 1960 Federal Constitution, came into force. It replaced the provisions on national committees with new local government regulations. Through these new regulations, the municipalities were recognized as the basis of the local government system. A municipality is defined as a self-governing community of citizens. Municipalities have a legal identity with their own independently managed property. According to the new regulations, citizens have the right to decide upon local matters either directly through referendums or through the municipal council. Elections to the municipal council are based on universal and direct suffrage. Municipalities possess the right to issue by-laws, a regulation which also applies to the execution of state delegated tasks. Municipal boundaries can only be changed with the approval of the municipality concerned. Moreover, the constitution allows municipalities to establish voluntary associations to ensure the efficient execution of municipal tasks. Municipalities and their associations are free to enter into international co-operation with other local governments and to join international associations of local government bodies.

The amended Federal Constitution established only a relatively broad legal framework for local government. The detailed regulation of local government organization and local tasks and responsibilities was left to the Republican Parliaments. This included, for example, precise regulations on the sphere of local tasks, delegated state tasks (which the municipalities administer on behalf of the state), regulations concerning local elections, and local government supervision. On this basis, the Czech government prepared in a matter of months a very far-reaching reform of local government and territorial state administration. With the Czech Act No. 367/1990 COL concerning local government and Act No. 425/1990 COL concerning district offices, the unified system of municipal, district and regional national committees was abolished and, in its place, a new local government organization and a district role were defined. Act No. 368/1990 COL determined the details of local elections; these provisions were amended in 1992 through Act No. 298/1992 COL on municipal council elections and local referendums. Also in this connection, Act No. 172/1991 COL on the transfer of state-owned assets to the municipalities ought to be mentioned. Together, these new acts established a new legal framework for local government at an early stage in the transition process.

This said, there can be no doubt that further legislation is needed. For example, there are still no detailed regulations providing institutional guarantees for independent local government, and the legal protection of municipal government against state interference is still insufficiently developed. Perhaps the main shortcoming of current regulations is that the 1990 Federal Constitutional Act made municipalities the core of local government, without explicitly providing for another self-government tier. This is an issue which will certainly need to be addressed in future. In short, then, further local government reform legislation is required; the impetus for reform, however, does not stem from the Czech Republic's emergence as an independent state but the need to complete the local government reform project.

Local government reform was accompanied by significant changes in territorial state administration. The regional national committees were abolished at the end of 1990, although the seven Czech regions survived as territorial units on the basis of the Federal Act from 1960 concerning territorial state organization. In practice, this has meant that there remain several state administrative institutions which are organized at the regional level. They include, for example, the regional military boards, police directorates, finance directorates, geodesic and cartographical boards, or the regional health offices. Since the abolition of the regional national committees, the only territorial state administrative bodies with a general competence have been the district offices. In 1992, the Czech Republic comprised 75 districts, served by 72 district offices (in the three urban centres, the tasks of the district offices are carried out by the municipal authorities). The district offices execute state tasks either as administrative offices of the first instance, or, in cases where tasks are delegated to the municipalities, as administrative institutions of the second instance. Many of the Czech Republic's approximately 5,800 municipalities do not have the necessary administrative capacities for the effective execution of delegated tasks. For this reason, the Czech government has named 381 'designated municipal authorities', which perform certain delegated functions on behalf of smaller adjacent municipal authorities. Despite the creation of designated local authorities, there has been a very considerable increase in the number of deconcentrated state organs at the district level during the last three years. These deconcentrated offices are not linked to the general district offices, and they are supervised directly by the relevant ministries. Not surprisingly, opinions differ very sharply on the desirability of this proliferation of deconcentrated state administration.

Another important development following the political changes of 1989 was the re-introduction of the institution of judicial review of administrative decisions from the beginning of 1992. Thus far, no special administrative courts have been established, but there are now special senates in the general courts charged with administrative jurisdiction. In most cases, it is the administrative senate of a regional court which decides administrative issues; however, appeals against decisions by central state bodies are dealt with by the Supreme Court of the Czech Republic.

With the exception of judicial review, the only substantial amendments to the Czech legislation on public administration passed after 1990 have concerned local government and the districts. By contrast, until recently, very little attention was directed towards the structures of government and central state administration, and, in particular, the public service; accordingly, little progress in these areas has been made. Two main reasons can be identified for the failure to address these crucial issues: firstly, the federal and state governments long considered economic reform and the privatization of state enterprises as their absolute priority; by comparison, the reform of public administration was very much considered a secondary issue. Secondly, continuous quarrels over the division of powers between the Federation and the two Republics meant that a great deal of reform energy was wasted. Often, it was unclear who had the power to act, and the mutual blockage of initiatives was not uncommon. All this led to a situation in which change in Czech central administration was more or less accidental, often rushed through and carried out under great pressure and without necessary co-ordination. Some republican ministries, such as the Czech Ministry for the Environment and the Ministry for Economic Policy and Development had their responsibilities redefined several times within a very short time span, with little sign of any rational and co-ordinated approach.

With the dissolution of the federal state, some of the impediments to purposive administrative reform have been removed. The uncertainty over the intergovernmental distribution of powers and responsibilities has been resolved, and, as a result, a much clearer picture of the tasks of Czech state administration has emerged. At the same time, the elections of June 1992 have produced a stable Czech government. With the transition period coming to an end, the government can now embark on a more long-term oriented strategy for administrative renewal.

III TOWARDS THE INSTITUTIONALIZATION OF ADMINISTRATIVE CHANGE

The basis for the further development of Czech public administration is a policy statement by the new Czech government of July 1992. This statement identifies administrative reform and decentralization as central issues on the government's political and legislative agenda. Administrative reform is recognized as an essential precondition for successful economic transition; moreover, improved administrative expertise, enhanced technical capacities, and a restored prestige of administrative institutions and their staff are considered vital prerequisites for effective democratic governance. Against this background, the Czech government has announced its intention to re-examine the departmental allocation of competences and ministerial structures as well as the territorial organization of public administration. As far as the latter issue is concerned, the government has re-affirmed the position of municipal governments as the basic institutions of territorial governance. But it also proposed to look into the question of self-governing institutions at the regional level or at the level of the historical lands, to which some central powers and resources might be transferred. For this purpose, the government has promised to create an appropriate legislative framework, which would allow for the constitution of such self-governing units. At the same time, the government has undertaken to prepare a draft Public Service Act to regulate the rights and duties of public servants, and issues such as public service career structures, entrance requirements and remuneration. The importance of this policy statement should not be underestimated. It demonstrates that, at last, administrative reform has been put firmly on the political agenda, and that its significance for democratic government and successful economic transformation has been acknowledged. The government has committed itself to reforming, modernizing and democratizing public administration as soon as possible, and it can, therefore, ill-afford to simply let the matter drop in future.

One of the first tangible results of this new emphasis on administrative reform has been the setting up of an Office for Legislation and Public Administration of the Czech Republic, headed by the Vice-Prime Minister, which began its operations in November 1992. As regards public administration, the office is, in particular, responsible for preparing a coherent project for administrative reform; for assessing reform proposals submitted by individual ministries; and for reporting to the government on the progress of reform, especially as far as the implementation of the individual measures approved by the government is concerned. In other words, the new office is intended to act as the central unit for the development of a coherent administrative reform strategy and for monitoring its implementation. The office is also charged with co-ordinating foreign administrative assistance, something which has thus far been lacking. The institutional combination of the responsibility for legislation and administrative reform represents a step in the right direction. The dismantling of the Czechoslovak Federation and the establishment of an independent Czech state obviously require far-reaching legal adjustments which directly affect the operations of public administration. Conversely, administrative reform often necessitates legal change. Thus, it makes sense to consider both issues in close connection.

Perhaps one of the central difficulties faced by administrative reformers is that public administration inevitably embraces both administrative, technical expertise and explicitly political concerns. Public administration is necessarily a sub-system of the political system (Ridley 1979, p. 3), and not just related to it through inputs and outputs. In other words, public administration is dependent on the political system for its basic structures, and its own values are, of course, influenced by politics. In this respect, the effects of four decades of subordination of public administration under the imperatives of the Communist Party, which acted as 'the leading political power in the state', have been highly damaging. Not only has it led to widespread demoralization amongst administrative staff, but it has also given rise to almost universal popular distrust of public administration and its officials. Perhaps less obviously, but even more worryingly, four decades of Communist state power have resulted in a general and deep-rooted discrediting of key concepts, institutions and instruments in administrative development. For example, the credibility of planning, competition, performance assessment and evaluation and even the concept of the law itself have partly been undermined in this process. Of course, such concepts were not unknown to Czechoslovak public administration, but they were often applied in such a way as to make them merely formalistic rituals. As a result, the real essence of such concepts has almost been forgotten, and it is now exceedingly difficult to find acceptance for many of the central prerequisites of a well-functioning public administration.

IV   OPTIONS FOR CHANGE

Against this background, a reform strategy for Czech public administration certainly needs to encompass central and territorial state administration; local government; the territorial organization of public administration; and, crucially, the re-building of an efficient and effective public service. Evidently, these problems are closely connected, and any broadly conceived strategy for administrative reform will, therefore, have to tackle a number of issues at the same time. They include:

— the general features of the administrative system, including the extent of its political independence, its technical expertise, and its effectiveness and efficiency;
— the modernization of central state administration, including deregulation and decentralization;
— the territorial organization of state governance, including, in particular, the relations between general-purpose institutions and specialized deconcentrated units;
— local government organization;
— the relations between local government and territorial state organizations;
— the character of the public service and its legal regulation;
— personnel policy, especially as regards issues such as expertise, loyalty, and staff morale, and professional development, training and education; and
— external controls over public administration.

Whilst it is necessary to consider these issues in close connection, in practical terms any reform programme will obviously have to determine priorities and decide on the sequencing of reform steps. But some issues need to be addressed immediately and simultaneously. First and foremost, it is necessary to reach a binding consensus on the general character of public administration, its principal tasks, structures and procedures. On such a foundation, it is then possible to work out individual reform initiatives. In some cases, such as local government reform, the Czech government is already committed to introducing reform legislation by a certain date, and undertakings of this kind obviously need to be taken into account in deciding on the sequencing of reform matters. It would be a fatal mistake, however, to wait until both a general reform framework and the details of all individual measures have been worked out before starting to implement priority initiatives. Such an approach would squander the reform opportunities which are currently available, and, ultimately, discredit the reform programme as such.

As argued above, what is most urgently needed is a clear idea of what kind of public administration and public service the Czech Republic should have. In my own opinion, the guiding principle should be a politically neutral public administration and a strong and independent public service. It is, of course, well known that even in developed countries with a long tradition of democratic public administration, the clear-cut demarcation between policy formation and execution is impossible, and the distinction between political and administrative roles highly blurred (Chapman 1988). Nonetheless, the idea of a politically neutral, modern and efficient bureaucracy should not be given up as a guiding principle. Only if the professional expertise and skills of administrative personnel can be improved, if the remnants of the notorious politization under Communist rule are to be removed, and if the political independence of public administration can be firmly established, is it realistic to expect a slow and gradual improvement of the popular prestige of public administration.

In this connection, new public service legislation and a new personnel management system are of central importance. Like other socialist countries in Central and Eastern Europe, Czechoslovakia did not have a developed legal framework for the public service; instead, employment relations were primarily determined by the General Labour Code which applied to all sectors, with only a few special regulations for certain groups of employees in public administration. A special Public Service Act is now under preparation in the Czech Republic. It is doubtful whether it makes sense to try to prepare a comprehensive and highly detailed public service law at this stage. For the moment, it might be a more realistic option to adopt a framework provision which stipulates certain fundamental principles of public administration and the public service which can subsequently be extended and detailed, either through amendments to the framework act itself, or through secondary laws based on the fundamental principles and guarantees laid down in the Public Service Act.

However, there can be little doubt that in itself the Public Service Act, albeit crucial for the reform of public administration as a whole, can only be of limited effect. What is needed is an entirely new system of public personnel management, which provides incentives for organizational and cultural change in public administration. At the heart of such a system needs to be a new approach to personnel recruitment. This includes, for example, the need to make sure that the public service becomes more attractive to university graduates and other qualified staff. In close connection with this, the whole issue of personnel training, education and development needs to be looked at in detail. In reforming personnel management, foreign experience can be of great help. However, it must also be realized that as far as personnel management is concerned, foreign practices cannot necessarily be applied in the Czech situation. For example, in the highly developed Western administrative systems, there is currently much emphasis on increased flexibility in the public service. Within Czech public administration, however, the situation is at present characterized by so much fluidity that the overriding aim needs to be to promote stability and consolidation rather than increase flexibility. Similarly, there are severe restrictions on the potential for introducing private-sector type personnel management techniques into Czech public administration. In this respect, it should be remembered 'that procedures and methods of government are different from business administration; businessmen cannot be expected to know how to run a government department any more than a civil servant can be expected to manage an industrial concern without a lot of training and experience' (Wass 1984).

Another key issue in administrative reform has to be local government organization. As was pointed out above, the government is already committed to adopting new legislation in this area by 1994. If this time-table is to be observed, then work in this area has to get under way as soon as possible. Vital concerns in this context include the relation between local (or self-governmental) and delegated tasks; the desirable extent of decentralization; and, importantly, the question whether there should be more than one level of local government. Perhaps the most crucial issue, however, is the territorial reform of local government. Since 1990, the number of Czech municipalities has risen sharply, as many larger localities have split up into individual authorities. This has led to a situation where there are around 5,800 municipalities with a total population of 10.3 million, and, unless action is taken, this trend towards the increasing fragmentation of the local government level is expected to continue. Of course, this development has to be considered against the background of the excessive centralism of the Communist state. Nevertheless, there can be no doubt that it hinders the sound territorial organization of public administration.

The territorial aspect of local government reform needs to be considered in close connection with the territorial organization of state administration. The essential problem here is the proliferation of deconcentrated units of state administration, whose number has risen sharply since 1990. Certainly, some of the new deconcentrated administrations have a sound rationale, at least during a transitional period which requires special administrative capacities for such tasks as property restitution or privatization. In the longer term, however, a substantial reduction of the number of central field offices is essential.

The latter point is intimately connected with one of the politically most controversial issues at present, namely the creation of a second local or regional government tier. The government's draft for a new Czech Constitution provides for higher local government units, but leaves undecided whether they should take the form of the historical lands or resemble modern regions. Both alternatives have to be evaluated very carefully, before any decision is made, and there are, obviously, close links between the territorial organization of state administration and the creation of a higher tier of local government.

As far as central state administration is concerned, the dissolution of the Czechoslovak state and the concomitant transfer of federal powers to the republican central administrations highlight the need for more efficient and effective governmental structures at the republican level. It is, therefore, imperative to take a close look at the central administrative organization. In particular, this needs to focus on:

— the interdepartmental allocation of competences;
— the division of labour between ministries and other central offices;
— inter-administrative co-operation and co-ordination at the central level in all stages of the policy-making process; and
— the position of the Office of the Government and of the newly created Office for Legislation and Public Administration in a new executive structure.

Finally, the Czech reform strategy must pay sufficient attention to improving the external controls over public administration. They need to be completed, and, at the same time, to be simplified, made more transparent and effective. Judicial control has to be extended, and there is a strong case for the creation of an institution along the lines of the Scandinavian ombudsman model. Control of legality needs to be complemented by more effective controls of efficiency and economy. This involves a thorough review of the structures and techniques for public auditing.

REFERENCES

Chapman, R. A. 1988. *Ethics in the British civil service*. London: Routledge.
Greenwood, J. and D. Wilson. 1989. *Public administration in Britain today*. London: Unwin Hyman.
Hesse, J. J. (ed.). 1991. *Local government and urban affairs in international perspective*. Baden-Baden: Nomos.
König, K. 1991. 'Verwaltung im Übergang vom zentralen Verwaltungstaat in die dezentrale Demokratie', p. 5 ff. in: *Verwaltung im Übergang*. Ein Cappenberger Gespräch.
Ridley, F. F. (ed.). 1979. *Government and administration in Western Europe*. Oxford: Martin Robertson.
Wagener, F. 1969. *Neubau der Verwaltung*. Berlin: Duncker and Humblot.
Wallerath, M. 1992. 'Aufgaben und Aufbau öffentlicher Verwaltung im Wandel', *Die Verwaltung* 25, 2, p. 157 ff.
Wass, Sir D. 1984. *Government and the governed*. London: Routledge.

THE TRANSFORMATION OF HUNGARIAN PUBLIC ADMINISTRATION

ISTVÁN BALÁZS

I THE HISTORICAL BACKGROUND

In 1990, the Hungarian political system underwent fundamental change. As a consequence, the socialist state organization, which had supported the former power structure and implemented its political will, needed to be replaced by an administrative framework that would be compatible with the principles of a pluralistic parliamentary democracy. Reflecting the evolutionary nature of change in the political system, the new shape of state institutions has only emerged gradually. This process, which is characterized by the dissolution of many established structures and the building up of new institutions, is still underway, but significant results have already been achieved.

In the case of central governmental institutions, perhaps the most important task has been to establish a clear division between the political leadership and the professional executive level. Of course, the new political leadership, when it got into power, could not really work without the experienced members of the former state administration. Whilst in Hungary there has been no systematic removal of high-ranking officials serving under the Communist regime, it has been necessary to identify those areas in the executive where the interconnections between the former single party state and public administration had been strongest. This included, for example, the internal security services or the *cadres* departments in central institutions. In such instances, it has been necessary to partly replace the administrative leadership, while preventing politically non-compromised staff from leaving the public service. A mass exodus of administrative key personnel could have destabilized the operation of public administration as such, and, perhaps, even have undermined the change in the political system.

As regards territorial governance, the typical socialist form of regional and local public administration was the Soviet-type council system; it was meant to implement in the sphere of public administration the principles of a party

Dr István Balázs is Director of the Hungarian Institute of Public Administration, Budapest.

TABLE 1 Key legal regulations on Hungarian public administration
adopted since 1989

Act xxxi of 1989 on the Modification of the Constitution
Act xxxii of 1989 on the Constitutional Court
Act xxxiii of 1989 on the Operation and economic management of political parties
Act xxxiv of 1989 on the Election of Members of Parliament
Act xxv of 1989 on the Election of the President of the Republic of Hungary
Act xvii of 1990 on the Representation in Parliament of national and ethnic minorities
living in the Republic of Hungary
Act xxxiii of 1990 on the Temporary regulation of the legal status of state secretaries
Act liv of 1990 on the Election of the representatives of local self-governments and
mayors
Act lv of 1990 on the Legal status of the Members of Parliament
Act lxv of 1990 on Local self-governments
Act lxvii of 1990 on Certain questions related to performing the task of mayors
Act xc of 1990 on the Legal status, office and certain tasks of the Commissioners of
Republic
Act c of 1990 on Local taxes
Act xvi of 1990 on Concession
Act xvii of 1991 on the Lifting of the competence of the government for controlling the
lawfulness of the operation of some social organizations
Act xx of 1991 on the Tasks and range of competence of local governments and their
organs, Commissioners of Republic and some organs under central control
Act xxiv of 1991 on the Local governments of the capital city and its districts
Act xxvi of 1991 on the Extension of the supervision by court on decisions taken by
public administration
Act xxiii of 1992 on the Legal status of civil servants
Act xxxiii of 1992 on the Legal status of public employees
Government decree 77/1992 (iv. 30) on Certain tasks of the Commissioners of the
Republic
Government decree 1026/1992 (v. 12) on the Modernization of public administration

---

structure based on 'democratic centralism'. The council system was characterized by the existence of a centrally controlled political élite, which, however, lacked real powers to take decisions. Thus, councils largely represented the illusion of democracy. Under the socialist system, the Communist Party controlled society through the council staff of counties and municipalities. As a result, the replacement of the council-based public administrative system with a sphere of independent local self-government was a key concern in administrative reform. It was partly for this reason that, after the ousting of the Communists, the reform of local government preceded attempts at modernizing other elements in public administration. At the same time, there can be no doubt that local government reform responded to a genuine demand in society. Against this background, it is not surprising that Hungary was the first among the Central and Eastern European countries to pass a new law on local government.

It was also the first to organize local elections, which took place only four months after the change in the central political leadership.

The establishment of a new system of local government has also had some distorting effects. As opposing political camps hold power at the national and local levels, local government issues were excessively party politicized already at a time when the new Act on Local Government was still in its preparatory stages in Parliament. At that time, local government was regarded as an absolute value; in fact, many saw it as the only democratic and effective form of public administration. In professional, political and even economic terms, local administration was regarded as the antithesis of state administration, which was equated with centralization, preventing the operation of democratic public administration. Such a perspective undermined the idea of a uniform public administration, and it also meant that it was very difficult to adequately prepare and complete the complex legislative work necessary for the effective operation of the new administrative system.

II THE PRESENT SYSTEM OF HUNGARIAN PUBLIC ADMINISTRATION

1 The constitutional position of central government and deconcentrated public administrative organs

In its present constitutional form, the Republic of Hungary is a parliamentary democracy based on the effective separation between the principal branches of state power. The current state structure is a result of the political compromises reached in 1989 between the then ruling Communist Party and the opposition forces. The main objective of that compromise was to prevent any part of the state gaining effective domination over the others. However, this carefully struck balance between the various branches of power has raised a number of practical problems. The source of the most pronounced difficulties have been the over-extended legislative competences of the Hungarian Parliament. In contrast to the former socialist state, in which Parliament played only a formal role and much legislative power resided in the government and the Presidency, Parliament under the new system has absolute legislative powers. Of course, changes in the social, political and economic system require an unusual amount of legislative work; but the current dominance of Parliament is due to the undifferentiated legislative powers which have been granted under the amended constitution. As a result, the National Assembly is faced with a situation in which it has to pass approximately one hundred new acts annually; this leaves, on average, only six hours to discuss an act, including presentations by committees and ministers. Such haste in legislation no longer really serves the interests of the constitutional state, but devalues its effectiveness by reducing the standard of legislation.

Another major problem is that certain institutions, such as the Presidency or the Constitutional Court, do either not have a precisely specified authority or their authority extends too far, leading to functional difficulties. As a result of the sweeping scope of Parliament's legislative powers, on the one hand, and the inadequate definition of the authority of some central state institutions, on the other, the autonomous competences of central public administration, and especially of the government, are too narrow. Compared to most advanced democratic-pluralistic states, the political and legal powers and related responsibilities of the Hungarian government and the Prime Minister appear insufficient. Moreover, the Hungarian government lacks the parliamentary mechanisms through which it could give decisive character to its policy and attempt to execute it despite obstructionist parliamentary policies. Historically, it is, of course, understandable why a constitutional solution has been chosen that obliges the government to use methods and instruments which differ from those typically utilized in liberal democracies. However, the experience since 1990 amply demonstrates the dysfunctional character of some of the current institutional practices.

At present, the Hungarian government, as the supreme controlling organ of public administration, is significantly smaller and more transparent than it was at any time during the socialist era. The government comprises thirteen ministries which are served by the Prime Minister's Office; in addition, key issues in the transformation process, such as privatization, relations with international organizations or the rights of national and ethnic minorities, are looked after by

TABLE 2   **Personnel in Hungarian public administration 1991/92**

Ministries	1991
Ministry of Interior	596
Ministry of Agriculture	445
Ministry of Defence	150
Ministry of Justice	291
Ministry of Industry and Trade	801
Ministry of Environmental Protection and Development	732
Ministry of Transport, Telecommunications and Water Management	1,321
Ministry of Foreign Affairs	1,325
Ministry of Labour	337
Ministry of Culture and Public Education	608
Ministry of International Economic Relations	395
Ministry of Public Health and Social Policy	365
Ministry of Finance	674
Other authorities with national competence	3,217
Personnel in central administration (total):	11,257 (1991)
State offices on sub-national level (staff):	44,570 (1992)
Local government staff:	38,750 (1992)

ministers without portfolio, who are cabinet members. The number of staff in central government has increased, but there have been important shifts in the departmental composition of the staff total.

As regards the system of deconcentrated organs of state administration in Hungary, a number of points are especially worth noting. First, mention should be made of the Commissioners of the Republic, who represent a genuinely new institution in Hungarian territorial governance. The Commissioners, who are central government appointees, operate in administrative regions which encompass several counties. At present, there is one Commissioner for Budapest and seven serve the countryside. Their main task is to control the legality of local government actions and decisions; this control, however, is purely of an *ex post* nature and is strictly limited to the control of legality. The Commissioners do not possess the right to simply repeal or change local government decisions nor can they suspend their validity. Should a local government refuse to act on the Commissioner's comments, the only course of action open to the Commissioner is to turn to the courts. As regards the execution of delegated state tasks by local government, it is the individual state ministries rather than the Commissioners that issue regulations on the professional rules for performing state administrative tasks and control their implementation.

Unlike the former council system, the new Act on Local Government distinguishes between state administration, on the one hand, and local administration, on the other. The administration of counties and municipalities (villages, towns, Budapest and its districts) is no longer part of state administration. Consequently, central departments have in recent years made increasing use of deconcentrated organs of state administration (field agencies), which are operated at the regional and county level by individual ministries. The growth in the number of these institutions is directly linked to the dissolution of the earlier council system, and in particular the weakening of the county administrations. Essentially, sectoral organs are being established to administer special tasks that cannot be performed effectively by county and municipal governments. In principle, state tasks can be delegated to municipal government, but not to counties. The chief municipal officer, the so-called notary, is both the preparatory and executive organ of local government and exercises state administrative competences. In the latter capacity, the notary acts independently from local government. But this solution has some important disadvantages. The notary is an employee of the local government's representative body, and there is thus a possibility for the locality to influence the notary in performing tasks related to state administration. For this reason, in certain areas such as public health, tax administration or consumer protection, state competences have been allocated to deconcentrated organs of state administration, which are independent of local government. However, in some cases it seems difficult to justify the establishment of new deconcentrated organs, especially when one considers the financial burdens on the state budget associated with the proliferation of deconcentrated agencies and the problems involved in their supervision and co-ordination. The government realized the gravity of the problem, when it recently instructed the Commissioners of the

**TABLE 3   The central organs of state administration
(since January 1992)**

1. *MINISTRIES*
   Ministry of Interior
   Ministry of Agriculture
   Ministry of Defence
   Ministry of Justice
   Ministry of Industry and Trade
   Ministry of Environmental Protection and Development
   Ministry of Transport, Telecommunications and Water Management
   Ministry of Foreign Affairs
   Ministry of Culture and Public Education
   Ministry of International Economic Relations
   Ministry of Public Welfare, Public Health and Social Policy
   Ministry of Finance
   Ministry of Labour

2. *ORGANS OF NATIONAL COMPETENCE*
   Office of Taxes and Financial Control
   State Banking Supervision
   State Insurance Supervision
   State Securities Supervision
   National Public Health and Medical Service
   National Office of Census
   State Property Agency
   National Headquarters of Penal Authorities
   Supervision of Consumer Protection
   Institute of Frequency Management
   Office of Economic Competition
   National Headquarters of Border-Guards
   Information Office
   Environmental Chief Supervision
   Transportation Chief Supervision
   Central Institute of Geology
   Central Statistical Office
   Aviation Directorate
   Hungarian Office of Standards
   Hungarian News Agency
   Central Office of the Hungarian Academy of Sciences
   Office of National Security
   Office of National and Ethnic Minorities
   National Office of Nuclear Energy
   National Chief of Supervision of Mining Technique
   National Office of Construction
   National Office of Settlement of Claims and Compensations
   National Meteorological Office
   National Chief Supervision of Work Safety and Labour

TABLE 3 *Continued*

National Labour Office
National Office of Historic Monuments
National Technical Development Committee
National Chief Police Headquarters
National Office of Patents
National Chief Directorate of Social Security
National Office of Physical Training and Sports
National Chief Directorate of Water Management
Supervision of Post and Telecommunications
National Headquarters of Fire Brigades
Customs and Revenue Office

Republic to co-ordinate the operations of the deconcentrated organs. However, this decision did not meet with universal approval; local government felt that this increase in the authority of the Commissioners could be a further step towards the establishment of regional governments, which would act as new power centres above them. Likewise, government ministries are reluctant to allow any interference in the operation of their deconcentrated field administrations.

2 The new system of local government

With the Act on Local Government of 1990, a new local government system was introduced in Hungary, which represented a radical departure from the former system of local councils. The Act follows the principles of the Charter on Local Government of the Council of Europe, and it provides the legal foundations for a local government system resembling those typically found in Western European democracies. At the same time, the Act represents, to a certain extent, a return to the experience of local government in Hungary prior to World War II. The basic principles of the new system include:

— County and municipal governments form part of an integrated system of public administration; however, they arrange for public matters with an autonomy guaranteed by law and protected by the courts.
— As a general rule, local matters are arranged by the elected organs of local government, i.e. the council and its committees, and, in the case of municipalities, the mayor; they are assisted by the county and municipal administration. In exceptional cases, local public matters can be arranged directly by assemblies of local citizens, who in those cases possess the rights of a local government.
— Municipal governments perform both genuinely local tasks, such as the organization and provision of local services, and delegated state tasks. Counties do not carry out delegated tasks.

TABLE 4   Deconcentrated organs of state administration

(a) *Eight Commissioners of the Republic*

Budapest, capital city
Bács-Kiskun, Békés, Csongrád counties
Baranya, Somogy, Tolna counties
Borsod-Abaúj-Zemplén, Heves counties
Fejér, Veszprém, Zala counties
Györ-Moson-Sopron, Komárom-Esztergom, Vas counties
Hajdú-Bihar, Szabolcs-Szatmár-Bereg counties
Jász-Nagykun-Szolnok, Pest, Nógrád counties

(b) *State administrative organs operating on the regional level*

Post and telecommunications supervisions
Water management directorates
Regional organs of ABKSZ
Environmental supervision
Directorates for the protection of nature
Directorates of national parks
Supervision of forests
Regional organs of forest management service controlled by the Ministry of Agriculture
Regional agricultural grading centres
Regional geological service
District supervision of mining technique
Receiving stations of the Office of Emigrants
Offices of Training

(c) *State administrative organs operating on the county (Budapest) level*

Transport supervision
Public road supervisions
Agricultural offices
Land offices
Animal health and food control stations
Plant hygiene and soil protection stations
Tax directorates
County institutions of ANTSZ
Sports directorates
Labour centres
Work safety and labour supervisions
Consumer protection supervisions
Statistical directorates
TAKISZ county offices
Offices of settlement of claims and compensation
Assets transfer committees
Police headquarters
County fire brigades
Customs and revenue guards

(d) *State administrative organs operating on the town settlement level*

Regional land offices
Town institutions of ANTSZ
Representations of labour centres
Town police headquarters

— The Act requires the municipalities to carry out certain mandatory tasks. For these, the necessary financial resources have to be made available by the state. The Act lays down a general and standard state subsidy and permits municipality governments to raise their own taxes. Also, they have the right to own property, are permitted to dispose freely of it and may become involved in commercial business activities.

— Municipalities are free to undertake tasks that are not explicitly reserved to other organs and which do not endanger the satisfactory performance of their mandatory tasks.

— Municipalities are also free to establish and operate their own organizations and they are only subject to legal controls. Only independent courts have the power to decide on the legality of local administrative action.

— Local governments have the right to issue mandatory regulations for the area they administer and exercise public power to ensure the implementation of legal regulations of a higher order.

— The Act emphasizes the equality of all local governments, i.e. counties and municipalities (villages and towns). This does not mean that all local governments enjoy the same rights and have the same obligations, although they all possess the same basic rights. Importantly, however, no local government can control or supervise any other local government.

— The Act does not recognize an independent, national policy-making role of local government; in contrast to the former system, local governments only have the right to local initiatives. Nor does the Act recognize any special regional local government rights. As a result, all types of local government are regarded as indeed *local* government.

The new regulations on local government distinguish between villages; towns, the capital city and the districts of Budapest; and county governments. Town government, village authorities and the government of Budapest and its districts each differ in their tasks and competences, and, of course, the counties' powers and responsibilities differ significantly from the municipalities. The basic element of the new system of local government are the municipalities. As a rule, villages with less than 1,000 inhabitants form common administrative offices under a rural district notary, though this does not affect their independence as local governments. As regards the distinction between villages and towns, this is not principally a matter of the size of the locality. Rather, the local government concerned must be able to support the claim for town status on the basis of the locality's development status and its regional importance. On this basis, the Minister of the Interior can recommend that town status be granted by the President of the Republic. Certain towns can be given county rights; such towns must play an especially important role in their regions and must have more than 50,000 inhabitants. In addition to the tasks and competences of local governments, towns with county rights also perform the tasks of county governments. As regards Budapest and its districts, they are local governments of special status, and their tasks and competences are defined

TABLE 5   Number of settlements and local governments in the Republic of Hungary (1 January 1992)

Capital, counties	Number of settlements			Number of local governments				
	Villages	Towns	Total	In villages	In towns	In districts of capital, in towns with county rights	Capital, county	Total
Budapest		1	1			22	1	23
Bács-Kiskun	105	11	116	105	10	1	1	117
Baranya	296	5	301	296	4	1	1	302
Békés	62	12	74	62	11	1	1	75
Borsod-Abaúj-Zemplén	333	15	348	333	14	1	1	349
Csongrád	52	7	59	52	5	2	1	60
Fejér	98	7	105	98	5	2	1	106
Györ-Moson-Sopron	167	5	172	167	3	2	1	173
Hajdú-Bihar	66	14	80	66	13	1	1	81
Heves	111	7	118	111	6	1	1	119
Jász-Nagykun-Szolnok	62	13	75	62	12	1	1	76
Komárom-Esztergom	64	8	72	64	7	1	1	73
Nógrád	119	6	125	119	6	—	1	126
Pest	167	15	182	167	15	—	1	183
Somogy	229	10	239	229	9	1	1	240
Szabolcs-Szatmár-Bereg	216	12	228	216	11	1	1	229
Tolna	101	7	108	101	7	—	1	109
Vas	206	7	213	206	6	1	1	214
Veszprém	211	9	220	211	8	1	1	221
Zala	250	6	256	250	4	2	1	257
TOTAL:	2915	177	3092	2915	156	42	20	3133

by a separate act. Lastly, county governments are performing certain local government tasks, which municipal governments cannot be expected to carry out themselves. These tasks include the provision of certain county-wide services. However, it must be noted that county tasks can be taken over by the municipalities if the latter can show themselves able to perform them. Like municipalities, counties enjoy basic rights granted by the constitution and the local government acts. On the whole, though, the role of the counties is merely a residual one.

Turning to the organs of local government, the supreme institutions are the representative body in the case of villages and towns and the general assembly in the case of county governments. Whilst the members of the town and village representative bodies are elected directly, the general assemblies of the counties are composed of representatives of the municipalities in the county. In the case of municipalities with fewer than 10,000 inhabitants, the mayor is elected directly; in larger villages and towns, the mayor is elected by the representative body, though not necessarily from amongst its members. The mayor's chief task is to control the local authority staff and to ensure the conditions for the effective operation of the authority. In exceptional cases, the mayor can also perform certain state administrative tasks (especially in civil defence and emergency management). The municipal notary is in charge of state administrative tasks, whose range differ between villages and towns. As far as the exercise of state administrative tasks is concerned, the notary acts independently from the representative body of the locality and the mayor. In the case of counties, the general assembly elects the county chairman and the county deputy chairman. The county chief notary is responsible for the lawful operation of the county administration. Neither the county chairman nor the county chief notary can perform tasks of state administration, even in exceptional cases, unlike, of course, the mayor and the local notary. Thus, at the county level, state tasks can only be administered by the deconcentrated organs of state administration.

Without doubt, the 1990 local government reform established one of the most liberal systems of local government in Europe. The reforms need to be considered against the background of decades of a highly centralized and anti-democratic social and political culture. Whilst the reforms represent a most definite break with the socialist council system and created an independent sphere of local government, some of their negative implications cannot be ignored. For instance, in administrative terms, it is important to note that as a result of local government reform, the number of municipalities nearly doubled from 1,584, under the former system, to 3,092. There are now a large number of very small villages, which often find it difficult to fulfil their mandatory tasks and to make effective use of their scope of discretion. In economic terms, the current system of standard and global state subsidies to local government does not seem economically rational in a situation of general resource scarcity. At present, over 55 per cent of total local expenditure is covered by state transfers; amongst the member states of the European Community, higher proportions are only found in the Netherlands (84 per cent) and Italy (63 per cent). The share of GDP allocated to local government in Hungary reached 15.1 per cent in 1991, whilst in the Netherlands, for example, it amounted to merely 1.1 per cent and in Italy to 1.8 per cent. Only in Denmark did the local budget reach a similar percentage of GDP (13.9 per cent). These figures, which underline the important position of local government in the national economy, are also supported by the fact that local governments appear to have received a disproportionately large share of former state assets. This has provided them with an entrepreneurial position that goes considerably beyond that normally associated with local activities in market-oriented economies. Of course, the generally favourable financial and economic conditions of local governments do not apply to all of them, but primarily to the counties and large towns and villages. Under the present system, however,

TABLE 6   Some key data on the economic position of local governments (in bn: Hungarian Forint)

	1990 actual	1991 expected	1992 estimate
GDP source (at constant prices)	1400	1294	1317
as percentage of previous year	95.7	92.4	101.8
GDP expenditure (at constant prices)	1352	1259	1264
as percentage of previous year	94.7	93.2	100.4
GDP source (at current prices) of growth of GDP	2079	2490	3030
Source in percentage (previous year: 100%)	120.1	119.8	121.7
GDP domestic expenditure (at current prices)	1999	2471	2964
Growth of GDP domestic expenditure	119.5	123.6	119.9
General government expenditure as percentage of GDP		1644	1871
(at current prices)		66.0	61.3
Central budget expenditure as percentage of GDP	642	850	938
(at current prices)	30.9	34.1	31.0
Local governments' budget	310	382	447
Local governments' budget growth	124.9	122.9	117.1
Local governments' budget as percentage of GDP source	14.9	15.1	14.7
Local governments' budget as percentage of GDP Domestic Expenditure	15.5	15.4	15.1
Local governments' budget as percentage of general government expenditure	23.3	23.3	23.9
State grant, shared personal income tax and vehicle tax total		241	282
Growth of these three resources			117.0
Proportion of these three resources as percentage of central budget expenditure		28.3	30.0

the central state does not have the necessary instruments to selectively support the small villages, most of which are economically not viable.

III   THE FUTURE OF HUNGARIAN PUBLIC ADMINISTRATION

Following a phase of reform, which emphasized, above all, the rights of local government, it is now necessary to focus on the complex vertical and horizontal ties needed to ensure an effective system of public administration. The Hungarian government has recently adopted a multi-year programme for the modernization of public administration. The basic objective of this programme is to examine the tasks, structures, procedures and personnel aspects of all branches and tiers of the administrative system, and, on this basis, to develop detailed proposals for improvement. In particular, the modernization programme addresses the following issues (for details see I. Verebélyi in this volume):

— the definition of the role of the modern state and modern public administration under the specific conditions of the Hungarian political, economic, social and cultural systems;

— the administrative implications of the transition towards a market economy, and, in particular, the consequences of marketization for the intergovernmental distribution of powers and competences;

— the question to what extent a highly decentralized system of public administration can be reconciled with the requirements for a uniform operation of the public sector;

— interadministrative co-ordination and mechanisms for improved internal and external controls of administrative activity;

— the interministerial allocation of tasks and competences;

— the intermediate level of public administration, and here, in particular, the role of the Commissioners of the Republic, the counties and the deconcentrated organs of state administration;

— opportunities for integrating, at least to a certain extent, the operations of municipal governments, with a view to maintaining the viability of small units;

— the system of local government finance, especially the system of central transfers;

— controls over the financial management of local government. In this respect, a system needs to be developed which takes account of the economic weight of the Hungarian localities;

— finally, it is proposed to take a close look at the operations of local administration, especially as regards their organizational capacities for service provision to the general public.

Beyond this, the modernization programme looks at the operation of the public sector as a whole, including both structural and procedural issues. This extends also to the question of public enterprises, the regulation of public works, the system of public contracts, without which structural reforms of public administration would not become fully effective.

As regards personnel policy, the recent adoption of two acts on public servants and public employees, which replace the old uniform labour code, has provided a first legal foundation for the establishment of a career public service, based on professional merit and political neutrality. In this connection, great emphasis is placed on the training and retraining of public administrators, and also elected officials.

The underlying idea of the modernization programme is to achieve continuous improvements. In other words, administrative reform is a permanent task. In this connection, values and experiences of other European countries have been taken into account, but it is also important to recognize the significance of Hungarian administrative traditions. Moreover, the specific conditions in the country require in many respects solutions that differ significantly from those found in Western European administrative systems.

REFERENCES

Balázs, István. 1992. *Central public administration and local governments in Hungary.* MKT, p. 21 (Hungarian).

Gajduschek, György. 1991. *Institutions between self-government and the inhabitants of the national period—the Hungarian experience.* MKT, p. 35 (English).

Horváth, Tamás M. 1992. *The development of operational conditions of local governments, further regulation requirements.* MKT, p. 29 (Hungarian).

Kökényesi, József. 1991. *The economic bases of local governments.* MKT, p. 50 (Hungarian).

——. 1992. *Legislative problems related to the basic acts influencing settlement, development, planning and related regulatory tasks.* MKT, p. 33 (Hungarian).

Kovárik, Erzsébet. 1991. *The development of public institutions as a category of constitutional law in Hungarian public administration.* MKT, p. 43 (Hungarian).

Péteri, Gábor. 1991. *Changes of concepts: legislation on local governments 1987–1990.* MKT, p. 14 (English).

Péteri, Gábor and Gábor Szabó. 1991. *Local government in Hungary: transition, renewal and prospects.* MKT, p. 21 (English).

Rékefi, Otto. 1992. *To the latest debate on the county.* MKT, p. 29 (Hungarian).

Szabó, Gábor. 1992. *Decentralization: the nature of deconcentrated organs.* MKT, p. 35 (Hungarian).

——. 1992. *Decentralization: theoretical approaches and the history of development.* MKT, p. 56 (Hungarian).

——. 1991. *The system of external relations of local governments as reflected by current law.* MKT, p. 30 (Hungarian).

Szente, Zoltán. 1990. *Parliamentary control over local administration in Hungary.* MKT, p. 25 (Hungarian).

Vági, Gábor, 1991. *Selected studies on settlements, local councils, local governments.* Gondolat Kiadó Budapest, p. 544 (Hungarian).

Verebélyi, Imre. 1988. *Local government-type reform of the system of local councils.* MKT, I/II, 181 + 131 (Hungarian).

Wiener, György. 1992. *Constitutions and local governments.* MKT, p. 82 (Hungarian).

ADMINISTRATIVE TRANSITION IN A POST-COMMUNIST SOCIETY: THE CASE OF HUNGARY

GÁBOR SZABÓ

I INTRODUCTION

Throughout Central and Eastern Europe, we have, over the past three years or so, seen fundamental economic and political-administrative changes. In economic terms, the principal development has been the move away from centrally planned economies towards market-oriented economic systems. In the political-administrative sphere, the dominant trend has been the emergence of pluralistic and democratic polities; at the local level, this has been accompanied by the abolition of Soviet-type local councils and the constitution of a sphere of independent local government, enjoying a comparatively high degree of autonomy in the state structure. These changes in the economic and political-administrative spheres have been widely discussed under such labels as liberalization, deregulation and privatization as regards the national economy; democratization and institutional transformation to describe political reform at the national and local levels; and, finally, reorganization, de-étatisation, decentralization and deregulation as far as public administration is concerned.

In discussing the transition experience in the post-Communist countries, the significant differences in the economies and political-administrative systems of the Socialist regimes in the former Soviet bloc have to be remembered. These differences partly explain the distinct national experiences in the transition phase. There is, therefore, only limited scope for generalizations about the nature of the transition processes in Central and Eastern Europe. In fact, it can be argued that, in a comparative analysis, attention should focus as much on *differentia specificas* as on those features and characteristics which the countries have in common (Elander and Gustafsson 1991; Hesse 1991; Péteri 1991). For example, in the political sphere, the hard-line regimes in the Soviet Union, Czechoslovakia, Romania or the German Democratic Republic were clearly very different from

Dr Gábor Szabó is Deputy Director of the Hungarian Institute of Public Administration, Budapest.

those found in Poland or Hungary, as the latter showed more openness to economic reforms and a greater degree of political tolerance. These country characteristics do not just reflect different historical experiences during the last four or five decades, but are sometimes indicative of many centuries of distinct national history. To varying degrees, these specific historical traditions have also left their mark on the political and economic development in the recent transition period. For example, a comparison of the countries of the so-called Visegrad Triangle, i.e. the former Czech and Slovak Federative Republic, Hungary and Poland, on the one hand, and the former Balkan states of Albania, Bulgaria and Romania, on the other, reveals very important differences in the dynamics of the transition process. Equally, economic, political and institutional change has taken a very different course in the European republics of the former Soviet Union, on the one hand, and the central Asian states, on the other. In short, then, whilst the post-Communist countries share important historical experiences, which make for a certain commonality in the transition challenges they face, there are equally significant differences, which narrowly limit the scope for cross-country generalizations.

But it is not just differences between post-Communist countries which need to be taken into account. Attention must also focus on diverse economic, political, social and cultural traditions within individual countries. In this respect, the Czech and Slovak Republics serve as the prime, and bearing in mind the separation of CSFR at the beginning of 1993 also the most realistic, example. Here, economic as well as cultural differences between, on the one hand, Bohemia and Moravia, which used to belong amongst the economically most advanced European countries, and, on the other hand, Slovakia, which formed an integral part of the Hungarian Kingdom and was economically far less developed, are of particular importance. But one might also mention, for example, the Ukraine, with the very pronounced economic disparities between its eastern parts, which belonged to the Russian Empire, and the western parts of the country, which formerly were part of the Austro-Hungarian Empire.

The following discussion concentrates on the transition experience in Hungary since the late 1980s, and it seeks to highlight some of the special conditions under which this transition process has taken place. These special difficulties, it is argued, help to explain some of the process's particular characteristics. Arguably the most important feature of the political, legal and economic transition has been its evolutionary character, which contrasts sharply with the experience in some other Central and Eastern European countries (Balázs 1991). The 'quiet revolution' in Hungary differed fundamentally from the 'velvet revolution' in the Czech and Slovak Federative Republic, or, even more evidently, the 'bloody revolution' in Romania. In Hungary, transition has meant step-by-step change, rather than the abrupt, revolutionary overthrow of the Communist regime. At least since the mid-1960s, the gradual introduction of market-type elements into the Socialist economic system and relative, though strictly limited political tolerance were slowly preparing the way for a peaceful evolutionary change from Socialism to capitalism.

II LEGAL TRANSITION AND THE ROLE OF PARLIAMENT

It is appropriate to begin the analysis of the Hungarian transition process by looking first at the role of the Hungarian Parliament. Evidently, political change and the need for legal-constitutional adjustment put a considerable burden on the legislative body. Over the last few years, the Hungarian Parliament has been faced with the task of achieving a complete renewal of the legal framework. This has involved the adoption of a great number of new legislative acts, and countless amendments to existing acts in order to provide a solid legal basis for a functioning pluralistic, democratic system and a market-oriented economy. Since the beginning of 1990, 100 new acts or significant amendments have, on average, been passed every year. Thus, in 1990, 104 new or substantially altered laws were adopted; the equivalent figure for 1991 was 93, and during 1992, 86 new or significantly altered laws were adopted. These figures compare with an average of just ten parliamentary acts per year during the 1970s and 1980s. The dramatic increase in Parliament's legislative activity has two main reasons. Firstly, political and economic transition has, of course, necessitated far-reaching legal adjustments. Secondly, the scope and function of the legislative body have changed fundamentally. During the Socialist era, Parliament played merely a subordinate role as, in fact, all important political decisions were taken outside the legislature, generally by central Communist Party organs. By contrast, the Parliament elected in 1990 has, by international standards, an exceptionally broad scope of functions, which enables it to fulfil its duties as the supreme representative and legislative body.

One of the most salient features of recent legislation has been the high number of amendments which are being adopted. This refers not only to amendments concerning legal acts inherited from the previous regime; but also to newly adopted laws that are subject to frequent amendments. There are a number of reasons for this. Clearly, the legislative agenda of Parliament is very crowded. At the same time, the preparation and implementation of new legal regulations place a great burden on government and public administration. As a result, the preparation of bills and acts is often insufficient, and the great speed with which new legislation is put on the statute book means that there is often not enough time to iron out problems in individual pieces of legislation. Thus, the need for amendments is built into new legislation. Moreover, the political struggle between the coalition government and the opposition parties means that compromises and concessions will often be reflected in legislative amendments. Sometimes, this leads to deliberately vague and unspecific regulations, which require further elaboration at a later stage. Finally, rulings by the Constitutional Court have repeatedly necessitated substantial modifications to existing legislative acts in order to bring them into line with constitutional law.

III ECONOMIC TRANSITION

In moving towards a market economy, Hungary has enjoyed definite advantages compared to other post-Communist countries. Some of the key legal institutions

TABLE 1   Major parliamentary acts on economic transformation

Act v of 1988 on the Economic Companies (amended).
Act xxiv of 1988 on the Foreign Investments in Hungary (amended twice).
Act xiii of 1989 on the Transformation of Economic Organizations and Companies (amended twice).
Act xl of 1989 on the Value Added Tax (amended twice).
Act i of 1990 on the Amendment of Civil Law Codex.
Act v of 1990 on Private Entrepreneurship.
Act vi of 1990 on the Floating and Circulation of Stocks and Bonds and on the Stock Exchange.
Act vii of 1990 on the State Property Agency and on the Management and Utilization of State Properties (amended).
Act xxii of 1990 on the Repeal and Amendment of Legal Acts (The Deregulation Act, amended).
Act lxxi of 1990 on the Amendment of State Enterprise Regulations.
Act lxxiv of 1990 on the Privatization of State Enterprises in the Fields of Retail Trade and Catering Trade.
Act lxxxvi of 1990 on the Prohibition on Unfair Market Activity.
Act lxxxvii 1990 on the Determination of Prices (amended).
Act iv of 1991 on the Incentive of Employment and on the Support of the Unemployed (amended twice).
Act xiv of 1991 on the Amendment of Civil Law Codex.
Act xvi of 1991 on the Concessions.
Act xxv of 1991: The First Compensation Act (amended).
Act xxxii of 1991 on the Arrangement of the Ownership of Ex-Church Real Estates.
Act xxxiii of 1991 on the Transfer of Certain State Properties to the Ownership of Local Self-governments.
Act xlix of 1991 on the Procedure of Bankruptcy Cases.
Act lx of 1991 on the Hungarian National Bank.
Act lxiii of 1991 on the Investment Funds.
Act lxix of 1991 on the Banking Institutions and their Activities.
Act lxxxvi of 1991 on the Company Tax.
Act xc of 1991 on the Personal Income Tax (amended).
Act i of 1992 on the Co-operatives.
Act xxii of 1992 on Labour Codex.
Act xxiv of 1992: The Second Compensation Act.
Act xxxii of 1992: The Third Compensation Act
Act xliv of 1992 on the Employee Part-owner Project

For key legal regulations, see p. 76.

associated with a market-type economy already existed in Hungary before the political changes of 1989/1990. For instance, throughout the Communist period, there were laws regulating enterprises and limited companies; these acts were not systematically applied, but as institutions they remained familiar. Modern income tax and value added tax systems were already introduced in the second half of the 1980s. Or, to give another example, a new modernized company code has already been in effect since 1988. Many other examples could be added, but the decisive point to note is that vital parts of the legal framework needed for a functioning market economy were in place before the Communists lost power. There can be little doubt that this fact has assisted the transition process, although this is not to deny that very substantial further economic reform legislation has been needed. Another factor facilitating economic transition has been the gradual adjustment of prices to world market realities, which began already in the early 1980s. Consequently, post-Communist price liberalization has not had such a drastic effect as in some other Central and Eastern European countries.

All this is not to ignore the contrast between a functioning market economy and Socialist planned economy interspersed with some market-type elements. The transformation of the latter into an unequivocally market-oriented economy involves both extensive legal deregulation and re-regulation, and a definite decrease of the state powers and competences in the economy. Apart from price liberalization, this includes, for example, the freeing of foreign trade (both export and import were previously state monopolies) or the removal of legal obstacles to the free acquisition of property. The aim of this and other measures that were adopted over the last three years or so, is to achieve a fundamental liberalization of the economy. At the same time, particularly as far as legal regulation is concerned, one of the overriding concerns has been to ensure that the new legal framework is compatible with the future membership of Hungary in the European Community.

But liberalization cannot just be equated with the withdrawal of the state from the economy. There are certain fields where increased state activity, or state activity of a new quality, is required, at least temporarily. This includes, in particular, the privatization of state property, on the one hand, and compensation for losses and damages suffered by individuals during wartime and the Communist era, on the other. Both tasks require state-led management, and the establishment of a State Property Agency (to manage the privatization process) and a National Compensation Office (with county branches) testify to this fact. At the moment, it is planned that these state institutions will be wound up once their original tasks have been achieved, although it is already clear that they will be active for much longer than many had initially expected.

IV   DEMOCRATIC REFORM

Turning from economic to political reform, it should first be noted that, in legal terms, the institutionalization of a modern, pluralistic and democratic political structure has been more or less completed. However, it has proved difficult to bring the spirit of these acts to life in the face of increasing popular alienation from the political process, the citizens' growing passiveness in public life and a widespread withdrawal from procedures of civil participation. The drastic decline in electoral turnout has often been cited as a prime example of this tendency.

In 1990, during the first free elections at the national and local levels, turnout reached more than 60 per cent in the national elections and around 40 per cent in the local elections. In 1991 and 1992, by-elections were held in a majority of constituencies, with turnout falling to approximately 20 per cent. The most notorious case of voter disaffection occurred in the Kisbér constituency. Here, a by-election for a seat in the National Assembly resulted in no less than eight election rounds, none of which satisfied the minimum requirement for electoral participation of 25 per cent stipulated in the National Election Act; in some rounds the participation did not even reach 10 per cent. As a result, the constituency did not have a representative in Parliament for more than a year. As far as local by-elections are concerned, citizen participation shows very similar patterns; if anything, participation rates are even lower in local by-elections. Unlike the National Election Act, the current Local Election Act, however, does not set a minimum quota for electoral participation in a second round. Consequently, at the local level, very low turnout has not translated into problems in filling the seats in local councils, although it is sometimes difficult to find candidates willing to stand in a local by-election.

Another manifestation of the citizens' progressive alienation from the political process is found in the growing popular disenchantment with political parties, Parliament and local councils. Empirical data show that there is a seemingly ever increasing animus against party politicians and parliamentary and local representatives. One of the main explanations for this increasingly hostile attitude is the economic difficulties experienced by many Hungarians. Up until the mid-1980s, Hungary's citizens enjoyed relatively high living standards compared with the other Socialist countries of Central and Eastern Europe; but during the last stages of the Communist era their living standards began to decline. The economic miracle that many expected from the transition to a market economy has thus far not materialized, and signs of an upward trend in economic development are still rare. If anything, the living situation of many Hungarians appears to have continued to worsen. At some point, the inflation rate reached almost 35 per cent (it has now fallen to around 25 per cent), and the unemployment rate has risen steadily (recently 12 per cent). The widespread feeling of disappointment and uncertainty which has resulted from these economic difficulties has translated into popular disaffection with some of the new institutions of democratic government and its representatives, most notably the political parties. Even the freely elected Parliament was roughly challenged, since recently the Society of People Living under Minimum Incomes has initiated – through a referendum – the dissolution of Parliament and the holding of new general elections.

This process of growing dissatisfaction and disenchantment developed in two stages. It affected, in the first place, the ruling conservative coalition, consisting of the Hungarian Democratic Forum, the Smallholders' Party, and the Christian Democratic Popular Party. Increasingly, the people had to realize that the coalition government could not bring about, at least in the short term, the economic miracle many had hoped for; on the contrary, there was a growing realization that things would have to get worse before they started to improve. In a second stage, popular discontent also began to affect the liberal opposition parties in Parliament, that is the Alliance of Free Democrats and the Alliance of Young Democrats, who had won the local government elections in most major towns and the capital. Increasingly, it became clear that the liberal parties at the local level, just like the ruling conservative parties at the national level, could not produce a swift economic recovery. As far as the other main parliamentary grouping, the Hungarian Socialist Party, is concerned, it is one of the successors of the former Communist Party and, hitherto, has had to take much of the blame for the errors of the Communist years; however, most recently some increase in popularity has been observed.

The crucial question is what the consequences of such popular alienation and dissatisfaction are for the future course of democratic reform. In particular, is there any real danger of a backlash against democracy, which might result in a form of totalitarianism as an attempt to avoid chaos? (Hesse 1991). Undoubtedly, a look across the post-Communist states of Central and Eastern Europe gives cause for concern. However, at least as far as the Hungarian case is concerned, there are also many signs to justify moderate optimism about the country's future, and their number is growing. For example, Hungary is not affected by shortages, and the shops sell a great variety of consumer goods, for which there is strong demand. The emergence of a vigorous middle class is anticipated. Investment by foreign and domestic investors is on the increase, and it should be noted that more than half of all foreign investment in the region goes to Hungary. Unlike other post-Communist societies, Hungary does not face internal ethnic minority problems, and there are no potentially disruptive separatist movements.

In short, there is a real prospect for a prolonged, but calm transition towards the ultimate aim of integrating Hungary into a common European house. To achieve this objective, it is necessary to internalize and defend certain basic standards of political culture generally accepted throughout the democratic world. In order to exploit the opportunities which democracy affords, it is, for example, necessary to develop commonly recognized standards of how to deal with the means of direct, representative and participatory democracy; and it is essential to develop acceptable practices in dealing with minority opinions and criticism from the opposition, the press, and other groups in society. In this respect, it is not enough to have the appropriate legal framework in place; what is needed is to transform the rules into proper practice and make them effective in everyday political life.

V INSTITUTIONAL TRANSFORMATION

Recent change in Hungarian public administration can be summarized under four main headings: reorganization, de-étatisation, decentralization and deregulation. These developments have affected both state administration, including territorial state administration, and local government, including the administration of municipalities (villages, towns and county towns) and counties. Re-organization has two dimensions: firstly, the reorganization of the system of public administration as a whole or as an individual tier or branch; and, secondly, the reorganization of an individual administrative institution. As figures 1 and 2 illustrate, there have been very significant changes in the basic structure of public administration as a whole. The most important have included the creation of the institution of the Commissioners of the Republic and the constitution of an independent sphere of local self-government. In the Soviet-type local government system, all local councils, or rather their executive committees, formed an integral part of a strictly hierarchical state structure. The activities of the councils were subject to the supervision and control of higher level organs, that is higher level councils or the Council of Ministers. This system of subordination of local councils was very similar to the subordination of deconcentrated state organs under central control. At the same time, local councils were subject to directives of the Communist Party.

With the introduction of a new local government system, this situation changed fundamentally. Local governments are no longer part of state administration, and the subordination of municipal councils under county council control was abolished. There is no longer any hierarchy between municipalities and counties; their relationship is characterized by equality, and county government has no supervisory function in relation to municipal governments. Both county and municipal governments are subject to limited legal controls. In the first instance, these are exercised by the Commissioners of the Republic, who represent a genuinely new institution in the Hungarian administrative system. Their rights in this respect are limited to noting if a local government, in the Commissioner's opinion, acts in violation of the law. If the local government in question fails to act on the Commissioner's notice, the only way of action open to the Commissioner is to take the local authority to court.

De-étatisation is, obviously, very closely connected to structural reorganization. With local government reform, the state withdrew from most local affairs, leaving their management to locally elected bodies. As a result, in some significant fields of public administration, the state no longer possesses an administrative capacity of its own, but is restricted to exercising legal control over local activities through the Commissioners of the Republic.

Territorial decentralization, as the third major trend in Hungarian public administration, is not, of course, a new phenomenon in the country's administrative history. Starting from the late 1960s, a growing number of tasks and functions were gradually decentralized, and this process of decentralization has been taken further during the transition period, through the strengthening of local government and the building up of decentralized state administrative capacities. As will be discussed below, such territorial decentralization has raised significant problems of horizontal differentiation, the appropriate division of tasks and co-ordination.

Finally, legal deregulation has had a very immediate impact on public administration. The first substantial deregulation programme was enacted at the

FIGURE 1   *The basic structure of public administration in the 1980s*

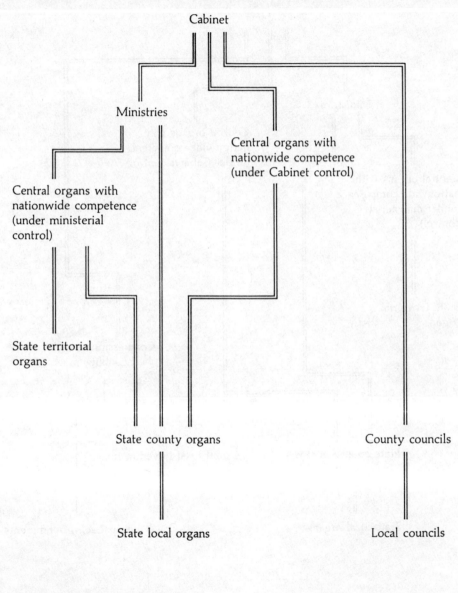

Cabinet

Ministries

Central organs with
nationwide competence
(under Cabinet control)

Central organs with
nationwide competence
(under ministerial
control)

State territorial
organs

State county organs

County councils

State local organs

Local councils

══════════════ = *subordination*

FIGURE 2   *The basic structure of public administration in 1992*

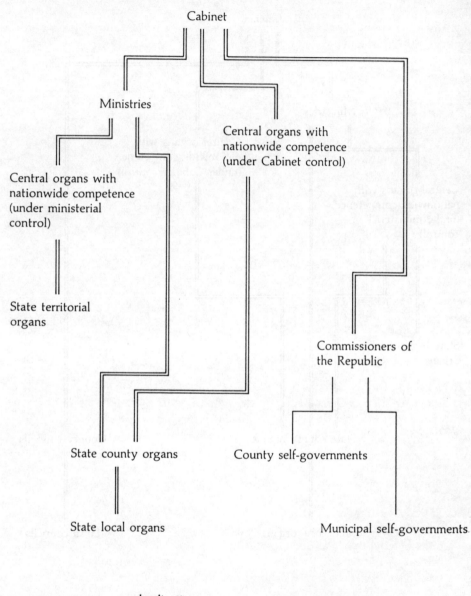

Cabinet

Ministries

Central organs with
nationwide competence
(under Cabinet control)

Central organs with
nationwide competence
(under ministerial
control)

State territorial
organs

Commissioners of
the Republic

State county organs   County self-governments

State local organs   Municipal self-governments.

============================ = *subordination*
———————————— = *legal control*

beginning of 1990, and from that time all legal regulations, including parliamentary acts and governmental and ministerial decrees, have been subject to review procedures which seek to assess the necessity of a proposed legal regulation. The recently adopted government programme for the modernization of Hungarian public administration also stresses the importance of legal deregulation. According to this programme, arrangements are to be made for repealing superfluous regulations and for simplifying other acts and decrees.

VI THE FUTURE OF HUNGARIAN PUBLIC ADMINISTRATION

As in the economic and political spheres, the re-shaping of public administration involved the adoption of several pieces of important reform legislation see the overview in I. Balázs' contribution to this volume. Amongst these, the Local Government Act of 1990 and the 1991 Act on the Scope and Functions of Local Government, the Commissioners of the Republic and Some Deconcentrated State Organs were of particular significance. Taken together, these Acts have already led to a considerable transformation in Hungarian public administration; there are, however, still many unresolved issues, which need to be tackled in the next stages of administrative modernization. As far as the central level of state administration is concerned, reorganization in this field has not, until now, been as comprehensive and fundamental as in the spheres of territorial state administration and local government. In the main, reorganization measures have focused on two matters. First, the departmental structure was modified. The number of ministries was reduced, a process which was accompanied by the partial interdepartmental reallocation of tasks and functions. The second major reform concerned the top ministerial leadership. All ministries now follow the same organizational model, which divides the ministry's leadership into a political sphere, consisting of the minister and a political secretary, and the administrative sphere, which includes an administrative secretary and his deputies (see figure 3). Turning to likely future developments at this level, the government's modernization programme attaches particular importance to the central level and aims at the streamlining of central competences, functions, structures and administrative procedures. In particular, the modernization programme envisages

— a review of the organization and operation of the government, which looks, in particular, at decision-making mechanisms and practices in cabinet; the tasks of governmental bodies, including the role and functions of the Prime Minister's Office; and the role of governmental supervision and control;
— the division of tasks and functions amongst ministries and between departments and other central organs with nation-wide competence; and
— the modernization of the ministries' internal organization and management.

Concerning territorial and local public administration, the main goal thus far has been the establishment of a genuine, democratically legitimated local government system (Elander and Gustafsson 1991). As was discussed above, local government reform has resulted in a fundamental redefinition of the position of local government in the political-administrative system. However, it has also raised a number of problems, which future reform efforts will have to tackle. Perhaps the most problematic aspects of the current system concern the county tier and the position of small local authorities in rural areas. In both cases, the regulations that were adopted in 1990 bear the marks of uneasy political compromises, and can only be understood against the background of the suppression of independent local government under the Socialist system. The constitutional requirement of a two-thirds parliamentary majority for the adoption of local government legislation ensured that the new legal framework commanded broad political support. On the other hand, the emphasis on solutions acceptable to both the governing coalition parties and parts of the parliamentary opposition implied that the legislation adopted was less reflective of a comprehensive, integrated and co-ordinated reform design than the need to accommodate and placate different constituencies and points of view in the government and the opposition.

At the county level, the oppressive role of county councils as the chief agents for the implementation of central policies and as organs of central control and supervision over the municipalities under Socialism was still very fresh in people's minds in 1990 (Horváth 1989). It is not surprising, therefore, that the county level was particularly open to attacks from all political forces, which resulted in the profound weakening of county government structures. Under the new local government system, the counties have only very limited administrative and executive functions, being restricted to public service provision in a few areas such as health policy, social welfare and education. Even in these instances, however, tasks can be taken over by municipal councils if they can show they are capable of performing them satisfactorily. Some of the former county administrative and executive functions were transferred to the Commissioners of the Republic. Their functions are essentially threefold. They exercise legal control over local government; act as a forum of appeal against local government decisions; and possess some co-ordinating powers in relation to the deconcentrated units of state administration.

At present, therefore, two types of general state organs exist at the intermediate level, the Commissioners, who have to maintain offices in every county, and the county administrations. Both are seriously deficient. The county councils, which are composed of delegates from the municipal councils in the county, can claim a qualified popular mandate, but they have only very limited, residual functions. The Commissioners, which are appointed by central government, lack any real local anchorage, but have, in principle, a broader executive scope. In practice, however, their executive functions are not really effective. The case for change at the intermediate level is, thus, compelling, and it can take two directions. It is either possible to strengthen county government and to transform the counties into real second-tier local authorities, resembling, for example, the German *Kreise*; or, alternatively, the Commissioners of the Republic could be given enhanced supervisory powers over the local level, along the lines of the French prefectoral system.

FIGURE 3   *Structure of the top leadership level in government ministries*

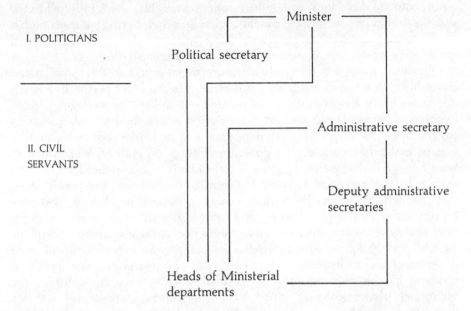

The second central weakness of the current local government system results from the position of small local authorities in rural areas. The system of joint local authorities, which existed during the era of Soviet-type councils, was politically clearly unacceptable under the altered political circumstances of 1990 (Szabó 1991). Instead, Parliament sought to enact regulations which would do justice to democratic ideals, whilst, at the same time, serving administrative efficiency. However, the system which was adopted does not really seem to produce effective outcomes. The proliferation of very small rural local authorities which resulted from the break-up of joint authorities represents a step backwards, especially if it is considered in the context of local government reorganization efforts in other European countries (Page and Goldsmith 1987; Hesse 1990/91). The fragmentation, or even atomization, of local government is one of its major deficiencies. At present, only larger local governments are really strong enough to be able to influence effectively state administration and central organs, and it is primarily these local governments which possess the necessary administrative capacities to play their active part in the intergovernmental system.

Decentralization raises the problem of horizontal differentiation between local government and deconcentrated state administration. First in the late 1960s and early 1970s and, again, in the first half of the 1980s, central authority was decentralized from upper-level administrative tiers to the lower levels, in particular local councils. This process was accompanied by the reorganization of the local level, which resulted in the amalgamation of many small villages into the above-mentioned joint councils. Since the councils were fully integrated parts of state administration, decentralization of this type did not raise specific co-ordination problems. After the change of political regime, one central question has been whether these formerly decentralized powers should remain in the – now autonomous – local government sphere or ought to be transferred to the deconcentrated organs of state administration. In other words, the question has been whether decentralization should take the form of devolution to local government or deconcentration within the state administration.

Obviously, there is both a technical-professional aspect to this question and an explicitly political element, and, at present, it is the latter perspective which dominates in the discussion. As was pointed out earlier, the local government elections of autumn 1990 resulted in a situation where the national opposition parties control the majority of larger local authorities. Under such circumstances, it is understandable that central government tends to prefer the execution of tasks through deconcentrated organs of state administration rather than handing them to local government. In fairness, it should, however, also be acknowledged that the deficiencies of the current local government regulations, and here especially the weakness of county government and the fragmented nature of rural local government, too, have a major influence on the government's attitude. Against this background, the proliferation of deconcentrated units of state government and an increase in their powers can be interpreted as a functional response to the requirements of territorial governments. By contrast, the opposition parties jealously guard local government competences and are determined to fight any proposals which, in their view, might weaken the local level and increase central controls. In this situation, further local government reform is unlikely to make real progress before the next national and local elections in 1994.

REFERENCES

Balázs, István. 1991. *The reform of the state in Central and Eastern Europe – summary and perspective*. Budapest: HIPA.

Byrne, Tony. 1990. *Local government in Britain*. Harmondsworth: Penguin Books.

Elander, Ingemar and Mattias Gustafsson. 1991. *The re-emergence of local self-government in Central Europe: the first experience*. Örebro: Högskolan i Örebro.

Gasser, Adolf. 1947. *Gemeindefreiheit als Rettung Europas*. Basel.

Hesse, Joachim Jens. 1991. 'Administrative modernisation in Central and Eastern European countries', in *Staatswissenschaften und Staatspraxis* 2, 197–217.

——. (ed.). 1991. *Local government and urban affairs in international perspective – Analyses of twenty western industrialized countries*. Baden-Baden: Nomos Verlagsgesellschaft.

Horváth, M. Tamás. 1989. 'A túlélés kockázata'. *Tér és Társadalom* 4.

Ingvartsen, Olaf and research team. 1981. *Economic and political trends in Danish local government*. Copenhagen: National Association of Local Authorities.

Kilényi, Géza. 1990. 'Hungary's road to a democratic state of the rule of law' in V. Lamm (ed.), *Democratic changes in Hungary – Basic legislations on a peaceful transition from Bolshevism to democracy*. Budapest: Law Research Centre of Hungarian Academy of Sciences.

Page, Edward C. and Michael J. Goldsmith. 1987. *Central and local government relations*. London: Sage Publications.

Page, Edward C. 1991. *Localism and centralism in Europe – The political and legal bases of local government*. Oxford: Oxford University Press.

Péteri, Gábor (ed.). 1991. *Events and changes – The first steps of local transition in East-Central Europe*. Budapest: Local Democracy and Innovation Foundation.

Szabó, Gábor. 1990. 'The Hungarian local government system in transition' in B. Jalowiecki and A. Kuklinski (eds.), *Local development in Europe – Experiences and prospects*. Warsaw: University of Warsaw.

——. 1991. 'Localities in transition: Re-emergence self-government system' in Takács K. (ed.). *The reform of Hungarian public administration*. Budapest: HIPA.

——. 1992. *Szétpontositás: Elméleti megközelitések és fejlödéstörténet*. Budapest: HIPA.

——. 1992. *The forms of decentralization in a unitary state with special regard to the role and functions of local self-government*. Budapest: HIPA.

Takács, Klára (ed.) 1991. *The reform of Hungarian public administration – Collection of studies published by the Institute in 1991 in English and French language*. Budapest: HIPA.

Verebélyi, Imre. 1987. *A tanácsi önkormányzat*. Budapest: Közgazdasági és Jogi Könyvkiadó.

OPTIONS FOR ADMINISTRATIVE REFORM IN HUNGARY

IMRE VEREBÉLYI

I INTRODUCTION

The tasks faced by administrative reformers in Hungary differ in important respects from those typically associated with administrative reform in the developed Western countries. In the latter, reform initiatives tend to focus on particular elements of established and, for the most part, well-functioning administrative structures; the main reform intentions are usually de-bureaucratization and administrative rationalization. By contrast, in countries such as Hungary, which have experienced a radical change in their political system, it is not just selected elements of public administration, but the administrative framework as a whole which needs to undergo fundamental change.

The comprehensive reform of Hungarian public administration that is therefore required is, of course, intimately linked to the radical changes in the political and economic system of the country. Gradually, a centrally planned economy, which was characterized by state ownership and state-socialist co-operatives, is being replaced by a market-oriented economy in which private ownership is expected to dominate. At the same time, after the dismantling of the centralized structures of the one-party state, Hungary has embarked on the establishment of a modern constitutional state based on the principles of democratic pluralism and functional decentralization. Clearly, both political and economic reform have profound implications for public administration and shape the reform agenda to a large degree; in addition, there is, of course, what might be called the routine task of de-bureaucratization and rationalization.

The comprehensive administrative reform agenda associated with democratization, pluralization, and economic liberalization has to include both central and local government as well as intergovernmental relations. At each level, reform projects must look at tasks, structures, procedures, and, importantly, personnel. It should be noted that between 1990 and the end of 1992, significant first steps

Professor Imre Verebélyi is Administrative State Secretary in the Ministry of the Interior, Budapest.

have been taken in all these areas; it is, therefore, misleading to argue that, as far as public administration is concerned, the first years of post-Communism were wasted. Fundamental structural reforms have been initiated, the main direction of which was outlined in the government's 'Programme for National Renewal' of 1990. Since then, a number of substantial legal measures for reforming public administration have been adopted, and many essential organizational decisions have already been implemented. After this first wave of reform, the principal challenge now is to complete the work that has been initiated, to make adjustments where it seems necessary and to stabilize public administration.

The tasks of completion, adjustment and stabilization are highlighted in a special administrative modernization plan and research programme which has been adopted by the Hungarian government in 1992. As far as completion is concerned, this implies, first of all, the detailed work which is still necessary to fill in the basic framework that has been created by the fundamental reforms undertaken between 1990 and 1992. This includes, in particular, the continuation of the process of democratization, a further strengthening of the legality of public administration and its control, and additional measures aimed at striking the right balance between centralization and decentralization, concentration and deconcentration. In this respect, the implementation issue needs to be given particular attention; this refers, above all, to improved mechanisms for inter-governmental co-ordination and integration.

A second type of challenge that can be grouped under the task of completion concerns the development of material and personnel administrative capacities. Reforms cannot stop at creating an appropriate institutional and legal administrative framework; it is at least important to secure the necessary material preconditions and personnel capacities required for the effective functioning of public administration. First and foremost, the skills of public servants need to be adapted to the new tasks they are confronting and the new political and economic conditions under which they are operating; at the same time their mentality and way of thinking have to change. The second determinant of administrative capacity, material resources, is, of course, always limited when compared to demand; and it is not just in Hungary that it is difficult to obtain parliamentary approval for increased expenditure on public administration. Against this background, it is imperative to stress the tangible benefits of administrative modernization in terms of the potential savings through a more efficient public administration.

Turning to the second major reform task, adjustment and partial correction, it needs to be acknowledged that in reaction to the previous regime, some of the first reforms to introduce a democratic institutional framework failed to strike the right balance. For example, the restrictions placed on the scope of action of public administration through the constitutional state turned out to be excessive; likewise, decentralization has been carried too far in some respects; and in international comparison, it would seem that executive power and the in-dependent professional functions of central and local public administration are underdeveloped. This is in no way to argue that the initial reforms were fundamentally misguided; it is simply to say that in certain areas adjustments are needed. Calls for powerful representative bodies, close restrictions on public administration, a weak central government and the strongest possible local autonomy during the first phase of institutional reform were understandable, given the experience with 'democratic centralism'. However, they have resulted in a situation where the government's power to act is too narrowly restricted, whilst a number of executive tasks have been delegated to the legislature. In other words, Parliament is not only responsible for legislation, but also, in part, for executive tasks. Similarly, at the local government level, the functions of the mayor and the chief local executive are not clearly distinguished, but the role of the local councils is defined too extensively. As regards intergovernmental relations, the local government system is now highly decentralized; however, mechanisms for vertical integration (for example through state supervision) and hori-zontal co-operation (for example through local associations) are largely under-developed.

Of course, these questions are not just of a technical-administrative character, but have strong political implications. The question is, therefore, whether politicians are able to afford to strengthen what is not a universally popular public administration. In particular, are the government and the opposition prepared to restrict the over-extended role of representative bodies, to address the excesses of local autonomy, and to loosen the legal chains of the 'judges state' which now threaten to undermine the effective and efficient functioning of public administration? Similarly, the government needs to decide whether it has the political will to risk conflict with departmental interests by tackling ministerial decentralization and by transferring some of the responsibilities of deconcentrated state offices to local self-government.

In essence, adjustment and correction imply the attempt to strike a workable balance between the power of representative bodies and a professional administration; legality and the efficiency of administration, decentralization and centralization; and, finally, decentralized local government and deconcentrated state administration. In this process of adjustment and correction, Hungarian public administration can draw on a comparatively rich academic expertise. Today, there are domestic academic specialists and experienced practitioners for almost every administrative issue, and their expertise can often be supplemented by experts from abroad. However, without the support of government and Parliament and without political perseverance in the case of implementation, progressive professional ideas will only enrich the shelves of academic libraries and, perhaps, the professional knowledge of future generations.

II DEMOCRATIZING PUBLIC ADMINISTRATION

Democratization has been the first main element in the process of transforming Hungarian public administration. This has implied that public administration has been firmly subordinated under democratically legitimated decision-making organs and individuals. They have assumed a determining role *vis-à-vis* the central and local administrations, which prepare their decisions and are responsible for their implementation.

The fundamental acts of Parliament adopted to ensure effective democratic controls over public administration maximized the role of representative institutions and elected officials; at the same time, there was a tendency to place the greatest possible limitations on the previously overpowering administration. This emphasis on limiting the scope of administrative action can at least in part be explained by the political mistrust for administrators, an understandable legacy from the previous regime. However, it would seem that under the label of 'democratization', executive power and public administration have been restricted to an extent which is scarcely compatible with the requirements of a modern state. Conversely, legislative and executive powers have been partly merged in Parliament. As a result, Parliament has become overburdened and thus finds it difficult to fulfil effectively its primary legislative task. Political and economic reform inevitably place very high demands on Parliament's legislative capacity; the fact that the legislative body is also responsible for what would normally be considered executive-type regulatory tasks means that it suffers from an acute work overload.

Whilst the government and state administration are subject to excessive restrictions on their scope of action, the opposite is true of the local government level. With the 1990 reforms, a local government system has been created in which the local level enjoys very substantial opportunities for separation and autonomy in relation to central government, state administration, and even Parliament. As at the central level, however, the powers of the democratically legitimated institutions and individuals over local administration have been over-emphasized. In other words, at the local level, too, the scope of action of the executive organs is unduly restricted.

Whilst in some areas, then, the concern with establishing effective democratic controls over public administration has resulted in excessive constraints, in other respects steps for further democratization are urgently required. For instance, the creation of the institution of a Commissioner for Citizens' Rights could be an effective means of protecting the rights of the individual citizen against public administration. There is also a need for improving the representation of national and ethnic minorities in the representative bodies which control central and local public administration. Another issue which should be addressed concerns the preparatory procedures for administrative decision-making. In this respect, it needs to be examined how the role of the public in the preparation of administrative decisions might be strengthened. Moreover, greater emphasis needs to be placed on co-operative behaviour in public administration. Citizens should not be treated as subjects, but as partners of a public administration which exists to serve the citizens' needs.

Next to measures aimed at enhancing public representation, participatory mechanisms should also be improved. For instance, in the direct management of central and local services, users need to be given a more active role than they play at the moment. Here, organizational and legal possibilities for such a more direct and active involvement need to be created. They could, for example, include the establishment of joint bodies composed of regulators, providers and users and the granting of rights of consultation, joint decision making and control to such bodies.

It should be clear from the above discussion that the basic legal framework for the comprehensive democratization of Hungarian public administration is, for the most part, already in place. What the experience of the last two to three years shows is that this framework needs to be completed in certain respects and that a certain amount of adjustment and fine-tuning is now required. At the same time, the material preconditions and the personnel capacities necessary for implementing the existing legal regulations need to be improved. The programme for the modernization of public administration which was mentioned above focuses, by its nature, on the strengthening of the democratic institutional framework from the perspective of public administration itself. Whilst this constitutes an important aspect of democratization, it is not in itself sufficient. This is why, parallel to the modernization programme, other initiatives aimed at the further democratization of state and society, in particular at the local level, need to be launched. In this connection, it would, for example, make sense to examine the local and national electoral system, the scope of activities of elected bodies and individuals, and, in particular, the potential role of self-organizing and community associations and their relations with other institutions of democratic government. Perhaps most importantly, it is necessary to improve access to information on local democracy, the role of local representative bodies, their committees and independent local organizations. The democratic development of local government as one of the fundamental tasks should, as far as possible be detached from the conflicts of national and party politics. This would certainly be made easier if local, national and general elections were not held at the same time.

III   THE LEGAL FRAMEWORK AND THE LEGALITY OF PUBLIC ADMINISTRATION

Legality implies, first, that public administration carries out its activities in the way permitted by the provisions of law and, secondly, that these provisions comply with the requirements of a state governed by the rule of law. To meet both requirements, Hungary needs to join the pertinent international agreements, ratify them, and revise domestic regulations which are inconsistent with international standards. During the first period of political change, the creation of new legal structures took priority over the systematic review of the enormous amount of legal regulations inherited from the previous regime. Partly because it has been over-burdened with creating new laws, public administration has fallen behind with reviewing existing regulations; and only a comparatively small number of these rules and regulations have been declared unconstitutional by the Constitutional Court. Consequently, a substantial part of the current body of law is incompatible with the requirements of the state based on the rule of law. In recognition of this fact, the government's administrative modernization programme stresses the need for a comprehensive review of existing legal regulations especially concerning their compatibility with democratic standards of legality.

Another legal issue requiring attention concerns the responsibility for law-making. It is increasingly evident that governmental and ministerial legal regulation cannot and should not be simply transferred to the sphere of parliamentary legislation. During a period of systemic change and within certain well-defined areas, the government should have the right to pass decrees concerning matters that are in urgent need of legal regulation. To prevent any abuse, government regulations should only have a temporary character. This could be achieved, for example, by making the authorization of legal regulation through government conditional upon the adoption of an act of Parliament within a period of one or two years. Perhaps more importantly, the constitution should clearly identify the scope and subjects of parliamentary legislation, with the implication that unlisted areas would fall under the regulating competence of the government or individual ministries.

Both current Hungarian constitutional provisions (which, in themselves, have scope for further improvements), and international agreements concerning the legality of public administration often allow for more than one legal arrangement. In the attempts to satisfy the requirements of a state governed by law, however, there has been a tendency to impose maximum legal restrictions on executive power, especially as far as judicial review procedures are concerned. At present, there are too many review and appeal levels, often with suspending powers. This kind of multiple 'over insurance' contradicts the concept of reasonableness in the practical application of law; more worryingly, it harms the true interests of citizens turning to public administration. Therefore, the type of review procedure applicable in a particular matter needs to be identified more clearly and the procedures need to be simplified. As regards conflicts between public institutions, a number of improvements seem vital. In particular, the courts should be given wider scope in settling disputes between local governments. This is especially important if, in future, the law might require inter-municipal agreements in certain matters, but individual local governments fail to reach consensus. It should also be examined to what extent the jurisdiction of the Constitutional Court in local government affairs could be narrowed and competences be transferred to ordinary courts.

Whilst judicial review procedures need to be made more efficient and effective, it should be acknowledged that the general standards of law application by public administration in Hungary are high. Notwithstanding the occasional transgression of their roles by the new, inexperienced democratic bodies, the basic legality of administrative activity was not undermined. This said, however, there have been proceedings against unlawful administrative activity, and although they have been relatively few in number, they do, of course, profoundly affect the parties involved. It is, therefore, important to think about ways of further strengthening mechanisms to ensure the legality of public administration.

This might include, for example, improved legal training for officials; and further directions and other professional information for a unified application of the law.

At the same time, however, further organizational measures are necessary to improve the material conditions as well as personnel capacities in the administrative courts. The need for legal interpretation partly reflects the often vague, imprecise or incomplete wording of legal acts, especially those adopted at the beginning of the transition period. Constitutional and ordinary laws often bear the marks of the difficult political compromises through which they were achieved. The involvement of the constitutional courts and the ordinary courts of justice in interpreting these laws, is, thus, almost inevitable.

Turning to developments in public administration itself, it is reasonable to expect that the relative importance of hierarchical control will diminish, especially in economic administration. This handover of operative control will be accompanied by a growing need to control compliance with the law, though this will have a much narrower scope than operative control. Instead of the previous emphasis on hierarchical control, the actions of public authorities will increasingly be directed towards mediation. This is especially the case since, in other policy areas too, authoritative administrative action will diminish in response to the liberalization of the activities of individuals and institutions. It is therefore likely that the scope of public administration will widen where it provides recommendations and acts as a co-organizer or contracting party. Such modes of action will also have to play a major role where the state's hierarchical and authoritative interference seems no longer adequate, but public authorities still need to have the capacity to co-ordinate the private actors.

Still, the exercise of public authority remains a central task of public administration. It is, therefore, necessary to win acceptance for the exercise of public power in the course of implementing the rules and regulations. The best way to ensure public acceptance of authoritative action is that the legislator only requires public administrative authority in specified and well-justified areas and within precisely defined boundaries. Popular dissatisfaction with public administration usually grows when the authorities interfere with private activities in cases that cannot be convincingly justified with reference to the public interest. Thus, all public servants who have immediate contact with the public should be encouraged to identify regulations which, in their opinion, ought not to be applied, because they are (no longer) appropriate.

IV   TERRITORIAL AND LOCAL GOVERNANCE

One of the key tasks of administrative modernization is to re-examine and, where necessary, to readjust the degree of decentralization and deconcentration in policy-making. It would be mistaken to suggest a general direction which such a readjustment ought to take. Depending on the task in hand, a higher or lower degree of centralization or a higher or lower degree of deconcentration may be desirable. As was noted above, the local government system is one area where such a re-examination is of particular importance. The Hungarian Act on Local Government of 1990, which put into effect the provisions laid down in the European Charter of Local Government, signalled a decisive break with the Socialist Council system. However, few doubt that the Act exaggerates certain local autonomies, and it clearly fails to provide for the adequate co-ordination, integration and supervision of Hungary's more than 3,000 municipalities.

In the previous Soviet-type local government system, local councils operated as part of state administration; thus, local councils had administrative responsibility for many tasks which in the majority of Western democracies are carried out by deconcentrated state organs rather than local government. Following the creation of a sphere of independent local government, separate from state administration, the number of deconcentrated state services and administrative institutions, therefore, increased. Some local governments, particularly at the county and town levels, felt that they have lost rather than gained competences as a result of local government reform; and indeed, it is evident that some central ministries have exaggerated the need for deconcentrated state organs. In future, there needs to be a much more careful analysis as to which tasks should be handled by deconcentrated state organs and which tasks could be carried out by local governments, either in the form of delegated tasks or as genuine local government responsibilities. In this connection, the recently adopted modernization programme envisages that all governmental and administrative rules and regulations that were adopted prior to the change in the political system but are still in force, will be reviewed. Based on old centralizing concepts, they often place undue restrictions on local autonomy, which are incompatible with the municipalities' new status. Finally, decentralization will be strengthened by the gradual improvement in personnel capacities at the local level.

One very important issue to be addressed concerns ways and means to improve the co-ordination between local governments and deconcentrated units of state administration. Closely connected to this is the question as to how co-operation amongst deconcentrated units of state administration can be strengthened. One possible solution here is certainly improved horizontal co-ordination between deconcentrated institutions operating in the same area. The other is horizontal integration, which might mean the integration of different deconcentrated institutions into the office of the regional Commissioners of the Republic. Overall, the aim is to overcome, first, the separatism between the different branches of deconcentrated state administration and, second, the rigid separation and lack of co-ordination and co-operation between local government and state administration. What is ultimately needed is a certain degree of 'regional harmony' of the different administrative organs operating in the same area and partly dealing with the same issues.

As regards local government tasks and responsibilities, a number of comments seem appropriate at this stage. First, mandatory local government tasks, either at the municipal or the county level, need to be defined more precisely through parliamentary legislation. Concurrently, the discretionary competences of local government should be protected and strengthened. Where a local matter requires state involvement, the state should not simply transfer responsibility from local to state organs, but seek to guard the national, state interest through central control, special supervisory arrangements, financial incentives or disincentives. Once such an approach is adopted and once the potentials of central assistance and inter-municipal co-operation are fully realized, it will become obvious that the scope for self-government tasks is considerably wider than is often assumed. Nonetheless, not all tasks can be handed over to the local level. Where more extensive resources, particular professional skills and a nation-wide approach are needed, it is the state rather than self-government which should act. Moreover, there is a case for direct state administration in cases where there are conflicts of interest between local government and individual citizens. Local governments should manage public issues of such a magnitude that they can be solved within the municipality or county without directly affecting the interests of another local government; obviously, it is difficult to establish precise boundaries here.

Another local government issue that should be looked at concerns the position of towns with county rights. Here, one suggestion which has been put forward is that fewer towns with county rights are needed, but that those given such a status should play a more dynamic role than they have done so far. In the case of larger towns with county rights, it seems well worth examining the particular advantages which 'town associations' might offer. Here, one could envisage that the major cities with county rights and surrounding villages would be bound together by a local government in the form of a town association, which might be established compulsorily, without losing their independent status. Thus, in line with Hungarian historical traditions, the largest towns with county rights would be distinguished from other, smaller ones with the same rights. As regards the latter, it might make sense to allow them to elect members to the County Assembly whilst, at the same time, keeping their own county rights, too. The county government representing these small and medium-sized towns, including all those with county rights, could reacquire those regional services and tasks which were delegated to the towns, without good reasons, under the Soviet-type council system.

As regards the government of the capital Budapest, the potential advantages and disadvantages of different structural models must be carefully evaluated. Essentially, one can distinguish three models. The first regards the capital as an entity in which the individual districts keep their autonomy, but where there would be more areas for compulsory co-operation and more responsibilities for capital-wide authority than at present. A second model currently discussed would concentrate governmental activities in the capital-wide authority, whilst the districts would mainly be restricted to management activities; they would have a much narrower scope of functions than at present. The third model under consideration treats the town centre (the city) and the outer districts separately. The town centre would have a unique legal status and would enter into special co-operative associations with the outer district. Apart from examining these alternatives, it is also necessary to review the present boundaries of the capital and the administrative structure of the agglomeration as a whole.

Turning from municipal to county government, it is now widely accepted that the local government reforms weakened county government more than could be justified. The reforms exaggerated the principle of subsidiarity, and the important role of the counties in the development of their area and in distributing central funds were ignored. Therefore, one of the central questions in local administrative reform is how and to what extent this intermediate level can be strengthened. In functional terms, there are three major types of functions that could enhance the position of the counties: first, tasks which would support municipal government, especially in the smaller towns and villages; second, duties to be transferred from the deconcentrated state organs to the counties; and third, responsibilities which would be decentralized from Parliament or central government organs. As regards the latter, one could think in particular of the distribution of central funds and other distributional tasks on behalf of central government. Functional reform at the county level should avoid establishing hierarchical relations between municipal and county governments. This said, the following county functions should be analysed:

— the counties' territorial development function, including territorial planning and infrastructure;
— their obligation to maintain a wider range of – mainly intermediate level – institutions;
— their role in protecting interests, especially in relation to central state politics and/or the deconcentrated state organs and also in international sub-central co-operation;
— their assistance function *vis-à-vis* villages and towns, including the initiation of inter-municipal associations and certain co-ordinating functions;
— the possible delegation of state administrative functions to the head of the county administration as a first level state administrative authority. This, however, is disputed by many who argue that such functions should remain with the appropriate deconcentrated state organs.

In connection with the reform of county functions, the election procedure for the County Assemblies also needs to be re-examined. Some argue that if a county can essentially be viewed as equivalent to the voluntary or compulsory association of municipalities, then the county representatives should be elected by the representative body of the municipal governments. This is, of course, the current system, which might, however, be improved. Another solution, based on the premise of considerably strengthened county functions and a clear institutional separation between counties and municipalities, suggests that the county assemblies should be directly elected like municipal assemblies.

Both the future of the counties and the further development of deconcentrated units of state administration are very closely linked to the question of how the institution of the Commissioner of the Republic will evolve. At present, the Commissioner has a limited role in the legal supervision over local government, performs certain state administrative tasks prescribed by law and is responsible for co-ordinating deconcentrated units of state administration. The Commissioner also acts as a second instance authority, although this function will have to be re-examined in the context of the simplification of the judicial review procedures discussed above. The tasks and instruments assigned to the Commissioner need to be regulated unambiguously through an Act of Parliament, which should aim at enhancing and specifying the Commissioners' supervisory powers and co-ordinating functions. In this connection, it is particularly necessary to specify the cases in which the Commissioners of the Republic can interfere, either with local government or deconcentrated units of state administration, and their direct administrative responsibilities.

The tasks and structures of the deconcentrated units of state administration need to be reconsidered by branches of activity. It is likely that there is a considerable scope for merging the activities of so-called inter-area organizations, i.e. offices which operate in more than one county; here, state line services such as water supply, or directorates of public roads can be expected to be particularly affected. There might also be scope for merging deconcentrated units, currently serving only one county, into larger offices, operating in larger territories. In the course of the internal reform in the deconcentrated institutions, an attempt should be made to separate service-type functions from those linked to the exercise of public authority and control. Where deconcentrated organs have similar functions in the same area, the possibility of merging such offices should be examined. In the case of those deconcentrated units that still remain, it should be examined whether they cannot jointly carry out certain functions. Here, one might think, for example, of maintaining common joint offices for customer contact. Finally, it should be explored whether the establishment of formal or informal co-ordination and consultation forums, composed of local government representatives, the deconcentrated organs and the Commissioner's office could help to improve horizontal co-ordination, and what type of issues they might usefully address.

In re-examining territorial governance and the local government system, organizational size and viability will obviously be major considerations. In the first instance, this concerns the appropriate size for Hungarian village administrations. The structures of representation can be adapted to quite small communities, with some necessary fine-tuning; but for implementation purposes, the representative organs of small villages must be able to draw on the administrative capacities of larger organizations. There are several ways in which the latter aim can be achieved. The state can encourage the establishment of voluntary administrative associations for joint management and service provision; here, the provision of financial incentives is of particular significance. There should also be the option, however, of forming compulsory associations. These could either be restricted to certain individual functions, or form fully blown joint administrative offices. There exists, of course, already a system of rural district offices, and they have proved very useful. However, one third of the smallest villages, with a population of less than 1,000 inhabitants, have thus far not decided to join such offices, but instead have established their own village administrations. Public service delivery in villages and towns should be examined under the aspect of which type and quality of services can be provided by individual local governments and which types and qualities need some kind of joint administration. In those cases where joint administration seems clearly called for, there should be legal means for insuring that such associations are formed. In the course of the administrative modernization programme, it should be decided how the law could regulate the village contributions towards the maintenance of a joint administrative apparatus, in those cases where villages do not voluntarily agree to join a common administrative authority.

Politically, the most sensitive question is how the representative institutions of small settlements can be associated. In this area, voluntary association should certainly be the guiding principle, and, as a rule, compulsory association should not be possible. Once a local government has been formed, it must only be merged into a larger unit if it agrees to do so. But more thought is needed to determine what constitutes a reasonable minimum size of municipality in the first place; in cases where such a minimum size is not met, central government must be given the powers to be able to dissolve a local authority. As regards the distinction between villages and towns, more demanding criteria for conferring the status of town should be specified.

As was pointed out above, the representative bodies of local governments have at present a powerful position compared to the mayor; at the same time, the relations between local administration and the mayor are characterized by the unequivocal subordination of the former under the latter. To a large extent, such a structure relies on co-operation and consultation to work effectively, and, in practice, such co-operative links have not always developed. Partly, representative bodies have found it difficult to co-operate with the mayor, and, partly, local administrations, which have been inherited from the old council system, have been distrusted by the new political leadership. As regards the relations between the local council and the mayor, opportunities for strengthening his role in management issues ought to be explored.

Decisions on centralizing or decentralizing measures should not be based on considerations of power but organizational effectiveness and efficiency. In this connection, it should, again, be remembered that central influence can be brought to bear without requiring the complete centralization of decision making. Alternatives include (a) deregulation of local government issues through acts of Parliament or governmental or ministerial decrees; (b) to make central financial assistance dependent on certain conditions; (c) to make the approval of local government decisions a necessary prerequisite for their enactment; (d) to create opportunities for appeal against local government decisions; (e) to ensure proper state supervision over local government activities, for example through chief supervisors, school inspectors, audit offices, or in extreme cases, the dissolution of municipal committees; (f) central influence on local government appointments (this can include central responsibility for vocational training and examination); (g) the need for local government to prepare reports and accounts for central inspection; (h) state administration in cases where local authorities fail to carry out their duties and responsibilities. Obviously, however, the substance of inter-governmental relations is much wider than state supervision over local government. Parliament and central government also decisively influence local autonomy through financial and economic means.

V CENTRAL GOVERNMENT AND THE PUBLIC SECTOR

Turning to central administration, a basic structural division within the ministerial departments has already been established. It is, however, of a temporary nature, and needs to be put on a more permanent basis. In particular, the final legal regulation of the relations between the minister, the political and administrative state secretaries, and the administrative apparatus of the ministry should only be adopted on the basis of a detailed study of the present system. Organizational and operational rules have to be adjusted so that the harmony of hierarchical and co-ordinating relations between the different professional sections in the ministries can be maintained. Unnecessary management and transmission levels need to be eliminated. Next to the line departments, the expert systems, which support the ministerial decision-making process ought to be given a special role.

The introduction of the institution of the political and administrative state secretaries was successful. However, it is necessary to re-examine the division of tasks between the minister and the state secretaries. Within the ministry, the department and offices structured on line or activity principles should be kept under the direct supervision of the deputy secretaries wherever possible. Departments dealing with issues of general administration may exceptionally be directly subordinated to the administrative state secretary. He should also be responsible for overseeing the process of administrative modernization in his department and the institutions that fall under the department's control. In special circumstances, it might be justified to place sectoral departments under the direct control of the political state secretary and the minister. In such a case, care must be taken to avoid the simple by-passing of the administrative state secretary.

Concerning central government tasks, it was mentioned earlier that the state thus far has only a weak role in regulating and supervising local government. Here, a strengthening of the central state seems unavoidable. As far as regulation is concerned, both legislation and executive-type government decrees should be used more extensively in securing a uniform framework in which local governments can operate. At the same time, the system of central financial transfers to local government must be changed. At the moment, it leaves too little room for flexibility and fairness in adapting to different circumstances and needs; the emphasis is very much on standard and automatic payments.

There are, however, the more far-reaching questions concerning the role of autonomous or semi-autonomous institutions in the public sector. One of the key concerns of reforms in the transition period has been the rejection of étatism and an emphasis on the development of autonomous institutions, be they market institutions, social institutions or those operating in the public sector. Clearly, a modern society needs a strong underpinning of individual and community autonomies; these autonomies, however, must ultimately fit into the necessary entity of the state. And they are always to be subordinate to the regulatory and supervisory powers of the democratic state, representing the public interest. Thus, the modern state fulfils both a subsidiary role, in that it should only act where there are no individual or autonomous institutions to whom a task could be entrusted; at the same time, the state remains the ultimate supervisor and regulator. Withdrawal of the state from certain areas does not mean that autonomous institutions will be able to take its place automatically. As long as the economic, social and local organizations are comparatively weak, de-étatisation can lead to performance problems. One of the key requirements of public sector modernization is, therefore, that the subsidiary state assists in the building up of self-governing institutions. In other words, the state should help and motivate economic and social self-organization. In this respect, the state has a vital role in ensuring certain preconditions for the effective functioning of self-organizations by providing an appropriate legal framework, an institutional infrastructure, and, where appropriate, financial incentives. Also, the state can steer the development of such institutions towards the public interest. Finally, state action can be of crucial importance in overcoming transitional difficulties in making self-organizations work.

The supervision of self-governing organizations and the protection of the public interest is an exclusive state function. The state safeguards compliance with the law; guarantees security based on law; ensures the citizens' fundamental rights and duties; provides access to fundamental public services through compulsory instructions aimed at state or self-governing institutions; maintains internal order and unity; organizes international relations; collects and distributes revenue in order to fund activities of public interest. Evidently, subsidiary and exclusive state functions are always present in all states, although, of course, their quality and extent differs historically and between countries. The essential state functions are in need of protection and development. Clearly, the modern history of developed democracies disproves the earlier notion that 'the stronger the state, the weaker society'. The starting point of the Hungarian modernization programme is that the state needs to be strengthened in its proper functions and that this does not weaken but, in fact, strengthen, society.

At present, in Hungary, there is a definite growth in certain state functions. The reasons include weak self-organizational mechanisms and the need to administer the transfer of a vast amount of state assets; to settle compensation claims; to deal with the flood of refugees into Hungary; to combat an increasing crime rate; to come to terms with the consequences of a civil war on Hungary's border. In the main, these are transitional phenomena, and, therefore, they do not imply the long-term extension of state functions. This temporary increase in state tasks should be seen in connection with a modernization programme which is aimed at reducing state functions and, at the same time, increasing the efficiency in carrying out such a core of public tasks.

What is needed, therefore, are strong defences against state intervention wherever it is not strictly justified. Whenever the executive branch of the state acts in the market as owner, customer or entrepreneur, it must not limit the inviolability of private property, the freedom of trade and industry, and the autonomous regulation of market supply and demand beyond what is strictly necessary to serve the public interest. The state exercising public power must be clearly distinguished from the state acting as a property owner; in its latter role, the state must be treated exactly like all other participants in economic life. The market of public assets and public works must be regulated separate from the private markets. With the help of a strict system of public contracts, it needs to be assured that public assets are used to attain certain public interest objectives, and are not utilized so as to injure private interests. The same purpose is served through appropriate regulations for the role played by public enterprise. Finally, a differentiated legal framework for the regulation of public institutions providing non-profit-oriented services to the public needs to be devised.

The duties and responsibilities of public administration are primarily determined by the role of the state in society. Accordingly, the review of the tasks of public administration ultimately necessitates a careful examination of the role of the state. Such a review of administrative tasks is likely to result in a process of regulation, deregulation, and re-regulation. In other words, there is a need for more precision in the definition of duties and responsibilities in some areas; a need for partial administrative disengagement in others and, on occasions, a need for even more far-reaching adjustment.

VI TOWARDS AN EFFICIENT AND COST-EFFECTIVE PUBLIC ADMINISTRATION

There can be little doubt that the efficiency and effectiveness of public administration has a direct impact on a country's social and economic performance. A productive, adaptive, efficient, and professional public administration is a key factor in social and economic development and modernization. To achieve such an administration, a number of steps have to be taken. To start with, public administration can really only function efficiently, if the tasks which it is given to carry out can actually be managed by administrative means. There are many areas where public administration can act, but administration cannot, by definition, organize efficiently tasks which are alien to its role. And even where public administration can play a part, other means of action, be they of an economic or social character, should not be ignored.

To function efficiently and effectively, administration must also be provided with the appropriate responsibilities, a rational organizational framework and well-qualified staff. In Hungary, two years ago, the functions were successfully re-defined, but this was not followed by a reform of responsibilities. The fundamental organizational framework for a renewed public administration has been established, but efficiency in administrative operation is lagging behind. Quality development, in terms of democratization, legality, centralization, decentralization, and efficiency, must be complemented by quantitative developments. Administrative simplification and rationalization have a role to play here, but, obviously, rationalization cannot be the main objective of administrative modernization. A cost-saving public administration does not mean a cheap administration. Costs are only to be saved in those areas, where the reductions do not endanger effectiveness and efficiency. In order to improve both, even cost-saving initiatives may not always be able to avoid cost increases. The cost-saving potential of such initiatives will rarely exceed a few percentage points of the total cost of public administration; the larger questions concerning the administrative performance are not really addressed through cost saving. Rationalization is, therefore, very much a supplementary purpose, and subordinate to quality issues in the modernization of public administration.

International comparisons show very clearly that present staffing levels in Hungarian public administration and personnel costs cannot be considered exaggerated. At the ministerial level, the number of staff is low; there may, however, be some scope for staff reductions in certain deconcentrated state institutions. As regards local government, there has been an upward trend since local government reform.

Cost-saving programmes find their main target not in the running costs of public administration itself, but in external administrative activities. In performing its external activities, public administration acts as a manager of finances. Here, cost-saving potentials exist in procurement, tendering, the more efficient organization of programmes, better evaluation techniques, and the application of up-to-date methods for asset management and financial controls.

THE CRISIS OF PUBLIC ADMINISTRATION IN RUSSIA

MICHEL LESAGE

I INTRODUCTION

Until 1989, public administration in the USSR was one of the instruments used by the Communist Party of the Soviet Union to implement its policy. Economic power lay in the hands of the state, under the leadership of the Party while the higher ranks of the administration were in charge of directing all its activities. The main characteristic of the administration was its complete subordination to the Party apparatus, facilitated by the fact that the administration did not have its own system for recruiting civil servants; this was controlled by the Party too. There were no legal guarantees of tenure of office for civil servants. Their only protection was a form of social solidarity which enabled them to maintain their positions and also, to some extent, resist political power.

The reform of the political environment, which was initiated in 1988, produced the collapse of this administrative system and, as a direct consequence, the present crisis in Russian administration, which acknowledges no master and no rules.

II THE BLUEPRINT FOR REFORM: THE XIXth PARTY CONFERENCE

The XIXth Party Conference in June 1988 believed that it was possible to reconcile the leading role of the Party with democracy:

> The main orientation of the reform of the political system is to ensure the completeness of the power of the Soviets of the People's Deputies as the basis of the system of the socialist state and of self-government in our country. The policy of the Party – economic, social, national – must be implemented first of all through the organs of the people's representation (Resolution on *The Democratization of the Soviet Society and the Reform of the Political System*).

The reform involved a new relationship between the Soviets, elected by the people, the executive committees in charge of the administration, and the leading

Michel Lesage is Director of the Institut de Recherches Comparatives sur les Institutions et le Droit, Ivry sur Seine, and Professor at the University of Paris.

Party organs. Most of the new concepts which were adopted in 1988 still form the basis of the administration today and, as such, they are also responsible for certain dysfunctions which prevent the system from being fully effective.

Several decisions, having a positive effect, were intended to give greater weight to the Soviets elected by the people. The liberalization of the electoral system was to produce more 'candidates' than 'mandates' and to give the electors a real opportunity to choose their representatives. It would be possible for Deputies to leave their professional occupations and to dedicate all their energies to controlling the administration. Rules to prevent the filling of the Soviet by members of the administration sought to establish incompatibility between the mandate of the Deputy and the administrative functions of the executive committees and departments.

But the attempt to guide the activities of the Soviets and to maintain the principle of Party leadership complicated the structure of the new system. The chairmanship of the Soviet was no longer to be the prerogative of the President of the executive committee, rather a new position was created whereby the President of the Soviet would also, in principle, be the First Secretary of the Party committee. Thus the XIXth Party Conference established a duality of power: on the one hand, the Soviet and its President; on the other, the President of the executive committee, now replaced by the head of the administration and therefore contributing to the inefficiency of the politico-administrative system. The Communist Party has disappeared since, but the duality of powers remains and has even been reinforced by the procedure of designating the head of the administration and by decentralizing the system.

The XIXth Party Conference considered self-government and decentralization of the administration to be fundamental elements of the democratization process and the 'struggle against bureaucratization'. For the Conference, local affairs had to be reorganized according to the principles of self-government, self-finance and self-sufficiency; within the administration, functions and attributions had to be redistributed in a way which ensured the maximum initiative and autonomy of the localities. A third element of the reform concerned the formation of a socialist rule of law to include: guarantees of rights and freedoms; responsibilities of the state towards the citizen and of the citizens towards the state; enhancement of the authority of law and its strict observance by all Party and state organs, associations and citizens. But none of these principles were implemented along the lines intended by the Conference. At the top, the Congress of the People's Deputies of the USSR, elected in the spring of 1989, escaped from the control of the central committee of the Party, and, in the spring of 1990, the new Supreme Soviet of the Republics – in the RSFSR (Russian Soviet Federated Socialist Republic) Congress of People's Deputies – came under the control of the centre. The 'parade of sovereignties' and the 'war of laws' between the Federation and the Republics finally led, in August 1991, to the disaggregation of the Communist Party of the Soviet Union, and, after the failure of the *coup d'etat*, in December 1991, to the disappearance of the USSR itself.

Central Soviet administration no longer exists and no longer extends to 15 separate Republics. There are now 15 different administrations in the 15 states of the ex-USSR. But the 'parade of sovereignties' was not limited to the relations between the Union and its Federal Republics. The same phenomenon was to be observed in the relationship between the Russian Republic and its 'autonomous units'. One after another, the Republics proclaimed their sovereignty. This movement was encouraged by Boris Yeltsin who was elected President of the Supreme Soviet of the Russian Republic in May 1990. He proposed to the Republics in August 1990 that they should 'take as much power as they could swallow'; the Russian Republic would be reconstructed from base: The 'RSFSR will be competent only in areas which are delegated to it'.

The result, however, was that the new authorities elected in the localities during the spring of 1990 did not recognize the jurisdiction of the central government and considered themselves as 'sovereign', trying to implement only their own decisions, without taking into account the rulings of the central authorities.

III   THE NEW STRUCTURE OF TERRITORIAL ADMINISTRATION

Even when Russia was still a Federal Republic within the Soviet Union, its Supreme Soviet initiated a reorganization of the territorial administration. For the first time since 1917, a distinction was introduced between the state and the local administration. The Soviet system postulated the unity of the state; thus all territorial authorities, from the regions to the villages, were organs of the state.

The amendment of article 138 of the constitution introduced the concept of 'local self-government' for the levels of districts, towns, boroughs and villages. At these levels,

> self-government is exercised by the population through the corresponding local Soviet of People's Deputies as a main link in the system of local self-government, organs of social, territorial self-government of the citizens and also local referendum assemblies, meetings of citizens and other forms of direct democracy (amendment of 24 May 1991).

This constitutional provision replaced the executive committee in charge of local administrative services with the 'local administration' and its 'head of administration' who was responsible to the Soviet, which could now adopt a critical attitude towards him and towards other civil servants of the local administration (article 147).

The law on 'local self-government', adopted by the Supreme Soviet on 6 July 1991, specifies the structures and organizational principles of activities of 'local organs of power and administration', the economic and financial bases of self-government and the competences of the local Soviet and the local administration. But the rules on local resources are still very imprecise and those on competences are repetitive for the different levels of administration.

The law established the principle that the head of the administration should be elected for five years, and should be responsible to a Soviet, also elected by the people for five years. The Soviet itself elects a President who chairs its sessions and organizes its work.

The regional level remained a part of state administration. The law on the administration of regions and territories by the Soviets was adopted on 5 March 1992, at which stage Russia was already a full state. The Soviet of People's Deputies is the 'representative organ' of state power in the territories and regions (article 1.1). The administration of the territory or region is a function of the 'executive organ' of state power. The territory or region must have a statute which lays down the constitutional basis for the structure, functions and competences of the administration (article 4). In the same way as the law on self-government, the law on Soviets and the administration of regions establishes the economic and financial bases, the structure and organisational principles of their activities, and the competences of the Soviets and of the administration. The features are the same: vagueness with respect to the use of regional resources, and a list of aims, rather than a precise definition of competences. The head of the administration is again elected by the people.

In spite of the distinction between local self-government and regional administration, the same law applies to the election of the heads of administration, both in the state administration in territories and regions and local administration in districts, cities, boroughs, villages, i.e. the Law of 24 October 1991 defining the electoral procedures. On 30 September, the Presidium of the Supreme Soviet adopted an order on measures for the preparation and organization of the elections. These had originally been scheduled for 8 December, but in the framework of special powers accorded to the President of Russia, Boris Yeltsin, by the Vth Congress of the People's Deputies to fight the economic crisis, they were postponed.

IV   THE POWER OF THE PRESIDENT TO APPOINT THE HEAD OF ADMINISTRATION

The failed *coup d'etat* of 19–22 August 1991 accelerated the introduction of head administrators, but by way of nomination rather than by election.

On 21 August, the Supreme Soviet of Russia decided to establish the function of chiefs of administration in the territories, regions, autonomous regions and autonomous districts as leaders of the corresponding executive organs and successors of the Soviet's executive committees. Pending the adoption of the law on the administration of territories and regions, the Supreme Soviet gave the President of the RSFSR the right to dismiss the Presidents of the Soviets of territories and regions, and to appoint their chiefs of administration. The following day, 22 August, Boris Yeltsin promulgated a decree on 'problems of executive power in the RSFSR' in which he included the status of the chief administrators of the territories and regions. They were to be appointed by the President with the agreement of the corresponding Soviet. The decree placed the chief administrators within a unique system of executive power, headed by the President of the RSFSR (namely, 'The President and the Vice-President of the RSFSR, the Council of Ministers of the RSFSR, the chiefs of the executive power and the Council of Ministers of the Republics within the RSFSR, the chiefs and organs of executive power of autonomous and administrative-territorial formations, the other civil services of the executive and administrative organs constituting the unique system of the executive power in the RSFSR' (article 1, amendment of 30 September 1991).

These powers of the President have been renewed twice by the Congress of the People's Deputies – in November 1991 and December 1992. The Vth Congress, in its decree of 1 November 'on the organization of executive power in the period of radical economic reform' decided to 'ensure the stability of the system of organs of power and administration of the state in the RSFSR in the period of radical economic reform by forbidding general elections of representative and executive state organs at all levels' (article 1). The Congress invested the President with the right to appoint until 1 December 1992, in agreement with the corresponding Soviet, the heads of the administration, not only of the territories and regions, but also of the cities and districts. Two-thirds of the regional chiefs of administration were appointed prior to the Congress; the remaining third was appointed between November 1991 and January 1992.

In the spring of 1992, two chief administrators were dismissed for illegal acts and, on 7 August 1992, Boris Yeltsin approved a rule on disciplinary responsibilities. In November 1992, the administrator for the Krasnodar territory was dismissed after a critical vote in the Soviet.

In December 1992, the Vth Congress deemed it inappropriate to hold the elections of the chief administrators before the elections of the Soviets and asked the Supreme Soviet to adopt a law on the procedure of their appointment and dismissal. Until the election of the Soviets, it gave the President the right to dismiss the head of the administration without the agreement of the Soviet.

However, the Congress did not like the representatives nominated by the President since August 1991. The VIth Congress, in its decree of 11 April 1992 on the course of the economic reforms, recommended to the President that he should not exercise his function of nominating the presidential representatives in the localities, given 'the parallelism of their attributions and activities within the constitutional organs of power and the administration'. In spite of the attitude taken by Congress, the President appointed and protected his representatives. The VIIth Congress on 5 December was more forthright: it gave the President one month to abolish the institution of representatives.

V THE FEDERAL TREATY AND ITS IMPLEMENTATION

When the RSFSR proclaimed its sovereignty, it became formally a federation composed of 16 autonomous republics, 53 territories and regions (including Moscow and Leningrad which have regional status), 5 autonomous regions and 10 autonomous districts. During the summer and autumn of 1990, the autonomous republics were also attracted by the 'parade of sovereignties': Komi on

22 August; Tatarstan on 30 August; Oudmourtia on 20 September; Kalmoukia on 18 October; Tchouvachia on 24 October, etc. As already noted, this movement was encouraged by Boris Yeltsin

The Declaration of the State Sovereignty of the RSFSR, adopted on 20 June 1990 by the First Congress of People's Deputies, recognized 'the need for a significant extension of the rights of the autonomous republics, autonomous regions, autonomous districts and also of those of the territories and regions of the RSFSR', and considered that the legislation of the RSFSR on state national organization and territorial administrative organization had to identify the main problems preventing the realization of these rights.

In their own declarations on state sovereignty, the autonomous republics went much further. They declared themselves 'Socialist Soviet Republics', which meant that they wanted the same status within the RSFSR as the 15 federal republics within the USSR; indeed, some of them regard as the basis of their legal status not the constitution of the RSFSR, but the agreements between the USSR and the RSFSR. For example, the Declaration of Bachkortostan specifies that 'the relations of SSR of Bachkiria with the Union of SSR, RSFSR and the other republics are laid down by the Union Treaty, the Treaty with the RSFSR, and the other inter-republican agreements' (article 2).

After almost two years of difficult negotiations, an intermediate solution was adopted: a federal agreement between the Federation and its members, whose major characteristics were included in the constitution. The federal agreement is not the basis of the constitution, as some Republics argued, but its provisions have constitutional validity and cannot be modified without the agreement of the Republics and the regions.

The 'federal agreement', signed on 31 March 1992 by the Federation and 85 territorial authorities and approved on 10 April by the VIIth Congress of People's Deputies, is, in fact, composed of three different agreements: an agreement on 'the definition of areas of competence and attributions between the state organs of the Federation of Russia and the organs of power of the sovereign Republics within the Federation of Russia'; a second agreement with 'the organs of the autonomous regions, the autonomous districts within the Federation of Russia'; and a third one with 'the organs of power of territories, regions and the cities of Moscow and St. Petersburg'.

The first agreement was signed by 18 Republics. In July 1991, four of the five autonomous regions were transformed into Republics, increasing the total number to 20. But two of the 20 Republics did not sign the Federal Treaty, namely, Tartarstan and Tchetchen-Inguch. In November 1991, the Vth Congress did not recognize the elections in Tchetchen-Inguch, and its division was initiated by the decision of the Supreme Soviet to establish a Republic of Inguchetia (4 June 1992) which became the twenty-first Republic within the Federation of Russia.

The Republics of Tatarstan and Tchetchenia wish to stay within the Russian Federation, but on the basis of an equal treaty in which the 'sovereign' states of Tartarstan and Tchetchenia will delegate to the Federation a part of their authority. Negotiations with the central authorities are ongoing. Bachkortostan rallied to the federal agreement at the last moment, signing an additional clause which gave it an autonomous budget. Negotiations were opened between Russia and Bachkortostan to prepare an agreement on 'complementary definition of functions'.

The Federal Pact (and the corresponding provisions of the constitution) distinguish between the unilateral competence and the joint competences of the Federation and the three categories of territorial authorities of which it is composed. In the field of joint competences, the Federation must not adopt laws, but their principles. On these foundations, regions can then adopt regulations, and Republics can adopt laws. The range of joint competences with the Republics is larger than that with the regions. For example, for both Republics and regions, the establishment of general principles of legislation on administration, housing and the protection of the environment are matters of joint competence whereas judicial organization, administrative procedure, labour, family, and intellectual property legislation are within the joint competences of the Republics only.

The Supreme Soviet continues to adopt laws as before, and the implementation of the Federal Treaty is slow and controversial. On 13 August 1992, the three Presidents of Tartarstan, Sakha (Iakoutia) and Bachkortostan issued a joint declaration accusing the federal level of ignoring the legitimate rights and interests of the Republics (*Izvestia*, 14 August 1992; *Nezavissimaya Gazeta* 15 August 1992). At the beginning of 1993, the Governor (head administrator) of Nini Novgorod protested against what he considered to be an unfair distribution of resources of the state's budget when it was disclosed that four Republics (Techtchenia, Tartarstan, Bachkortostan and Iakoutia) did not pay taxes to the federal budget (*Izvestia* 4 January 1993).

The Republics concluded bilateral agreements between themselves, the agreement on 'friendship and co-operation' signed on 13 September 1992 between Tartarstan and Mari being the first. Tartarstan followed with an agreement with Bachkortostan and both are preparing agreements with Sakha Iakoutia.

Where ethnic conflicts occurred, the central authorities were sometimes obliged to intervene with the use of emergency powers. Thus, on 2 November 1992, the President of Russia imposed a state of emergency in the territories of the Republics of North Ossetia and Inguchetia, by the appointment of a temporary administration.

At the end of 1992, the Republics increased their political weight within the organization of central power: on 23 October, Boris Yeltsin established a Council of the Heads of the Republics, a consultative and co-ordinating body chaired by the President of Russia and comprising the Presidents of the Republics or Presidents of the Supreme Soviets of the Republics, in case there is no President. The Council's task is 'to prepare the main principles to implement the Federal Treaty, taking into account the specific features of each Republic and of the state administration of the Federal Republic'. In October, Boris Yeltsin tried to use the Council of Heads of the Republics to postpone the VIIth Congress of People's Deputies. In a decision of 14 November, the Council approved the proposal of the President of Russia to establish a multi-lateral working group with the participation of representatives of the Republics, territories and regions to prepare the laws of the Russian Federation, the decrees and ordinances of the President, and the decisions of the government concerning the mechanism to implement the Federal Treaty. During the VIIth Congress, the Council was invited to participate in proposing candidates for the position of President of the Council of Ministers. Thus it is through concerted action that the latter hopes to restore its authority over the Republics and regions which have managed to avoid the implementation of central power.

VI   GOVERNMENT AND CENTRAL ADMINISTRATION

Until 1990, the administration of the RSFSR was fully subordinated to the administration of the USSR. In many fields, the central administration had direct authority over the activities of the territories of the Russian Republic.

Beginning with the Declaration of Sovereignty of June 1990, the Russian government has fought to increase its own power in relation to the Council of Ministers and to reduce the competence of the central authorities. At the same time, the transition to a market economy led to a reorganization of ministries and state committees (for example, the decision of 30 July 1991 of the Presidium of the Supreme Soviet of Russia 'on modifications to the list of republican ministries and state committees of the RSFSR'). After the disappearance of the USSR, the RSFSR had to absorb its central administration.

On the eve of the *coup d'état* of August 1991, the central administration of Russia was composed of 20 ministries and 21 state committees (Decree of the President of Russia of 16 August 1991 'on some problems of the organization of the Council of Ministers of the RSFSR'), whose activities were co-ordinated by a first vice-president of the Council of Ministers and five further vice-presidents. The vice-president, ministers and Presidents of state committees required the agreement of the Supreme Soviet to be appointed by the President, on the proposal of the President of the Council of Ministers (amendment of the constitution, 24 May 1991). On 26 September, the President of the Council of Ministers, I. Silaev, left his post and has not been replaced.

In November 1991, the Vth Congress of People's Deputies gave to the President the right to reorganize the executive power. He decided not to fulfil the constitutional obligation of appointing a President of the Council of Ministers, but to lead it himself, with the assistance of a first vice-president of the Council (Bourboulis) and two further vice-presidents, one for economic policy (Gaidar) and one for social policy (Chokin). These four people are supposed to co-ordinate the activities of 20 ministries and four state committees (Decree of the President of Russia of 8 November 1991 'on the organization of the work of the government of the RSFSR in the conditions of economic reform'). A third vice-president (Chakhrai) was added on 12 December, responsible for legal policy and supervision of the administrations in charge of it.

But during the same period, Boris Yeltsin established his own structures, answerable only to him and working concurrently with the Council of Ministers. On 5 August 1991, he established the administration of the President firstly by an order concerning the supervision of the activities of organs of executive power in the regions, and co-ordinating the representations of the President in the Republics (14 August); secondly, he put a group of experts in charge of analysing socio-economic problems (13 September); and finally, he set up a State and Legal Directorate (GPU) for preparing the decisions of the President (12 December). On 19 July 1991, he furthermore established a Council of State, to which he appoints both 'state councillors' and ministers.

Responding to different social demands, Yeltsin made provisions for various services close to the centre of power, namely: a co-ordinating committee for the affairs of invalids (5 August 1991) on 19 November 1991, a state committee for civil protection, emergencies and the cleaning up of the consequences of catastrophes; a state committee for the protection of the Russian Federation's economic interests, also under the President of the RSFSR, etc. On 26 November, even an RSFSR state committee for standardization, metrology and certification was established under the President of the RSFSR! On 19 December, to limit this administrative disorder, five state committees were transferred to the jurisdiction of the Council of Ministers.

But the lack of co-ordination between the Council of Ministers, the administration of the President and his councillors, and the absence of control by Parliament created political tension with the latter. At the next session of the Congress of People's Deputies, Boris Yeltsin was obliged to make concessions and to lower the legal status of his councillors. On 30 November, he abolished the Council of State while maintaining the state councillors who, in May 1992, became simply the councillors of President G. Bourboulis, who is again the main councillor of Boris Yeltsin, and has changed his title five times in 18 months, i.e.: state secretary of the RSFSR, secretary of the state council (19 July 1991), state secretary of the RSFSR (7 April 1992), state secretary to the President of the Russian Federation (8 May 1992), chief of the group of councillors to the President (26 November 1992), and finally, adviser without title (14 December 1992).

Twice in 1992, on 12 May and 30 September, the President issued decrees to instil some order into the central administration ('On ordering the system of state administration', 12 May; 'On the system of central organs of the federal executive power'; 'On the structures of the central organ of the federal executive power'; 'On co-ordinating and consultative organs established by the President of the Russian Federation, the government of the Russian Federation, the ministries and services of the Russian Federation'; 'On ordering the composition of co-ordinating and consultative organs established by the President of the Russian Federation', 30 September 1991). But the absence of a single co-ordinating instrument, serving both the President and the Council of Ministers, prevented unity of action of the executive power.

The situation was made still more complex by the fact that the Council of Ministers was not the competent institution for problems of security and law and order. The law on security of 5 March 1992 established a Security Council, chaired by the President of the Federation of Russia and composed of four other permanent members (the vice-president of Russia, the first vice-president of the Supreme Soviet, the President of the Council of Ministers and the Secretary of the Security Council. The Secretary was appointed by the President with the agreement of the Supreme Soviet.) On 8 October, Boris Yeltsin established an interdepartmental commission of the Security Council, chaired by Vice-President Rutskov, to lead the struggle against crime and corruption. When, on 23 October, Boris Yeltsin also established the Council of the Chiefs of Republics, its secretariat was allocated to the administration of the Security Council. Similarly, in December 1992, co-ordination in foreign policy was linked with the same council by an interdepartmental commission for foreign policy of the Security Council, chaired by the Secretary of the Council himself. The absence of a single central body for co-ordination prevented preliminary control of administrative acts. In May 1992, the Ministry of Justice was required by the President to register the normative acts of the ministries. Of 125 normative administrative acts presented for registration since, only 102 were recognized as legal. Six instructions, three ordinances and 14 orders were refused registration. Some ministries were very slow to present their acts. The State Customs Committee first sent its instructions and orders to its local agents and only afterwards presented them to the Ministry of Justice for registration. Already, four normative acts of the administration have been declared illegal and have not been registered.

The Ministry of Justice is unable to intervene prior to the adoption of administrative normative acts to ensure the coherence of the legal system; neither is it able to prevent the implementation of illegal acts. Officials of the Ministry are convinced that one main condition for implementation after registration must be the official publication of an information bulletin or some specialized journal. But they can only propose that the government establish such a system.

VII   THE CIVIL SERVICE

Protection of citizens against the arbitrary power of civil servants is a traditional problem of Russian bureaucracy; another is the difficulty of implementing political decisions in the face of administrative inertia. A new economic and political environment – with the introduction of a market economy and the disappearance of the Communist Party as the main instrument in the selection, appointment and control of civil servants – has radically changed their situation and raised new problems which are far from being solved. A particular problem is the construction of an honest and flexible civil service, able to fulfil the goals set by the government.

The Law of 22 March 1991 'on competition and the limitation of monopolistic activities' forbids civil servants to participate in business activities. This prohibition was repeated in the decree of the President of Russia of 4 April 1992 'on the struggle against corruption in the system of state civil services'. On 3 July 1992, the first vice-president of the Supreme Soviet and the first vice-president of the government asked the state committee for an anti-monopolistic policy to support new economic structures in co-operation with investigations by the General Procurator. In May 1991 in Russia, there were already 700 instances of direct participation of senior public employees in business activities. Following the last investigation more than 2,000 instances of this kind were recorded. Studies of the Ministry of the Interior appeared to show that 1,037 were combining public service with business activities (S. Filatov, 'Power and business', *Rossyskaya Gazeta* 30 December 1992).

On 17 September 1992, the government of Russia established a commission, chaired by the President of the government 'to examine the problems and to define proposals with a view to fighting corruption in the civil service and organizing financial and legal control of economic activities in the most important sectors of the economy'. And at the end of 1992, the committees of the Ministry of Security and the Ministry of the Interior, in a joint session, examined the implementation of the President's decree of April 1992 on corruption. They identified 1,331 criminal actions and unmasked 400 people with links to organized criminal groups. At the end of 1992, according to the press service of the Ministry of the Interior, 3,000 cases of extortion were discovered, and 3,000 thefts of varying magnitude. The decree had been violated by 1,168 civil servants and one in four was fired (*Rossisskie Vesti* 30 December 1992).

The general situation in the civil service is a matter of concern to the government. As Maskhagomet Alaudinovich Bekov, Head of the General Directorate for the preparation of *cadres* for the civil service (known as 'Roskadry') explained, highly qualified civil servants went into business and were replaced by 'the ignorant, the inexperienced and the dilettantes' ('In deficit: cadres for public service' *Elconomiceskaya Gazeta* 27, July 1991),

The General Directorate was established by the decree of 28 November 1991, to organize the training of highly educated and qualified specialists for federal, republican and local organs of power and administration. Its function is also to analyse and improve the work of the administration and to draft laws and other normative acts concerning the tasks of state organs and administration. To fulfil this goal, the government has allocated to the Head of the General Directorate: seven centres for training *cadres*, some branch institutes for improving qualifications and a scientific information centre with a printing office. The Head of the General Directorate considers his main task to be to introduce into the state apparatus new working practices under market conditions. He is directly responsible for training the higher civil service: deputy ministers, heads of departments and divisions, and for regional centres for the training of local civil servants (*ibid*).

Roskadry prepared a law on the civil service which was presented to the Supreme Soviet on 10 October 1992. The draft was sent back to the committee of the Supreme Soviet because of problems relating to the work of the Soviets of People's Deputies and self-government. It was examined by the Council of the Republic on 24 November under the heading: 'Fundamentals of legislation of the Federation of Russia on the civil service', but several Deputies considered that the draft was conceptually flawed and it was rejected (*Rossyskaya Gazeta* 25 November 1992).

The draft tried to establish in the civil service 14 ranks organized into four groups: A–for higher civil servants (ranks 1-5); B–for principal civil servants (ranks 6-8); C–for responsible civil servants (ranks 9-12); D–for junior civil servants (13–14). Civil servants of ranks 1-5 ought to be recruited on the basis of the rules established by the constitution, the Supreme Soviet and the President; civil servants of ranks 6-12 through competitive examination; and ranks 13-14 by the usual labour legislation. The examination should be organized by a commission, but the criteria for the composition of the latter are still unclear. The draft contains provisions on the obligations and duties of civil servants, rules on promotion within the civil service and on the administration of the civil service.

> For civil servants effectively to establish a stable apparatus of public administration, independent of changes of leaders, cabinets etc. and not to be an 'oprichtchina', involving the whole of society in secret or dangerous entanglements, we must have effective democratic laws. Phantoms must disappear from the corridors of power

concludes Andriuchtchenko, a commentator on the draft (Eugenii Andriuchtchenko, 'Phantoms in the corridors of power', *Nedelja* 45, November 1992).

VIII   CONCLUSION

It was to be expected that administrative transformation in Russia would prove difficult. Not only was it necessary to introduce a whole new system of public administration in which the civil service would be independent of government but also, more generally, to introduce completely transformed political and economic structures. Moreover, reform of public administration and reform of the political and economic system were undertaken almost simultaneously, which caused tensions to arise. The negative impact of the political and economic reforms on traditional power bases, such as the Soviets of People's Deputies, and on the economic expectations and conditions of the population was such that opposition to the various policies quickly arose. The consequence for public administration, as has been shown above, was that many attempts at reform became subject to the struggle for power between the Russian President, Boris Yeltsin, and the Congress.

The description of the process of administrative transformation in Russia highlights a number of obstacles to the effective implementation of policies for reforming Russian public administration. In attempting to reform a country's system of public administration, it is preferable to build upon a certain degree of political consensus as to what shape such reform should take. However, as the Russian case amply demonstrates, in the absence of political stability, it is particularly difficult to reach consensus on the overall direction of the reform and on the ways and means of implementing corresponding policies. Even where reforms are introduced under such circumstances, compliance is difficult to achieve in a prevailing atmosphere of political uncertainty.

In terms of analysis, it has not proved particularly difficult to identify the causes of the crisis in Russian public administration. In terms of prediction, however, the degree of instability currently existing in Russia prevents even a tentative appraisal of the direction which the reform of public administration may take. Until the struggle between the Russian President, Boris Yeltsin, and the Congress comes closer to a resolution, any long-term conclusions remain elusive.

ADMINISTRATIVE TRANSFORMATION IN EASTERN GERMANY

KLAUS KÖNIG

I INTRODUCTION

Public administration is connected with certain concepts of change. The category 'administrative reform' provides a common reference which enables discussions to be extended beyond cultural and linguistic barriers (Caiden 1969). Parallel to this, the term 'development' has often been the subject of attention in international debates on administrative matters. Behind this term are two concepts for explaining the administration of the Third World. In the first, the development of an administration is seen as a transition from traditional patterns to new differentiations; in the second, the administration of development is mentioned in connection with conditions of resource scarcity.

However, neither the terms 'reform' nor 'development' adequately describe the political-administrative changes in Poland, in what used to be Czechoslovakia, Hungary, Russia and the former German Democratic Republic (GDR). First, the systemic transition which is being tackled is more profound than a reform of the public service or the administrative territories in a Western democracy. Second, while self-critical words may be heard from Eastern Europe in connection with under-development, it would be unfair to put the development deficits evident in every industrial state on the same level as the poverty-related phenomena of developing countries. Since categories such as social change or modernization do not really help in this context either, it is necessary to seek an adequate alternative. A difficulty arises in that while extensive terminology exists to describe the transition from capitalism to socialism and the ultimate 'withering away of the state', there is hardly any concept to describe the reverse phenomenon – how to emerge from a socialist system and attain a system of public administration appropriate for a contemporary European society (König 1982; 1991).

The unification of Germany on 3 October 1990 has made abundantly clear that the change in its eastern parts represents not only a regime transition but

Klaus König is Professor of Public Law and Administrative Sciences at the Hochschule für Verwaltungswissenschaften, Speyer, Germany.

a transformation of the entire social and economic order and, therefore, a transformation of statehood. In this way, the transformation is also a specific historical process which cannot be compared with developments in the Third World or with modernization processes in western countries. 'Transformation' – as it is occurring in Eastern Europe – is defined first, as a comprehensive, systematic change which, secondly, does not simply and naturally take place behind the backs of the historical actors, but is driven by active policies. Thirdly, this transformation is characterized by certain similar relationships between the old and the new system. With regard to the German case in particular, one can refer to the legacy of the Prussian administrative state, on the one hand, and to industrialization, on the other. Fourthly, there is a formal-legalistic revolution with which to contend (Quaritsch 1992). In principle, the monopoly of the state over law and the use of force was not infringed. Socialism was displaced peacefully through new constitutional rules, regulations and laws.

At the centre of this transformation is the principle of statehood. According to Marxist-Leninist doctrine, the state was the 'main instrument' for bringing about socialism. The functional doctrine of the state set out the ideological scope of its administrative activities. This included, amongst others, the economic-organizational function. Accordingly, the economic system was formed as a plan and as an administrative system. For this reason, the transformation of statehood also implies the institutionalization of a social market economy (König 1992). The same is true for areas such as health care, education, traffic, energy, etc. On the whole, the public sector must be defined in a completely new manner. The basic principle of the organization of public affairs was the Marxist-Leninist maxim of 'democratic centralism'. Society, economy and state were subjugated to the control of the highest party leadership and horizontal as well as vertical unity of power existed for the state machinery. In contrast to this, transformation means that the separation of the legislative, the judicial and the executive functions, as well as the differentiation of federalism and municipal government must be established not only as a form of division of labour but also as a political differentiation. This list of systematic changes can be extended in many respects.

II THE DIRECTION OF THE TRANSFORMATION PROCESS

The starting point of the transformation is the 'real-socialist' administration as it existed in the GDR until 1989. The fact that the term 'public administration' was not used there should not give rise to concern. Given the principle of the unity of powers, the dogma of the unity of decision and implementation was inviolable. Thus 'public administration' as a term was rejected in favour of the term 'executive-ordering function', following the pattern of Soviet usage (Akademie für Staats-und Rechtwissenschaft der DDR 1988). Yet a country enjoying the levels of technical and industrial development of the GDR could not forgo separation of work. At least, for this reason, a certain institutional and functional differentiation developed between public representations, judicial instruments, etc., which made it possible to identify a state-administrative core with executive as well as decision-making functions. A separate body of administrative law emerged for this area – albeit ever so hesitantly and with a number of problems concerning the powers to implement it.

The prevailing characteristics in the real-socialist administration were instrumental étatism in administrative tasks, the development of *cadres* among the administrative personnel, the afore-mentioned 'democratic centralism' within the administrative organization and the transmission of the Party's will in the administrative process. Consequently, the transformation in the case of the GDR proceeded from a complex, and yet historically solid, condition. In contrast to other Central and Eastern European countries, including the Soviet Union, the political and administrative circumstances were not conducive to change. Thoughts on systemic reforms such as ministerial or territorial reorganization were smothered immediately. A dynamic contribution from the administrative sciences could not be expected, since these were based on authoritative structures and had an apologetic relationship with the decisions of Party and state (C. Schulze 1991).

However, even if the starting point for administrative transformation is fixed, its end remains uncertain and, as yet, in the future. In contrast to Poland, Hungary and other socialist countries, after being brought into line with the Basic Law, the constitutional reference points in the German case have become the state and administration of the Federal Republic. Nevertheless, even the statically regarded public administration of the old Federal Republic of Germany cannot be defined as the goal of the transformation, since that is still changing within itself. Therefore, we need to continue to examine the past and, at the same time, look into the future, in order to reach a classification concerning the nominal conditions of the transitory process in our fast-moving present. Using the concept of a classical-European administration, an attempt will be made to combine both perspectives in determining the direction of the transformation process.

In inter-cultural comparisons, the traditional public administration in Germany can be defined as a 'classical' administrative system (Heady 1984). It shares this definition with administrations in countries such as France and Austria and differs not only from administrations in developing or socialist countries but also – albeit to a lesser degree – from the 'civic culture' administrations of the Anglo-American sphere. An important aspect of the similarities is the administrative legal culture. In this respect, it is interesting to note how within the legal order of the European Community the legal structures of Great Britain, moulded by other traditions, are attempting to adapt to the codified continental-European legal system (König 1990). These are changes which have resulted from European integration. Therefore, the category of the classical-European administration combines national traditions with supra-national perspectives for the future and shows the direction the transformation of the socialist administration needs to take in a changing world.

III FROM INSTRUMENTAL ÉTATISM TO A LIBERAL AND SOCIAL STATE

According to Marxist-Leninist doctrine, the state in the GDR was the 'main instrument' for bringing about socialism (Akademie für Staats-und Rechtwissenschaft der DDR 1984). The scope for administrative tasks was defined according to party ideology together with a Marxist-Leninist functional theory of the state. Under the socialist administration, domestic functions were especially important, for example the economic-organizational function, the cultural-educational function, the regulation of levels of work and consumption, and the protection of the socialist legal order, socialist property and the socialist rights of the citizens (Marxistisch-Leninistische allgemeine Theorie des Staates und Rechts 1975). The system-oriented will of the party, then, defined the respective 'historic mission' of the state. Within this functional scope the state apparatus had to carry out the tasks of industrial production, maintenance and provision of health care, education, etc. (G. Schulze 1991a). In this process, the deductive structure of ideology, party decision and state order was often superseded by voluntaristic acts of a Stalinist command when defining administrative tasks.

In achieving the transformation from socialist to classical-European administration, it is, of course, important to establish a constitution and a democratic order of public tasks. For the transformation of the tasks themselves, the transition from central administrative economy to social market economy is characteristic. The economy in the GDR was not a self-regulating part of society, but stood under the command of the political-administrative system. In accordance with the orders of the party, the state made decisions concerning the production, circulation, distribution and consumption of material goods. This politically inspired, economic-organizational function of the state had to be overcome, a task since undertaken by the *Treuhandanstalt*, which is discussed below.

It would be insufficient to focus solely on the system-related differences in the economy, the organization of labour, and in consumption. Transition to the tasks of a liberal and social constitutional state affects all other political areas as well – from matters of culture to the health system, from environmental protection to social provisions. In all areas, differentiations according to the classical-European standard between individual interests, social self-organization and the defining power of the state need to be introduced. A differentiated machinery of state intervention needs to be put into force.

In many cases, classical-European administration as compared to socialist administration means a reduction of state activities. However, this does not imply that a liberal and social constitutional state functions on minimalist principles. A high level of state intervention illustrates the welfare state character of Western democracies, and such a level of state activity, especially in the case of social services, will help the transformation. In the new *Länder* such activity will also lead to the substantial tackling of tasks such as environmental protection, urban restoration or public infrastructure. The current lack of innovation is visible in many places in the former GDR. At any rate, the high level of service provision in the classical-European administration shows that the issue is not a withdrawal of the state but a re-definition of its powers.

IV FROM 'DEMOCRATIC CENTRALISM' TO ORGANIZATIONAL DIFFERENTIATION

A basic principle of the organization of socialist state power was the idea of the afore-mentioned 'democratic centralism' (Institut für Theorie des Staates und des Rechts der Akademie der Wissenschaften der DDR 1975). Originally, it was a Leninist Party organizational principle, and later became the doctrine for structuring the state. For this reason 'democratic centralism' in dialectic reasoning has been claimed repeatedly to uphold the firm unity of central leadership and planning as well as the initiative of the working people and self-responsibility of the economic units and territories. In terms of socialism as applied in the GDR, however, 'democratic centralism' was a criterion by which to assess to what extent Marxist-Leninist power, leadership at the highest party and state level, commitment to party decisions, and party and state discipline were implemented in 'the executive-ordering area' (Kazenzadek 1966).

In this respect, the state and administration of the GDR were indeed moulded in principle by a unity of powers and, in basic doctrine, by a unity of decision-making and of implementation. While a certain separation of labour existed between legislative and judicial organs, for example, there was no separation of powers. In terms of the classical-European administration, however, separation of powers between the legislative, judicial and executive levels has to be established. A number of steps towards such a goal have already been taken. However, further efforts are required before parliamentary and judicial powers are established as a means of controlling the administration according to democratic and constitutional patterns. The executive needs to become aware of the fact that one set of party leaders has not simply been replaced with another.

The principle of 'democratic centralism' applies not only to the horizontal differentiation of executive functions but also to the vertical division of administrative levels (Akademie für Staats-und Rechtwissenschaft der DDR 1984). Federalism and local autonomy are constitutional realities which shape the administrative organization of the Federal Republic of Germany, and are incompatible with a doctrine of controlling a state from a unified centre. In the 1950s, the *Länder* of the GDR and the rest of the traditional system of local government were dissolved. Counties and communities became the 'local organs of state power' and the principles of double subordination applied to territorially lower administrations. The implications of this organizational principle for regional and local administrations were that executive organs became subject to the public representatives by whom they were elected and also subject to higher-level executive organs, including those at ministerial level. According to official doctrine, this double subordination was intended to secure unified leadership by a central state organ and, at the same time, was to provide for the respect of local conditions and requirements by state authorities in the territories. In practice, the vertical level proved to be the more important control as the standards of higher-level authorities were decisive, even to the extent of subjective interpretation and arbitrary intervention.

Since unification, steps have been taken in the former GDR to establish a local level. Here the old socialist administration is now moving into the direction of the classical-European administration too. The ratification of the European Charter of Local Government in 1985 demonstrated that local autonomy is not only a specific German issue; the determination of the relationship of the state to the communities in terms of local autonomy is a matter of European concern. For the communities and counties in the Länder of the former GDR much remains to be done beyond the constitutional solution in the area of local and municipal law, public finances and administrative performance until an adequate level of autonomy is achieved.

Of more concern is the European perspective on regional government, since decentralization is not a fundamental characteristic of the classical-European administrative model. Nevertheless, the historic opportunities for autonomy are favourable in a 'Europe of the Regions'. It is becoming more and more obvious that the cultural, social, economic and political resources of a sub-national region are better used when forms of self-government are granted as well. Therefore, it may be assumed that federalism in its German form is also within the perspective of a classical-European administration. With the organizational structuring of Brandenburg, Mecklenburg-Western Pomerania, Saxony, Saxony-Anhalt, Thuringia, as well as Berlin as a unified city, the state employs regional potential which will be of national as well as supra-national benefit.

V FROM THE TRANSMISSION OF COMMANDS TO RATIONAL PROCEDURES

The basic concept of all procedural and decision-making patterns of a socialist administration is the transmission: the transfer of the will of the Marxist-Leninist party by the state machinery. Whether respective orders in the GDR were system-formulated decisions of the political caste or voluntary Stalinist acts of high-level *nomenclaturists*, it did not change the subordinate structure of order and obedience. Nevertheless, an extensive advisory system had been established in the Party, and in state, economic and cultural bodies which also applied to the administration; namely through advisory meetings of members of ministerial councils with regional and county councillors, etc. On examining these advisory mechanisms more closely, they may be better described by the term 'consultative authoritarianism' (Ludz 1968).

Socialist law could not fundamentally change this situation even to the extent that it developed a form of administrative law (Pohl 1991a). According to Marxist-Leninist definition, 'lawful' was only that which corresponded with the will of the working class and its party. The definition of 'lawful' drew no reference from matters existing contemporaneously with or even beyond the Party (Brunner 1979). Quite simply, a selective use was made of legal positivism, in terms of regulations, sanctions, etc. The phrase 'to lead by law' demonstrated that the main focus of attention was on the instrumentalization of the law in order to influence administration, economy and society (Mit Recht leiten 1974).

Therefore, transformation in this context requires that a structured legal system, encompassing a constitution, laws, regulations and ordinances, be established and prevail for the administration and, moreover, that this structure should not be capable of being rendered ineffective by the decision of a party or leaders in power. Using the principle of socialist legalism, Marxism-Leninism had developed a decisive doctrine which made it possible for party ideology and will to be given preference over written norms at any time. According to the historic situation this doctrine fulfilled multiple functions concerning the control of legal-administrative matters, including functioning as an opportunistic principle, as an interpretive rule, and as a method of control. Such arbitrariness needs to be removed through the adoption of constitutionally decisive rules, namely: supremacy of the law, reservation of the law, legal methods, interpretive principles, etc.

The socialist administration in the GDR was characterized by a multitude of legal cultural deficits (Pohl 1991b; Bley 1991). Transforming this situation requires, in the first place, the establishment of a legal basis for an administrative jurisdiction; secondly, the assurance for the citizen that not only can interests be safeguarded collectively but also that both individual rights and a system of individual legal protection exists; and finally, the establishment of the principle that administrative law is binding for everyone.

As with law in the GDR, so too did finance prove to be unreliable in controlling administrative decisions (Riese 1970; Akademie der Wissenschaften der DDR 1989). Neither the law nor public finances contributed to a satisfactory rationalization of administrative decisions. Monetary language did not provide clarity in public matters. Rather, both state and administration were typified by a predominance of management of material resources over the concerns of the monetary sphere.

This brings us to the Leninist formula of transforming the whole state economic mechanism into one great machine, into an economic organism which works according to the pattern of hundreds of millions of people guided by one single plan. To this effect, the GDR established a people's economic plan, which encompassed the social and economic control of the state according to materialistic socialist understanding (Hoss 1991). The failure of planning over decades – not only at the national level, but also at the level of district, county and communal administration – is not only of economic interest but deserves special attention in respect of public administration (Rytlewski 1985).

In replacing this pattern of planning and moving towards the classical-European model of administration, (and note that even in the GDR the concept of the 'great machine' was not fully utilized), a number of changes have to occur. It is important that public finances come under technical control: that a valid budget, effective audit control and solid technical planning should be established, and that more sophisticated forms of accounting such as medium-range financial planning, territorial development, and result and performance controls are tackled. Moreover, all of this should be done with the non-Marxist-Leninist premise that state and administration cannot solve the problems of mankind, that they are not the general agency for happiness on earth.

VI ATTEMPTS AT PRIVATIZATION: THE *TREUHAND* EXPERIENCE

As the states of Central and Eastern Europe leave socialism behind them, they have been trying to find a means of achieving the transition from a centralized state-planned, controlled economy to a market-oriented economic order. Currently, it is not possible to predict which economic 'model' states such as Poland, Hungary, and Russia will adopt following their respective transition periods (Nagels 1991, p. 32). Yet both Marxists and non-Marxists agree that private ownership of the means of production – interpreting ownership in the wider sense of public law terms – constitutes a key factor to systemic change. Accordingly, it is worthwhile paying attention to how the difficult process of privatizing socialist property is being carried out in such states. Of particular interest in this respect is that, in the former GDR, a central institution has been established to implement that transformation – the Agency Responsible for Privatising Formerly State-Owned Industry in the GDR – more commonly referred to as *Treuhandanstalt* or *Treuhand*.

The *Treuhand* has its origins in a decision taken by the then GDR government on 1 March 1990 (Beschluss zur Gründung der Anstalt zur treuhänderischen Verwaltung des Volkseigentums (Treuhandanstalt) vom 1 Marz 1990, GB1. DDR I, p. 107). On being established, the *Treuhand* assumed trusteeship over the GDR's national property, the legal responsibility for which lay with a variety of business plants, agencies, collective combines and economy-controlling organs as well as other business units listed in the GDR national economy register. On the same date, an ordinance was passed transforming nationally owned collective combines, business facilities and institutions into corporations (Verordnung zur Umwandlung von volkseigenen Kombinaten, Betrieben und Einrichtungen in Kapitalgesellschaften vom 1 Marz 1990, GB1. DDR I, p. 107). The legislative foundation for that radical change was the GDR government's Act on the Privatization and Reorganization of State-owned Property of 17 June 1990 (Gesetz zur Privatisierung und Reorganisation des volkseigenen Vermögens (Treuhandgesetz) vom 17 Juni 1990, GB1, DDR I p. 300), the former GDR's *Treuhand* Act, so to speak. The Unification Treaty concluded with the 'old' Federal Republic of Germany on the 23 September, 1990 laid down that the *Treuhand* should continue to exist as an institute directly subordinate to the Federal Government. Thus, its equity holdings in the transformed corporations are indirect federal government holdings.

According to the Unification Treaty, the *Treuhand's* main function is the privatization of state-owned property, as stipulated in section 2, para. 1, of the

Treuhand Act (Hax 1992). This includes the following objectives: enabling the largest possible number of enterprises to compete effectively, safeguarding jobs and creating new ones, assisting the recovery of enterprises and their structural adjustment to market requirements as well as promoting the development of efficient corporate structures. Beyond these objectives, there is a multiplicity of further tasks, ranging from managing property owned by the GDR political parties and mass organizations to the rationalization of agricultural producers' cooperatives.

Two commitments deserve particular attention. The first is that the *Treuhand* must liquidate businesses which are no longer viable. Inevitably in such cases, opinions as to the prospects for revitalization of a plant or business will differ, provoking conflicts, particularly with those threatened by the loss of their jobs. The second commitment is the assignation of property to public ownership, mostly in the form of reassignments to communal bodies. Measured by Western standards, the local administrative authorities in the former GDR owned relatively few communal facilities and amenities and, from nursery school to sports and cultural centres, they sponged on the nationally owned enterprises and cooperatives.

At its outset, the *Treuhand* was regarded as the world's biggest holding company – having some 4 million employees, 40,000 plants and business facilities, and a landed property totalling almost 60 per cent of the former area of the GDR. As of 1 June 1992, the revenue from privatization totalled some 29.3 thousand million DM, capital investment commitments reached the amount of 138.5 thousand million DM, and commitments for employment of 1,169,983 persons had been made. In particular, the *Treuhand* paid attention to the establishment of small to medium-size businesses, as the *de facto* elimination of that sector of the economy is considered to be central to the GDR economy's lack of competitiveness. By the same date, 25,000 items of property of the GDR trading organization, 17,000 pharmacies, 550 bookshops, 600 cinemas, etc. had been privatized.

In the light of the strong presence of multi-national concerns in West Germany, endeavours were made from the outset not to let the privatization of national property develop into a matter between purely German partners. Advertisements seeking foreign investors were published all over the world. By June 1992, foreign partners had bought 350 enterprises and plant divisions or had acquired equity investments in them. This included commitments to employ 99,277 persons and to make capital investments totalling 10.8 thousand million DM.

Re-assignment of property to local authorities also made progress, as many rural districts, cities and other localities submitted applications to the *Treuhand* for such property reassignment. Ownership of a large number of nursery schools, sport centres, vocational schools, polytechnic institutions, hostels for apprentices, cultural centres, outpatients' clinic departments, restaurants, hotels, water supplies and engineering services, local public transport services and, above all, land for economic activities has been re-assigned to local authorities.

Aid for business revitalization was granted by the *Treuhand* in various forms – financial support, loans, guarantees, etc. – in all totalling over 77 thousand million DM in 1991. At the same time plants employing over 220,000 persons were closed down. About 1.2 million people are currently employed by about 4,500 enterprises in the hands of the *Treuhand*. In a great many of these, serious problems are being faced. The *Treuhand* is making efforts to minimize the social consequences of restructuring by assuring the establishment of social compensation plans, by promoting staff qualification programmes and by supporting job-creation schemes. Nevertheless, this has not prevented the *Treuhand* from being seen as a kind of negative symbol for the damaging cost of transforming the GDR's moribund economy.

Systematic change in the former GDR and in the new federal Länder has been and continues to be a peaceful process. Neither government authorities nor industrial enterprises were taken by force of arms. Although demonstrations, token strikes, and symbolic plant occupations occurred, these did not surpass the scope of what may equally be experienced in times of crisis in the West German shipyards or steel industries. The state monopoly over the formulation and enforcement of law was not violated in principle. One may call this a formal and legalistic revolution. Accordingly, the task to be fulfilled by the *Treuhand* entails a gigantic legal work, if only on account of the number of cases concerned. Given the great pressure of time under which the economy of the former GDR has to be transformed into a social market economy, it is clear that such an achievement could and can be fulfilled only with a great deal of legal pragmatism, albeit pragmatism founded on high legal and executive standards.

Nonetheless, many fundamental legal issues may be raised relating both to the *Treuhand's* terms with potential buyers and its administration of enterprises in a fiduciary capacity. Particularly controversial are decisions to close industries viewed as non-viable, and some such decisions have resulted in legal challenges. However, a solid assessment of the legality of the *Treuhand's* activities awaits future treatment from legal historians.

VII FROM *CADRE* ADMINISTRATION TO PUBLIC SERVICE

Finally, there remains the personnel factor in the process of transformation (Derlien 1991; König 1992). Through use of the *cadre* system of administration, socialism created its own type of state functionary responsible to the Marxist-Leninist Party (Balla 1973; Lipp 1978; Ule 1990; G. Schulze 1991b). *Cadres* are persons who, based on their political and technical knowledge and abilities, are commissioned to guide collectives of workers to bring about social processes and tasks or, as scientifically trained specialists, to co-operate toward this outcome (Ehlert, Joswig, Luchterhand and Stiemerling 1973). A basic qualification of the administrative *cadre* was his political-ideological suitability. While a technical qualification appears in the definition of *cadre* (Glaessner 1977), it remained a secondary requirement for state officials, in contrast to the professio-nalism required of a civil service. (The latter had been abolished by the Soviet military administration in 1945.) One must imagine a selection mechanism in which, from secondary school to earning a university degree, from acceptance into an entry-level position in the administration to the attainment of a top-level position, political-ideological qualifications took precedence over expertise. Such a process can only lead to the systematic thinning out of expertise in the higher echelons, no matter how talented individuals may be.

In Poland, the former Czechoslovakia, Hungary and Russia, the transformation of the administration has led to the traditional problem of regime change, i.e. old and new faces working in governmental and administrative positions. In the case of the GDR, German unification has provided an additional – in some respects, an alternative – option to deal with this problem, that being the transfer of personnel from West to East German departments. Given the transfer of the West German legal and economic system to the East, such an option has also proved to be a necessity. Thus, there are three questions to be addressed: first, what is there to say about the old *cadres*; second, how about the newly recruited forces from East Germany; and, third, how is the transfer of personnel from West Germany to be evaluated.

Cadres in top-level positions had already left the administration by the time the democratic government of the GDR was installed, either because they had been dismissed according to GDR law for state officials or they had found alternative positions in business or industry, especially in companies of the old state economy. The question of taking on or dismissing the old *cadres* first arose with German unification. Both quantitative and qualitative problems had to be confronted. Quantitatively, administrative personnel from East Germany were needed for the large-scale organization of the state machinery. Numerically, a sufficiently large transfer of personnel from the West was not an available option. On the other hand, the public service, employing some 2,125,054 persons in August 1990, was overstaffed by Western standards (Weiss 1991). Statistical comparisons between different administrative systems are difficult to make, however, it is noteworthy that in the old Federal Republic 7 per cent, as opposed to 12 per cent in the GDR, of all residents have been employed in public service (Weiss 1991; Renger 1991). Moreover, the distribution in the GDR was unsuitable according to western standards, if only because of the strongly equipped workforce of the central administration as opposed to the poorly equipped local authorities.

Problems also arose from a qualitative perspective, given the existence of the *nomenklatura* (Volensky 1980) and the *cadres* of a Marxist-Leninist-Stalinist regime. Transformation was not just a political problem, however. If consideration is given to how personnel recruitment in the socialist system took place, the phrase 'politicized incompetence' (Derlien 1991) largely reflects the existing state of affairs, namely, that professional qualifications according to western standards simply could not be assumed. Although the Unification Treaty laid down that 'in the interest of administration and of employment' members of the pre-existing public administration were to remain in employment, the principle was valid only for those administrations which were transferred. If an administrative organization was abolished, a temporary lay-off took place. For those who found no further employment, special ordinary and extraordinary dismissal rules were applicable. According to these rules, the employment relationship could be terminated because of inadequate professional qualification or insufficient demand; or because of violations against the principles of human rights or the rule of law, or on account of past work for the state security police. Since the public service was retained, changes had to be made in traditional civil service law and a new category of personnel had to be created, called the 'accession civil service' (Goerlich 1991). As the *cadre* career was not tied to western career qualifications, this new category is based upon a probationary period in a job which corresponds to that of the western public service. At present, an extensive network of programmes for adjustment training is in place.

Although specific data concerning the qualitative effect of the transformation upon the old administrative *cadres* exists, there is as yet no overall balance sheet of the ongoing transition process. Consequently, the following comments merely point to certain trends. Employment in the administrative service in the former GDR has diminished at the central state level. In considering such information, it should be noted that in the new federal administration no place exists for the old ministries of the GDR. By contrast, employment in the regional and local administrations, now in the new *Länder* and communities, has increased. It is difficult to provide precise data on members from the *cadre* administration affected by temporary lay-offs. Estimates run between 200,000 and 250,000 persons. Heads of personnel in central departments have expressed the view that a great many of the *cadres* found employment in other departments, for example in the new *Länder* and labour administrations. The same holds true for employees of the old districts. However, there are branch-specific cases: on the one hand, the most obvious is the diplomatic service of the old GDR, which has been abolished in its entirety; on the other, large enterprise administrations, such as post and railways, continue to exist, though here the question of over-staffing arises. More than 90 per cent of the employees of the administrative services in the former GDR come from the old *cadres*. Nevertheless, both horizontal and vertical mobility exist, and some have had to accept employment in lower grades. Even if the *nomenklatura* has largely been retired, no clear dividing line concerning ranks can be drawn. Whereas in the military sector, no colonel or general was admitted to the Federal Armed Forces, circumstances in the administration vary, especially if the still existing enterprises of the state economy are taken into account. Finally, extraordinary dismissals did happen, but not on a massive scale.

One of the problems of recruiting new administrative personnel from East Germany results from the effectiveness of the Marxist-Leninist regime in suppressing the emergence of a relevant oppositional élite (Derlien 1991). Today, access to employment in the public service is open to everyone. Dissidents however, were often excluded from higher education, so that their qualifications are often below those required for the position. In certain cases, attempts have been made to remedy this situation through the use of flexible employment laws, but basically one has to depend on the younger generation. With German unification, a 'perpetuation' of the old personnel relationships was taken into account as part of the bargain (Weiss 1991; Lecheler 1991). That may have been a suitable reaction to the historical situation. Still, it should not be forgotten how many peoples' life and employment prospects were ruined by an unjust system.

The transfer of personnel from West German to East German administrations is a part of our administrative history which deserves closer investigation and scientific documentation. That applies both to the first phase of consultation between administrators from federal ministries and their GDR counterparts, for example in agriculture or labour, and to the second phase of the building-up of public administration in the new *Länder*, which required continuous forms of personnel assistance, in which the different administrative levels and branches participated, especially through partnerships between *Länder* or communities, co-ordinated through a clearing-office in Bonn (Reusch 1991). Again, some data exist for this personnel transfer; for example, in August 1991, approximately 800 public servants from Nordrhine-Westphalia were in service in the 'partner *Land*' of Brandenburg (Meyer-Hesemann 1991). Again, however, no overall balance sheet exists as yet, since the process is still ongoing. With this in mind, the following may be noted: at its peak, personnel transfer included over 15,000 persons, with some estimates nearer the 20,000 mark. Personnel distribution differs according to the administrative levels, branches and ranks involved. A certain concentration of personnel transfer is to be observed at the ministerial level in the new *Länder*. With respect to horizontal differentiation, administrations relating to justice and the interior, including public security, on the one hand, and administrations concerned with finance and the economy, on the other, account for the bulk of the personnel transfer, a fact which reflects, the historical heritage of socialism. Among the career groups, the higher service, i.e., the highest career group within the civil service, dominates, the advanced service is next, whereas middle and lower services are less important (Linde 1991).

Such differences can bring about cumulative effects. For example, in 1991, the Ministry of Justice in Brandenburg had a Western employment rate of over 70 per cent in the higher service. In the Departments of the Interior, and of Finance and Economics, over 60 per cent of the civil servants came from West Germany. Looking at the higher ranks of the administrative élite, it emerges that early in 1992, in the Minister-President's offices of Brandenburg, Mecklenburg-Western Pomerania, Saxony, Saxony-Anhalt, and Thuringia, 15 of the 19 heads of departments, i.e. more than three-quarters, came from the West, and all five offices were headed by West Germans. That may lead to a new dualism of 'Ossis' (Easteners) and 'Wessis' (Westerners), overshadowing the old confrontation between Marxist-Leninist oppressors and the oppressed in the former GDR. One therefore has to ensure that the transfer of personnel does not give rise to a new feeling of 'colonial rule' in the government and administration of East Germany.

References

Akademie für Staats-und Rechtwissenschaft der DDR (ed.). 1984. *Staatsrecht der DDR Lehrbuch*. 2nd edn. Berlin (Ost): Staatsverlag.

——. (ed.) 1988. *Verwaltungsrecht, Lehrbuch*, 2nd edn. Berlin (Ost): Staatsverlag.

Akademie der Wissenschaften der DDR. 1989. 'Wesen und aktive Rolle des Geldes in der sozialistischen Plantwirtschaft', *Veröffentlichungen der Wissenschaftlichen Räte*. Berlin (Ost): Akademie Verlag.

Balla, B. 1973. *Kaderverwaltung: Versuch zur Idealtypisierung der 'Bürokratie' sowjetisch-volksdemokratischen Typs*. Stuttgart: Enke Verlag.

Bartsch, H. 1991. 'Aufgaben und Struktur der örtlichen Verwaltung', p. 109 in K. König (ed.) *Verwaltungsstrukturen der DDR*. Baden-Baden: Nomos.

Battis, U. 1991. 'Entwicklungstendenzen und Probleme der Einführung des Dienstrechts in den neuen Ländern', *Neue Justiz 89*.

Bley, J. 1991. 'Verwaltungsentscheidungen und Verwaltungsvollzug', p. 249 in K. König (ed.) *Verwaltungsstrukturen der DDR*. Baden-Baden: Nomos.

Brunner, G. 1979. *Einführung in das Recht der DDR*. 2nd edn. Munich: Beck Verlag.

Caiden, G. 1969. *Administrative reform*. Chicago: Aldine Publishing Group.

Derlien, H.-U. 1991. 'Regimewechsel und Personalpolitik-Beobachtungen zur politischen Säuberung und zur Integration der Staatsfunktionäre der DDR in das Berufsbeamtentum', in *Verwaltungswissenschaftliche Beiträge der Universität Bamberg*, Nr. 27, Bamberg.

Ehlert, W., H. Joswig, W. Luchterhand and K.H. Stiemerling (eds.) 1973. *Wörterbuch der Ökonomie: Sozialismus*. Berlin (Ost): Dietz Verlag.

Glaessner, G. J. 1977. *Herrschaft durch Kader*. Opladen: Westdeutscher Verlag.

Goerlich, H. 1991. 'Hergebrachte Grundsätze und Beitrittsbeamtentum', *Juristen Zeitung 75*.

Hax, H. 1992. 'Privatisation agencies: the Treuhand approach', p. 143 in: S. Horst (ed.) *Privatization-symposium in honor of Herbert Giersch*. Tübingen: Mohr-Siebeck Verlag.

Heady, F. 1984. *Public administration – a comparative perspective*. 3rd edn. New York/Basle: Dekker Verlag.

Hoss, P. 1991. 'Staatliche Pläne und Planung', p. 199 in K. König (ed.) *Verwaltungsstrukturen der DDR*, Baden-Baden: Nomos.

Institut für Theorie des Staates und des Rechts der Akademie der Wissenschaften der DDR (ed.) 1975. *Marxistisch-leninistische Staats -und Rechtstheorie*. 2nd edn. Berlin (Ost).

Kazenzadek, F. 1966. 'Demokratischer Zentralismus', in K.D. Kerwig (ed.) *Sowjetsystem und demokratische Gesellschaft: Eine vergleichende Enzyclopädie*. vol. I, col. 1158ff. Freiburg: Herder Verlag.

König, K. 1982. 'Kaderverwaltung und Verwaltungsrecht', *Verwaltungsarchiv 1, 37*.

——. 1991. 'Zum Verwaltungssystem der DDR', in K. König (ed.) *Verwaltungsstrukturen der DDR*. Baden-Baden: Nomos.

——. 1992. 'Zur Transformation einer real-sozialistisschen Verwaltung in eine klassisch-europäische Verwaltung', *Verwaltungsarchiv Heft 2, 229*.

Lecheler, H. 1991. 'Der öffentliche Dienst in den neuen Bundesländern-Die Lösung neuer Aufgaben mit alten Strukturen?' *Zeitschrift fur Beamtenrecht 48*.

Linde, J. 1991. 'Der Neuaufbau eines Landes: das Beispiel Brandenburg', *Staatswissenschaften und Staatspraxis 282*.

Lipp, W. 1978. 'Bürokratische, partizipative und Kaderorganisation als Instrument sozialer Steurung', *Die Verwaltung 3*.

Ludz, P.C. 1968. *Parteielite im Wandel*. Köln/Opladen: Westdeutscher Verlag.

Marxistisch-Leninistische allgemeine Theorie des Staates und des Rechts. 1975. Der sozialistische Staat, vol. 3. Berlin (Ost).

Meyer-Hesemann, W. 1991. 'Hilfen zum Aufbau von Verwaltung und Justiz in den neuen Ländern-dargestellt am Beispiel der Zusammenarbeit zwischen den Ländern Brandenburg und Nordrhein-Westfalen', *Verwaltungsarchiv 578*.

Mit Recht leiten (Lead with the law): Aktuelle Fragen der Durchsetzung des sozialischen Rechts in Betrieben und Kombinaten. 1974. Berlin (Ost).

Nagels, J. 1991. 'Die Staaten Zentral- und Osteuropas im Übergang von zentraler staatlicher Planwirtschaft zu marktwirtschaftlichen Systemen', in *Deutsche Sektion des Internationalen Instituts für Verwaltungswissenschaften: Verwaltungswissenschaftliche Informationen* 3/4, p. 32.

Pohl, H. 1991a. 'Entwicklung des Verwaltungsrechts', p. 235 in K. König (ed.) *Verwaltungsstrukturen der DDR.* Baden-Baden: Nomos.

——. 1991b. 'Verwaltungsrechtsschutz', p. 263. in K. König (ed.) *Verwaltungsstrukturen der DDR,* Baden-Baden: Nomos.

Quaritsch, H. 1992. 'Eigenarten und Rechtsfragen der DDR-Revolution', *Verwaltungsarchiv* Heft 2, 314.

Renger, M. 1991. *Einführung des Berufsbeamtentums in den neuen Ländern.* Regensburg: Walhalla-und Praetoria-Verlag.

Reusch, U. 1991. 'Starthilfe fur die neuen Länder. Aufgaben und Arbeit der Bund-Länder-Clearing-Stelle für die Verwaltungshilfe', *Deutschland-Archiv. Zeitschrift für das vereinigte Deutschland* 230.

Riese, H. 1970. *Geld im Sozialismus: Zur theoretischen Fundierung von Konzeptionen des Sozialismus.* Regensburg: Walhalla-und Praetoria-Verlag.

Roggemann, H. 1989. *Die DDR-Verfassungen: Einführung in das Verfassungsrecht der DDR.* 4th edn. Berlin.

Rytlewski, R. 1985. 'Planung', p. 986 in *DDR Handbuch,* vol. 2, 3rd edn. Cologne: Heymann Verlag.

Schulze, C. 1991. 'Staat und Verwaltung in der sozialistischen Reformdiskussion der DDR', p. 71 in K. König (ed.) *Verwaltungsstrukturen der DDR.* Baden-Baden: Nomos.

Schulze, G. 1991a. 'Aufgabenfelder der Verwaltung' p. 71 in K. König (ed.) *Verwaltungsstrukturen der DDR.* Baden-Baden: Nomos.

——. 1991b. 'Verwaltungspersonal und Verwaltungsausbildung', in K. König (ed.) *Verwaltungsstrukturen der DDR.* Baden-Baden: Nomos.

Treuhandanstalt (ed.) 1992. *Treuhandanstalt-Wegweiser und Zwischenbilanz.* Berlin.

Ule, C.H. 1990. 'Beamter oder Staatsfunktionär', *VOP: Verwaltungsführung, Organisation, Personal* 151.

Volensky, M. 1980. *Nomenklatura: Die herrschende Klasse in der Sowjetunion.* Munich: Molden Verlag.

Weiss, H.-D. 1991. 'Wiedereinführung des Berufsbeamtentums im beigetretenen Teil Deutschlands-Entwicklung und Darstellung des seit dem 3 Oktober 1990 geltenden Beamtenrechts auf der Grundlage des Einigungsvertrages', *Zeitschrift für Beamtenrecht:* 1.

Acts of the GDR government

Beschluss zur Gründung der Anstalt zur treuhänderischen Verwaltung des Volkseigentums (Treuhandanstalt) vom 1 März 1990, GBl. DDR I p. 107.

Verordnung zur Umwandlung von volkseigenen Kombinaten, Betrieben und Einrichtungen in Kapitalgesellschaften vom 1 März 1990, GBl. DDR I p. 107.

Gesetz zur Privatisierung und Reorganisation des volkseigenen Vermögens (Treuhandgesetz) vom 17 Juni 1990, GBl. DDR I p. 300.

Vertrag zwischen der Bundesrepublik Deutschland und der Deutschen Demokratischen Republik über die Herstellung der Einheit Deutschlands-Einigungsvertrag-vom 31 Aug. 1990, BGBl, II 1990, p. 889.

III COMPARATIVE OBSERVATIONS

ANALYSING INSTITUTIONAL CHANGE AND ADMINISTRATIVE TRANSFORMATION: A COMPARATIVE VIEW

THEO A. J. TOONEN

I INTRODUCTION

This contribution presents an effort to develop a public administration perspective on the ongoing process of institutional reform and transformation in Central and Eastern Europe. It is organized around three rather straightforward questions. The first refers to analytical issues. How should we study the subject at hand? We are dealing with a multi-dimensional and multi-level reform and transformation process. The Central and Eastern European experience has not yet generated any models and theories of its own which might drive the administrative analysis. The question is how one could arrive at a theoretically orientated perspective to explore adequately the ongoing, multifarious and turbulent administrative reform processes, without being unduly biased by 'western' presuppositions and preoccupations (section II).

The next question is: what may we learn from the developments? Which aspects of the administrative reform efforts merit attention from a comparative point of view, given the fact that the analyses so far, have been predominantly historical, economic and political in nature? What are striking features of the historical revolution in Central and Eastern Europe from the viewpoint of building a solid administrative system for guidance, evaluation and control in the public sector? Such a system, after all, is an indispensable cornerstone of the sustained development of the liberal market economies that serve as a guide for the ongoing reforms in Central and Eastern Europe (section III).

The observations in this paper refer predominantly to developments within the administrative systems of Poland, Hungary and the former Czechoslovakia as reflected in the country reports of the national experts represented in this volume. Empirical research and standardized data collection on the basis of an

Theo A. J. Toonen is Professor of Public Administration at the Rijksuniversiteit, Leiden, The Netherlands.

explicit public administration interest and a common theoretical framework are still rare. This analysis is part of an attempt to explore the topic of administrative reform in post-socialist countries and to formulate some issues and research questions from an administrative point of view. The third question is, therefore, whether we might be able to identify some needs, both in terms of research and of prescriptions for public sector reform that merit attention from a public administration perspective. Is there, on the basis of the material available, anything else that can be said other than the standard prescription that public sector management and training are still much needed in the aforesaid countries? (section IV)

II ASSESSING ADMINISTRATIVE REFORM IN POST-SOCIALIST COUNTRIES: ANALYTICAL PROBLEMS

Developments in Central and Eastern European countries are currently rather overwhelming and thus not easily categorized. The efforts to reform the administrative systems of the countries of the former Communist Bloc are dominated by an overall effort to 'privatize' state agencies, particularly in the industrial production sector. The current attention of scholars and researchers in the area of public administration is mainly focused on the question of how to 'reform' the respective administrative systems, which are mostly grouped together in one, undifferentiated category. A prescriptive bias dominates: how can we improve the system?

Rice (1992, p. 166) has presented an overview of what should be done to bring the public administrations of Eastern European countries into the post-socialist era. On the basis of several documents from Hungary, Poland, Romania and Bulgaria, he identifies five principles that are likely to guide Central and Eastern European societies in building their governments:

—the retreat from the discredited central government in favour of decentralization and privatization;
—the improvement of channels of communication between governments and their citizens in response to a demand for participation;
—the creation of a hospitable business environment and an adequate institutional infrastructure for a market economy;
—a concern for public welfare and social justice in terms of services and human rights;
—an efficient government administration at all levels within a setting of public review and internal and external accountability.

With this 'model' as the yardstick, Rice (1992, pp. 117–22) identifies a number of administrative needs and problems for public administration reform. To improve policy making, he primarily emphasizes the need to strengthen the capacity for economic projections and the development of strategies. The former central planning system was merely a bureaucratic device and not a system of forecasting in a market situation. Most basic statistical and other types of policy information are lacking or entirely missing.

Rice observes that the devolution of significant powers and responsibilities to sub-central governments has already advanced considerably, but that this radical shift also complicates the reform process in a number of ways. Questions about the desired central-local relationship have not been resolved, although formal pieces of legislation and local government reform offices have been established – Hungary and Poland in particular display strong activities in this field – but actual performance capacities at the local level are still far from clear. One of the problems is that, since the state enterprises formerly served as the main source of government revenue, a tax management and effective revenue-raising system, in the broadest sense, is largely absent.

Much in the same way, the various countries according to Rice (1992, p. 121) have so far largely ignored the need for civil service reform ' . . . even though it is their civil servants who must implement planned reforms ... Governments have apparently not conceived of their employees as a bureaucracy-wide civil service'. They have yet to develop comprehensive reform strategies. He suggests that to this end central government change agents are necessary. Central government directorates should formulate and implement comprehensive action plans to overhaul the civil service by (1) transforming the bureaucratic culture and organizational structure, (2) introducing mechanisms to assure accountability, and (3) expanding training capacity.

Such prescriptions are not uncommon, but they also raise questions. In most Western European countries, the administrative modernization process over the past decade has taken the form of a rather incremental approach, but has seldom been a centrally steered innovation process (Hesse and Benz 1990; Dente and Kjellberg 1988). Available evidence seems to indicate that successful institutional development is usually best perceived as an evolutionary pragmatic political process using and blending the social and political forces and dynamics within the system.

Comprehensive plans have seldom resulted in the desired administrative reforms in Western administrations. Effective reform must largely come 'from within'. Former Eastern Germany is likely to remain the only example where the transition from 'socialist' to 'post-socialist' is being tried in a comprehensive, synoptical way on the basis of a complete 'management buy-out' and subsequent 'reorganization' of the system. All other countries will necessarily be required to make the transition in a more incremental, step by step way. It remains to be seen which societies, in the end, are or will feel themselves better off. But it is certainly true that, with massive help from elsewhere in the world, the starting point for Central and Eastern European countries will be to rebuild themselves with what they have.

Some will find this proposition difficult to accept. The primary task of an evolutionary-orientated approach to administrative reform is to provide a solid assessment of the actual existing situation, its deficiencies and its growth or development potential. The development in the former socialist countries is, however, primarily defined in terms of a process of getting away from the previous situation instead of arriving at a desired state of affairs. The label 'post'-socialist, as such, indicates a preoccupation with what has been, without a perception of what should or will be. The future is left open.

For all three countries under observation here, a tendency is reported towards a degree of 'over-transformation' in terms of decentralization and massive streams of newly enacted legislation; distrust of the old regime and the rejection of both the 'old' central planning system and the former *cadres*, whatever their precise role, are identified with it. The people have a better idea of where they are coming from than where they are going to. Sometimes 'administrative reform' has become a goal in itself. Few people within the system – so far, but times may quickly be changing–will take the risk of 'defending' the previous situation, or show an interest that might be perceived as being associated with the Communist *ancient régime*.

The positive aspects of what was or is might, under the prevailing conditions, easily remain unarticulated. For the outsider looking at the situation, it is still very difficult to assess the precise nature and accuracy of the criticism and cynicism abundantly available with regard to both the past situation as well as the ongoing reform processes. The historically distinct character of the ongoing developments might imply that analysts have to concentrate on the innate characteristics of a transformation process which, from established Western theoretical perspectives – and their former 'Eastern' antipodes, are 'unknown'. These observations might easily be considered to be 'too romantic', 'too optimistic' or 'naive' for a strongly built and 'modern' public administration. As with developing non-western countries, however, one might envisage tendencies towards self-governance and self-administration of parts of the society outside the domains which we – i.e. 'western' analysts – would normally identify and recognize as government and administration 'proper'.

The ongoing reform processes can be studied from different administrative angles (cf. Toonen 1983; Kiser and Ostrom, 1982; Hood 1991). The economic orientation of both the reform efforts and the analysis stresses the need for building an efficient and responsive administrative system. With respect to the Polish case it is observed that the ultimate result of public administration reform is to achieve a pro-citizen mentality amongst the officials and a change for the better in society's attitude towards the administration. An interest in a more effective, responsive and responsible administration is the stated purpose of many western recommendations.

As time and developments progress, however, attention has shifted to complement a mere concern for economy and responsiveness with a concern for cooperation and rectitude in the public sector. Administrative scandals in Czechoslovakia as well as a growing critique of the Polish government have contributed to the awareness that the legitimation and acceptance of administrative systems rely not only on their effectiveness and efficiency in reaching goals, but also on the way in which goals are being reached and tasks are being accomplished. The achievement of a degree of joint decision making, fairness, reciprocity in public obligations and a proper discharge of duties in substantive and procedural terms, among the parties involved, are becoming increasingly important administrative concerns in the various reform processes.

The third angle which causes observers to worry and merits attention in an administrative analysis, is the robustness and sustainability of the reforms set in motion. Not enough attention is paid to the need to build administrative capacity to implement and follow through political and legislative initiatives. People are becoming frustrated by undelivered promises and are losing their faith in the process and the credibility of the operation in the longer term. Almost all observers, most explicity in Poland and Czechoslovakia, express their anxiety about the danger of stagnation of the reform process and a resultant fundamental political instability. There is a clear concern about the 'constitution' of the reform processes, not only in terms of its legal structure and containment, but more importantly in terms of the basic trust and feelings of reliability among the general population.

The different angles represent more or less distinct administrative value systems (Hood 1991). They also seem to refer to different worlds of action and administrative reform (Kiser and Ostrom 1982). The values of responsiveness, goal-orientation and effectiveness refer to the 'world of operational choice' and the management of day-to-day actions and decisions, within a given framework of rules and institutions. Issues of accountability, reciprocity, public obligation and procedural legitimation refer to the 'world of collective choice' and situations of joint decision making, policy formulation and implementation. The sustainability of the reforms, the question of reliability, trustworthiness and resilience of newly erected institutions refer to a concern about the soundness of the 'constitution' of the reform processes.

1 Multi-dimensional and multi-level problems

Every sound administrative system will have to satisfy the three different value complexes at more or less the same time. The different value systems and underlying questions apply not only to stable liberal democratic market economies, but to transitionary systems as well, as the various reports clearly indicate. The only difference is that in stable situations and institutionally well developed and established administrative systems the different functions and corresponding core values are usually served by more or less separate institutions and procedures. They are conventionally studied and evaluated accordingly by different theories and disciplines. To simplify: constitutional courts deal with constitutional issues, policy makers and legislatures deal with questions of collective decision making, and public managers, executives and civil servants deal with operational issues. Each type of issue requires more or less its own consideration, logic and approach. Constitutional questions are different and are therefore separated from operational management decisions.

The analytics of the ongoing transition process in Central and Eastern Europe are much more complicated than in more stable environments. The complexity and turbulence of the reforms are caused partly by the fact that, with respect to any concrete decision or development, almost all dimensions have to be considered at the same time. This often causes the different value systems to be in conflict and to overload any specific situation with analytically rather different considerations. Decisions on privatization, for example, serve in the Central and Eastern European countries different value systems at the same time. Privatization is defended for reasons of efficiency and economy. But privatization is also aimed at bringing about 'constitutional' changes in, for example, the economic or property rights structure. In the case of 're-privatization' or the restitution of private property to former owners, the 'constitutional' and 'operational' considerations are further complicated by questions of equity, fairness and rectitude.

On the other hand, efficient privatization at the operational level presupposes the existence of a market-like infrastructure (property rights, banking systems, public enforcement agencies, etc.) at the 'constitutional' level. The difference in meaning of privatization within the various perspectives, implies that western knowledge and expertise in the area are often not easily transferable. Where Western efforts to 'privatize' in say Britain are usually aimed at increasing the efficiency of the economy, privatization efforts in Central and Eastern Europe are largely aimed at constructing a market system. This strongly limits the lessons that British 'privatization' may hold for Central European countries. Other examples come easily to mind: many Western business firms and companies are interested in 'privatizing' firms or factories in one of the post-socialist countries precisely because these occupy a monopoly position. The 'hospitable' part of the business environment in the post-socialist countries, is 'constitutionally' just the opposite of what the privatization philosophy entails.

The confusion of the various dimensions and levels of analysis is also reflected in proposals to privatize public transport 'because the government can make no profit out of it'. Instrumental operational considerations often dominate constitutional questions. Constitutions, legal procedures and courts, on the other hand, are given a role in the operational management of the political process. This might be understandable in the short run, but the constitutional rule of written constitutions and independent courts might easily be evaded, if not threatened, when they are systematically drawn into solving policy and operational issues. Developments with respect to the role of the Revisional Chamber in the case of Hungary provide a case in point.

The reason that courts become easily involved in the world of operational action and collective choice has to do with their well-developed organizational and operational skills and capabilities. However, operational capacities within the system are sometimes easily overlooked because of veiling 'constitutional' contexts. The problem, for example, is not that people in the post-socialist countries do not know how to compete or how to deal with 'competitive and market-like situations'. They have always been competing: not for the favour of clients or citizens, but for suppliers of goods and services, their party bosses, government officials, etc. A desired capacity comes often in a different guise. Instead of writing off whole 'lost generations' in the respective countries, one may try to find ways to organize the institutional infrastructure and the relevant policy incentives away from hierarchy towards a responsiveness by which people can and will learn to apply their already existing competitive skills in the new (constitutional and policy) setting.

2 Framing and reframing

Whether we like it or not, the existing situation in Central and Eastern European countries requires an analytical capacity in which, in principle, it is possible to 'think the unthinkable' and, potentially, recognize 'the efficiency of inefficient approaches'. We need a sufficiently broad theoretical view and analytical framework. The topical issue in western public administration and organization and management sciences, i.e. to be able to (theoretically) frame and reframe the administrative problem at hand from various perspectives, is particularly relevant in the present case. 'Foreign models' and experiences are valuable and inspiring for the various countries, but cannot be applied directly and without modifications.

In Taras's opinion ' ... it is better to fight against the causes of existing evil, than to search for a hypothetical good'. Indeed, we do not need a model to guide us in 'the search for a hypothetical good', but — apart from empirical evidence — an analytical and theoretical framework that allows us adequately to conceptualize the various dimensions of the complicated multi-level and multi-dimensional reform process at hand. The starting point of such a framework has to be that the market economy is only 'free' within a public and legal set of enforceable rights and constraints (Riker and Weimer 1992). Privatization presupposes a very elaborate and collectively maintained and publicly enforced 'economic constitution'. The success of introducing the mixed market economy critically hinges upon the development of a reliable public infrastructure in terms of legal systems, regulatory agencies to safeguard competition, promotional agencies for economic and regional development and for scientific and technological development, as well as the exploration of potential markets for export and of the provision of some kind of basic welfare administration.

III ADMINISTRATIVE REFORM IN CENTRAL AND EASTERN EUROPE: COMPARATIVE OBSERVATIONS

From a comparative point of view, there is at least one point that cannot but surprise any Western European administrative observer when he looks behind the curtains of the formerly 'centrally planned' administrative systems of Central and Eastern Europe. Employment rates in public administration and particularly the segment identified as 'the civil service' are extremely difficult to compare. But the reported figures of, for example, Poland, with a total of 158,000 civil servants of which 53,000 are employed at national level and out of which about

10,000 work for the central ministries, are somewhat surprising for an outside observer. Rice (1992, p. 121) equally observes that compared to western standards, the central government civil services in Eastern Europe are surprisingly small, with staffing levels in government ministries ranging from 8,000 in Hungary, to 25,000 in Romania.

Lack of accurately defined comparative data means that it is hard to draw firm conclusions. Many services are conducted outside the 'proper' civil service. A surprise reaction is unavoidable, however, if one recollects that a relatively small country like the Netherlands has over 150,000 national civil servants without ever having had the ambition to be a centrally planned economy. Indeed it gives rise to the counter-intuitive thought that ' . . . rather than looking for ways to streamline these core civil services, the countries of Eastern Europe may need to consider strategies to expand and improve them (Rice 1992, p. 121).'

Experiences like these underline the fact that it would be difficult but very necessary and profitable to probe into the comparative facts and figures and the 'nuts and bolts' of comparative administrative systems and civil service reforms in Eastern European countries. Obviously the required retrenchment policies have to mean something else than the 'downsizing' of the civil service which is the main definition of reducing government intervention in western countries. If the figures are at all comparable, then, also from a comparative 'western' point of view, the charge of excessive outlays on public administration in terms of money and personnel are part of a misconception. In some cases public administration will have to grow instead of diminish.

It also means that one has to rethink the 'off hand' initial prescription that administrative modernization in Eastern Europe would imply the mere decentralization of administrative systems and the handing over of power from the central to the local authorities. Looking more closely at the situation in the different countries, one sometimes gets the impression that the real problem was that not only were there no local authorities, but, even worse, initially there was hardly any effective central power to hand over to them.

In one of the initial comparative assessments of administrative developments in Central and Eastern Europe, Hesse presents a somewhat gloomy overall analysis. The shared characteristic of the transformation process of these administrative systems is the development from a one-party rule to pluralist, multi-party systems with democratically elected and accountable governments; the principle of 'democratic centralism' is being abandoned in favour of the deconcentration and decentralization of political power under the rule of law; and it is universally accepted that administrative effectiveness, efficiency and flexibility need to be increased. According to Hesse (1991, p. 199)

> . . . the task of modernizing public administration goes much beyond . . . responsibilities in the majority of the industrialized countries of the Western hemisphere. The challenge with which public administration is faced is to redefine its role in society, or, more concretely, its relations with politics, the economy and the civil community . . . Administrative restructuring and reorganization must be pursued with the same vigour as political and economic reforms, and they require a similarly sustained effort.

The situation varies, however, from country to country. There are no standard solutions.

1 Czechoslovakia

Czechoslovakia witnessed the quickest 'velvet revolution' of all countries, but in a way the two Republics are now lagging behind in modernizing their state structures. Despite the fact that much energy has been absorbed by trying to concentrate on resolving fundamental constitutional problems, one should not overlook another important explanation. The Communist regime in Czechoslovakia was amongst the most strict and conservative, particularly since it suppressed the '68 liberalization movement. They also stayed in power to the very last minute, until at the end of 1989, the regime gave way to a surprisingly swift take over.

Soon after the take over, several ministries were abolished in an effort to reduce central state control over the economy, but perhaps also to take away power from the federal government. New institutions were created for revitalizing the economy. Over the following year the entire federal state system has come under consideration. Federalization, or rather efforts in favour of its realization, had already led to a transfer of powers and responsibilities from the federal level to the Republics. Local government had already ceased to be part of the state administration. Discussions and ongoing constitutional and administrative reforms became burdened if not entirely stalled by the long-standing historical distinctions among Czechs and Slovaks and inherent centripetal tendencies.

The breaking up of Czechoslovakia may be understood as a classic case of the struggle between autonomy and influence or co-determination of the component parts of the state, in this case the Czech and the Slovak people. The striving for 'autonomy' by the Czech and particularly the Slovak Republic goes back a long time in history and has more often been dealt with, but not resolved, under the Communist regime by mere repression. The division of the territory by the Czechs and the Slovaks originates in the 1970s and the changes of November 1989 merely serve to expose them. More than a dissatisfaction with the old regime, the striving for autonomy, particularly by the Slovaks, seems to follow from a distrust of the centre over joint decision making; the central authority of the Federation has long been seen not as a centre of decision making but as being dominated by one of the two component parts, the Czechs. In addition, the Slovaks were more adversely affected, economically speaking, by the administrative transition. Their economy had faired relatively well under the Communist regime, being the regional centre of heavy steal (arms) industry.

The continued striving for 'autonomy' by both parties was caused less by a dislike of the *ancient regime*, than by the fact that the federal structures were invariably *not* perceived by at least one of the participants (the Slovaks), as just or fair with mutual administrative arrangements for joint decision making. This rift could be exploited by conservative forces aiming at strengthening their regionalized power bases.

The outside world might have tried to prevent the developments by giving selective and 'velvet' support to those symbols, institutions, projects and persons representing the remaining world of collective choice. Perhaps President Havel might have been more effective in building joint decision-making structures, if at the operational level he had something more to offer than a relatively widespread trust in his personality and charisma.

The striving for 'autonomy', i.e. the separation of the Czech and Slovak Republics, might actually stabilize the situation and need not result in a total stagnation and conflict of the reform processes in the two Republics. Experiences in Spain and Belgium come to mind, where the granting of autonomy has stabilized the 'constitutional' situation, thus opening avenues for pragmatic joint policy making in the operational world of action, thus gradually contributing to efforts to talk from 'community to community' and to try to develop different and mutually acceptable forms of co-operation.

The process of (con)federalization, and eventually the breaking up of the Federation in January 1993, has complicated administrative reform efforts primarily because it absorbed most of the political energy. With all the attention concentrated on various constitutional issues at the federal and state level, the two Republics now both face the need to build their structures for joint decision making and effective operational management within their newly established states. Particular attention has to be paid to developing integrative institutional arrangements at the intermediary levels between the national and local levels of the two Republics. Operational administrative capacity to deal with the implementation of a stream of legislation seems required, with a view to enforcing agreed legislation, but also towards injecting realistic and feasibility considerations into an otherwise somewhat inflationary legislative process.

2 Poland

In Poland, the most notable developments are perhaps the (re)establishment of a system of democratic local government and the seemingly stagnating reform processes, due to institutionalized (should one say bureau-political?) rivalries and conflicts among the major institutional and political actors that comprise the national government. Both the functional and the territorial institutional differentiation entails a sharp break with the previous system of uniform, hierarchial and highly centralized state administration. This is true, despite the fact that, for example, centrally appointed governors of the (regional) *voivodships* still perform substantial supervisory functions.

At the national level, crumbling identification within the ranks of Solidarity has not been very favourable for designing and implementing a comprehensive plan for civil service reorganization. Nor has it been replaced by other integrative forces, although sometimes informal networks of civil servants are thought to be able to take over that role and act as an integrative force in a rather fragmented governmental system. It is questionable whether a strong presidency will be able to overcome the problems. From the outside, it sometimes seems as though the main problem is not so much the highly plural political game which is being played, but the lack of appropriate rules for the game of pluralistic politics. The game has to be played with inadequate constitutional, political and cultural rules for the game of consociational politics and joint decision making which is based upon accommodation and mutual adjustment.

In Poland it is equally observed that the conflict between 'autonomy' and 'co-determination' among rival political factions is resulting in stagnating reforms. Some maintain that one might even have to await the return of political stability in order to be able to make some progress. The ongoing difficulties do not start from scratch either, and need to be understood in the light of the reforms of the years of Communist rule. The difference with Czechoslovakia, in terms of our comparative framework, is that the difficulties originate at another level or institutional world of action. The inertia, paralysis, incompetence, bureaucratism, arrogance and corruption, as observed by country specialists, seem to originate less in the world of constitutional action and more in the world of collective choice. Although the problems may spill over into a constitutional crisis in terms of sustainability, trust and the break down of the system, the observed problems at the operational level of government seem to be particularly caused by problems at the level of joint decision making. It is noticeable that the once-held fundamental principles of legality, justice, and equality of opportunity are more and more questioned. Letowski therefore prescribes a basic code of administrative conduct, rules of a moral nature such as that the agency does not lie, does not prevaricate, keeps its promises, behaves honestly and decently. The values of the world of collective choice and joint decision making deserve attention owing to the lack of effective institutional arrangements to that end.

The problems of the actual legislative process, and the civil service or local government reorganization and decentralization exemplify the problems of joint decision making surrounding contemporary Polish administration. Within the institutionally and politically fragmented system the historical development has led to a situation in which the administrative hierarchy is missing and more importantly – one in which little or no constitutional provision for conflict resolution and will formation has yet been developed. The great speed of legislation, the problem of the binding nature of 'ministerial law', the use of the legally wrong 'tools' for dealing with citizen affairs (instructions instead of statutes), the way in which 'emergency powers' are being demanded and the administrative battles between government, ministries, Parliament and President are all serious threats to the future development of the system.

At the same time the problems all sound familiar. The system of joint decision making in Poland displays in an extreme and enlarged form all the problems of ministerial collegial government which can also be found elsewhere. The Council of Ministers is obviously too weak to act as an integrating force, and the same is true for the President and Parliament which have not been able to tip the balance to either's advantage. Where a collegial ministerial and cabinet system already creates serious problems of interdepartmental co-ordination, this is *a fortiori* true for Polish government, where the informal culture and routines of consociational and consensual politics and administration have also had no time to develop. In such a system the 'hands-on manager' who is politically pressed to undertake activities and 'solve problems' is almost forced to use whatever means are available within the existing situation. The goal starts to justify the means. Achieving results becomes more important than the way in which these results are achieved, which often leads to counter-productive outcomes.

The abuse of legal 'instruments' by goal-directed politicians, keen to score, is, in such a context, a familiar phenomenon in other administrative systems as well. In the operational world of action, the law is a binding act and therefore a vehicle for resolving problems of administrative uncertainty and incoherence. In such a system emergency powers may also provide a temporary solution, but are likely to be used instrumentally for too narrow and *ad hoc* purposes since they do not rest on a broader constitution which ensures the use of the special mandate for a broader purpose, thus eroding the 'instrument'. The desire for interministerial co-ordination or even a ministry for home affairs or the civil service centrally to direct the required reforms is predictable from a comparative perspective. From the experiences of other systems with collegial administration it is to be expected, though, that these will not do the job, since 'co-ordinating' ministers very often acquire the responsibility but seldom the power to co-ordinate their colleagues. The reason is simple: such a provision would erode the principle of collegial ministerial government since one of them would become the superior.

Experience with hierarchical non-consensual reforms — as in for example Thatcher's UK — suggests that a strong commitment from the Prime Minister is necessary to implement radical administrative reforms. The question is, however, whether such a centralized and non-consensual reform would fit in the rather diverse Polish political structure and culture and would generate enough support to last in the long run. In this case, outside instigation of a sustained but incremental and more consensual reform process could take the form of exerting external pressure on some strategic operational goals so as to force opponents into joint action. For a while an outside community like the EC could play the role of 'external coordinator', by generating pressures that indirectly and directly require goal-driven opponents to co-operate and co-ordinate their activities *vis à vis* the common (external) challenge. In the process, one might be able to generate sustainable, reliable and robust 'constitutional' routines, procedures and techniques for mutual problem solving.

Offering a perspective on future economic co-operation with the European Communities in exchange for the requirement to meet European financial and economic standards might provide such pressure and 'external co-ordination'. The promises of the European integration process have more often, and for several EC countries, turned out to be able to integrate and coordinate fragmented national decision making and foster effective informal co-ordination and mutual adjustment at administrative and political levels.

At the subnational level of the Polish administration, decisions are needed concerning proper relationships between various public and private actors. The regional government level has to be defined either as some kind of prefectorial system, which is responsible for the co-ordination of national executive functions in the region or as a territorial council which represents certain regional interests and may act as a partner in carrying out state functions as well. A mixed model – on the basis of comparative experience – would not be a bad solution for shaping complex Polish intergovernmental interests. But clarity about the role of regional government seems warranted.

The problems of local government seem to originate particularly in the operational world of action. Legislation has been issued. The problems reported indicate that a degree of politicization and 'confessionalization' of administration is frustrating its operations. From a comparative perspective it might be helpful to point to systems such as the Netherlands or Belgium and Italy where local-state-Catholic Church relationships were a prominent feature of the local government organization. Given the Catholic principle of 'subsidiarity', local authority in these systems usually means more than simply 'local government'. In the Catholic administrative doctrine a network of non-profit 'privatized' subsidiary organs may play an important role in carrying out local state functions. In that case a different concept of 'local *governance*' instead of 'local government' is called for. It has not prevented the development of strong local administrative systems in countries facing similar social features.

The politicization and party-political appointments in the local administration, again, exemplify a lack of trust in joint decision-making institutions and will not easily evaporate. Rather than criticizing the practice, one might consider the creation of institutionalized opportunities for political appointments in the higher ranks of the local administration while basing the award of these positions strictly on the grounds of merit.

3 Hungary

The most stable progress, so far, seems to have been made in Hungary, which has the longest history of market-orientated reform experiences. The legal foundations for a pluralist liberal democracy seem to have been laid. The most basic and also controversial change in Hungarian public administration concerns not so much the internal national government organization, but its relationship with the other levels of government. In 1990, the legal conditions for far-reaching regional and local autonomy and self-government were created as a reaction to the democratic centralism of Communist rule. Local and regional administration have been put under the control of elected councils. As elsewhere, the durability of reform of economy and public administration is threatened most by a stagnating economic development.

In Hungary, the administrative modernization and adaptation to a liberal market economy seem to be relatively well under way. The problems which are reported may be identified in terms of the 'operational world of action': the goal-directedness, the economy and the frugality of the system. A flood of legislation is being observed, to the extent that one may wonder about its effectiveness, suitability and enforcement. This is true, despite the fact that an equally abundant number of deconcentrated state services for supervising the implementation of national legislation has emerged in the region.

The relative success of developments so far seems to be due to the fact that the Hungarians entered the modernization process at the end of the 1980s 'with their feet down running'. Again the roots of current developments are to be found in the past under the Communist regime. The 'Hungarian secret' seems to consist of three pre-existing conditions. First, already in the 1960s and 1970s, Hungarian government implemented a local government reform characterized by scale-enlargement and decentralization. A relatively strong local government system and the determined application of it is an important feature of the ongoing reform and modernization process. Secondly, even under the central planning of the *ancient regime*, Hungary used to be the regime most liberated from central planning, including as many liberal-economic elements as was politically possible. The Leninist-state and economic system was liberated to the utmost degree. Finally, Balázs observes that, just prior to the transformation, a new generation of bureaucratic 'mandarins' – technically well skilled and politically with a low profile – had risen to a position just below the top. When the established ministries were politically beheaded they were ready and able to take over, thus limiting the human resource problems which faced so many other administrative systems when faced with changes of regime. Thus a situation emerged, which is quite the opposite of Czechoslovakia, where leadership had to be brought in from the outside and was confronted with an administrative system which had not been reformed at all and needed to be fully 'reorganized'.

The 're-emergence of history' gives rise to all kinds of differential institutional logics and developments. It is this continuity, not the quick shift ('big bang') which has brought about what seems to be the relatively most stable ongoing reform process in the direction of a liberal market economy. The main problems in Hungary are being created by the decline of economic resources due to the economic stagnation following the transformations which revealed the gross inefficiencies – both economically, as well as in terms of human and environ-mental resources – of the previously 'centrally planned' economies. The trust of citizens in the transformation has been undermined by the fact that the reforms have not resulted in an immediate increase in welfare, but rather the contrary.

Also in other areas the arrangements for joint decision making and collective action among different administrative units are under pressure. Intergovern-mental relations now seem to suffer from an initial tendency to move away and by-pass the county level which under the *ancient regime* performed many disputed intermediary tasks. This has left an institutional vacuum which is still not properly filled. In aspects of local government one may observe the tendency to feel the shortcomings of overstretched concepts of local 'autonomy' and a move back to stressing the need for developing adequate interrelationships among different planes of government.

The most fundamental problem the Hungarian administrative system seems to face, however, is the alienation of citizens and the lack of civic interest in participating in elections and other forms of collective choice procedures.

Western nations may learn from the historical developments in Central and Eastern Europe that states do not easily lose the diffuse, general trust and confidence – regime legitimacy – of their citizens. Once it is lost, however, the impact is dramatic and it will be difficult to get it back. A regime shift is a necessary, but not sufficient measure. Regaining this trust primarily requires time.

IV ADMINISTRATIVE REFORM IN CENTRAL EUROPE: CONCLUSIONS

What conclusions may one draw from the previous analysis? One may want to take issue with the observation that ' . . . all the same, public administration across these (post-socialist) countries is more notable for similarities than differences both in its shortcomings and the stages of reform' (Rice 1992, p. 117). Administrative reform never starts from scratch. The analysis provided here suggests that there is no watershed or 'big bang' between the Communist and post-Communist era from the viewpoint of the recreation of an effective public administration system. The relative advantage (of Hungary) and dis-advantage (of Czechoslovakia) in terms of the ongoing reform process, are clearly rooted in events, preconditions and decisions sometimes dating far back into the history of Communist rule.

Given the magnitude of the changes and transformations at the end of the last decade, the degree of continuity and influence of the past comes as somewhat of a surprise. The ease with which countries seem to adapt to a capitalist mode of production so far seems to be determined as much by the historical circumstances during the Communist era as the decisions of the post-socialist reformers.

The common challenges which the different countries face entail at least the disentanglement of public administration and the civil service from party bu-reaucracy and membership. Whole sections of the administrative systems, previously responsible for the 'democratic centralism' of the centrally planned and controlled economy, are being eliminated, while, at the same time, new administrative capacities for economic market development have to be created. Planning and monitoring procedures need to be reorientated from the imperial categories of the internal 'central plan' towards external performance and public service delivery. Effective mechanisms for the protection of citizens against arbitrary or unlawful actions by administrators need to be installed.

In coping with these challenges, the systems have to deal with various puzzles. Removing civil servants closely connected with the previous Communist regime (as in Poland and Czechoslovakia) is prone to the accusation of politicizing public administration under a different label. Neither will the ideal of liberal democracy, based on the rule of law, feel comfortable in the company of a requirement that civil servants are not allowed to be members of a given political party, even if this is a Communist party in name.

Perhaps some new talents may be drawn into the civil service. Resources for attracting new people are scarce, not only in terms of pay, but also in terms of all other kinds of incentives: prestige, image, infrastructure. This is not only because the private sector has so much more financial appeal. Just as important is that, again contrary to what one might have expected under Communist rule, the administration and its employees were treated as a necessary evil which would vanish when the state was transformed into Communist self-government. Quite different from what one might expect from a 'state-oriented system' of government, employees were already in low esteem before the changes, had the least protection by the state and were not respected by the citizens.

One has to find ways to restore pride and self-esteem in relation to working for and within the public sector. The existing rank and file members of the different civil service systems, which have been trained, recruited and socialized under a completely different set of bureaucratic and decision-making premises, will have to go through a time-consuming and difficult process of adaptation to the changing role of public administration in their societies.

In several cases, the danger sometimes seems to become more acute, that economic developments might not give the Central and Eastern European countries quite the time nor the incentives necessary for such infrastructural changes. There is little possibility of 'buying-off' frustrated interests. The redistribution issues which are inherent in any reform process have to be resolved in the present context of declining resources or, at best, in the short run, stabilizing resources. This often turns the reform efforts into a zero-sum or even negative-sum process. The call for strong political leadership to avoid chaos is, internally and externally, potentially dangerous. This is particularly true for the societies under consideration here. They have not yet had the time to develop a basic democratic, self-governing infrastructure. The same applies to a political culture and societal reflexes in which strong but checked and balanced leadership may develop.

The various countries sometimes seem to be half way through the reform, which results in situations in which the parties representing the conservative anti-reform interests may use the already introduced procedures and rules of democratic decision making to protect their interests and strengthen their vested positions. In one country – Hungary – an 'incomplete' constitutional structure seems to create fewer difficulties than in another country – Poland – where the 'flexibility' of the constitutional structure owing to lack of appropriate informal consociational devices contributes to stagnation and deterioration.

The retrenchment of state organization, i.e. denationalization, in favour of market organization has proceeded to a certain degree, but it is now generally considered to have slowed down considerably. Lack of (foreign) capital and investors is a frequently mentioned cause. Also, there is still much variation in the degree of state influence considered necessary or desirable. Furthermore, entrepreneurial skills to run complex, large-scale business organizations are almost completely lacking.

Stagnation of the reform processes and a corresponding destabilization of the political and social situation are explicitly expressed concerns particularly in the Polish and Czechoslovakian cases. The initial concern with respect to the developments behind the former 'iron curtain' was about the 'rationalization', 'decentralization', 'administrative modernization' and the 'upgrading' of system and personnel. This followed from an understandable, but in retrospect clear underestimation of the problems at hand. The main contemporary concern is, or rather, should be, that the current developments in the formerly socialist countries primarily ask for the capacity for stable and sustainable administrative development. Almost all country reports refer to, or reflect, a certain fear of social and political destabilization, stagnation of the reform efforts and a risk of escalating into potentially dramatic directions.

Instead of the design of a 'responsive and efficient system of governance and administration', the situation in the respective countries seems primarily to call for the constitution of a reliable, stable and adaptable system of self-governance, joint decision making and the corresponding forms of public management and administration. Some progress has been made and political prerogatives for developing an effective administrative system have been installed. The situation is far from stable, however.

On the basis of their comparative study of politics and society in Western Europe, Lane and Ersson (1991, p. 321) conclude that the degree of political instability is a function of the perceived (im)balance within these societies, which depends on the different social groups and interests in terms of subgroup autonomy on the one hand and the influence on national government on the other: 'Political stability in the long run perspective is related on the one hand to social cleavages and their conflict implications and on the other to the decision making system, in particular to the distribution of influence and autonomy between major groups within a society' (p. 322).

Lane and Ersson also observe that people and organizations in western societies demand both increased institutional and increased individual autonomy and that this demand is related to the perceived distribution of influence within centres for joint decision making. Citizens and organizations demand more autonomy when they experience government as unresponsive, inefficient, unfair or unreliable. When channels for co-determination and joint decision making do not work or are mistrusted, citizens ask for more autonomy.

When citizens feels that their activities in a certain field are no longer 'autonomous' they will try to influence government or other institutions for joint decision making in which they trust. If such an option is not available, this will easily result in a striving for autonomy regardless of the repercussions. Others that adopt a slightly different perspective of joint decision making will easily perceive this as an unproductive 'overtransformation'. This is basically what, in different forms, has been happening in all the countries under consideration here.

In cases where resources decline and the trust in public and other institutions for collective action is low on the basis of past experience, as is the case in present day Central and Eastern Europe, the situation is unstable indeed. It is predictable that people will strive for individual and institutional autonomy, even if this autonomy is shrinking too. Granting a certain degree of institutional autonomy may contribute to the overall stability of the system. Stability does not require a 'strong centre'. The development of several viable, strong and trusted collective decision making centres with ample opportunity for co-governance by the respective social, political, economic and administrative interests might alleviate the pressure for 'autonomy' which is anxiously identified by the Polish, Hungarian and Czech researchers.

The collective distress and psychological stress of the individual citizens have been reported more than once as important constraints on possible reform measures. It is obviously something that needs to be taken very seriously. Indeed, there is much more to privatization than economics or legal instrumentality. More than to economics, political and administrative structures and processes, attention must be paid to the needs and fears of the citizens in the ongoing reform process. For more than one reason, it worries me, that as a western analyst I cannot easily get to grips with this problem.

REFERENCES

Dente, B. and F. Kjellberg. (eds.) 1988. *The dynamics of institutional change*, Beverly Hills: Sage.

Hesse, J.J. 1991. 'Administrative modernisation in Central and Eastern European countries', *Staatswissenschaft und Staatspraxis* 2, 2, 197–217.

Hesse, J.J. and A. Benz. 1990. *Die Modernisierung der Staatsorganisation*. Baden-Baden: Nomos.

Hood, Ch. 1991. 'Public management for all seasons?, *Public Administration* 69, 1, 319.

Kiser, L.L. and E. Ostrom. 1982. 'Three Worlds of action: a metatheoretical synthesis of institutional approaches', in: W. Ostrom (ed.). *Strategies of political inquiry*, Beverly Hills; Sage.

Lane, J. and S.O. Ersson. 1991. *Politics and society in Western Europe*. London/Beverly Hills.

Rice, M. 1992. 'Public administration in Post-Socialist Eastern Europe', *Public Administration Review* 52, 2, 116–25.

Riker, W.H. and D.L. Weimer. 'The economic and political liberalisation of socialism: the fundamental problem of property rights', *paper for the Social Philosophy and Policy Center, Bowling Green State University, Ohio*, April 1992.

Toonen, Th.A.J. 1983. 'Administrative plurality in a unitary state', *Policy and Politics* 11, 3, 247–71.

CONSTITUTION-MAKING IN EASTERN EUROPE: REBUILDING THE BOAT IN THE OPEN SEA

JON ELSTER

I INTRODUCTION

The present report has two purposes. On the one hand, it aims at enhancing our understanding of the momentous political transitions that are currently taking place in six core countries of Eastern Europe: Bulgaria, The Czech Republic, Hungary, Poland, Romania and Slovakia. (All general references to 'Eastern Europe' are restricted to these countries and to the former Czechoslovakia.) On the other hand, it offers a first step towards the construction of a framework for the analysis of the constitution-making process. I begin with the latter, more general task, and then proceed towards more particular analyses, first of Eastern Europe taken as a whole, and then in some more detail of the Polish case. Although the main topic is constitution-making, I shall inevitably have to touch on various related matters, notably decisions by the Constitutional Courts, party formation, government formation, and electoral laws, which, in most countries, are not enshrined in the constitution. Also, I shall have to discuss the Round Table Talks that were an important pre-constitutional or quasi-constitutional stage in several countries.

I approach these matters neither as a constitutional lawyer nor as a historian, but as a political scientist. The emerging constitutions are well worth studying from the legal point of view. Often, they were put together in a hurry, and contain technical flaws or inconsistencies that call for juridical analysis for which I have no competence. Historians have already started to retrace the process of the downfall of Communism in the various East European countries. As I have only a superficial historical knowledge of the region and do not read any of its

Jon Elster is Edward L. Ryerson Distinguished Service Professor of Political Science and Philosophy at the University of Chicago. The present article was originally written as a report to the IRIS project, University of Maryland. He is happy to acknowledge the generous IRIS support for his work on Eastern Europe. He would also like to thank Christopher Clague, Lucian Mihai, Claus Offe, Wiktor Osiatynski, Cass Sunstein and Michel Troper for their comments on an earlier draft.

languages, I could not think of emulating their efforts. However, my focus, just as theirs, is on *process*. I want to understand the mechanisms of constitution-making at a more abstract level, at which general patterns might emerge. Here, the many simultaneous transitions in Eastern Europe offer a gigantic natural experiment. The countries have a number of similar features, and they share both a pre-Communist history and the recent Communist past. (The best survey of the region I know of is Bogdan (1990). He shows compellingly how the histories of the countries in the region have been intertwined with each other for a thousand years or more, creating deep- seated shared memories — especially of conflict and strife.) At the same time, they differ in level of economic development, form of religion, the prevalence of ethnic conflict and many intangible but palpable aspects. This mix of similarities and differences suggests that it might be possible to tease out some causal hypotheses.

Many countries have had their moments of constitution-making. I survey some of them in Part II, with special emphasis on the Federal Convention in Philadelphia 1787 and the Assemblée Constituante in Paris 1789–91. However, the situation in Eastern Europe is unique. The countries in the region have to make the transition to constitutional democracy at the same time as they are engaged in three other tasks of daunting difficulty. First, they are committed to a transition to a market economy. Second, they often have to engage in a process of state building or, as it has turned out in several places, of state dismantling. In countries ridden with ethnic conflicts that were artificially restrained by the harsh rule of the Communist Party, the initial hope of integrating different ethnic groups and nationalities has proved to be spurious. Instead, there has been either violent conflict (in the former Yugoslavia) or a peaceful dissolution (in the former Czechoslovakia). Third, many of the countries have found themselves in the throes of violence as they tried to come to terms with the Communist past. Demands for retribution, 'lustration' (publicizing the names of collaborators with the former regime) and restitution have taken up much energy that could have been devoted to other, more forward-looking tasks.

The constitution-making process has both influenced and been influenced by each of these tasks. I shall consider them in reverse order, and begin with the interaction between constitutionalism and backward-looking justice. To some extent the constitution itself may have been influenced by the fear of the founders — many of whom have been former Communist officials — of being targeted for retribution. Thus art.41.7 of the Romanian constitution says that 'Property is presumed to have been acquired legally', which is an unusual sort of provision. To make sense of it, we might look to a decision made by the Czechoslovak government on 26 September 1991, that in the future successful bidders for state-owned business would have to prove where their money comes from. The measure was intended to block the use of 'dirty money' that had been illegally accumulated by members of the former *nomenklatura* or black marketers. There is a presumption of guilt: the government is under no obligation to show that the funds have an illegal pedigree. Instead, citizens will have to prove that their money is clean. The Romanian clause may have been intended to pre-empt similar measures.

This is, admittedly, a speculative claim for which I have no direct evidence. The influence of constitutional thought on the processes of restitution and retribution is much more important and indisputable. In Hungary, the Constitutional Court has several times struck down laws on restitution and retribution voted by Parliament. In Czechoslovakia, the controversial 'lustration law' was in part struck down by the Federal Constitutional Court in a decision made immediately before the country's break-up. In these cases, the Court has invalidated decisions based on retroactive legislation, collective guilt, or inverse burden of proof. The decisive factor has not been this or that clause of the constitution, but rather the willingness of the courts to take the spirit of constitutionalism seriously.

Consider next the interaction between constitution-making and conflicts between ethnic groups and nationalities. With the exception of Hungary and Poland, such conflicts exist throughout the region. But this statement needs to be qualified. Although Hungary has very few internal minorities, about three million people with Hungarian as their first language live outside the borders of the country. (For a discussion of such 'external minorities' and their impact on the politics of the 'home country' see Elster 1991.) The constitutional expression of these conflicts has been an extended debate over the rights of ethnic minorities and national groupings. In Bulgaria and Romania, the presence of respectively Turkish-Muslim and Hungarian minorities has been a major hurdle in the constitution-making process. The first draft of the Romanian constitution contained an outright ban on ethnically based parties, aimed directly at the Hungarian opposition. In the final version, this provision was eliminated. A clause of this kind was, however, incorporated in the Bulgarian constitution (art.11.4).

In the former Czechoslovakia, the main issue was the organization of the federation rather than individual rights. I have more to say about this question in Part II below. Here, I shall only observe that the pre-existing constitutional set-up, inherited from the Communist period, gave the Slovaks a veto in the making of the new constitution. With the exception of Romania, this reflects a general feature of constitution-making in the region. The process took place within the framework of the existing Communist constitutions, thus effectively giving them a life after death — in fact *only* after death, since they never mattered before the fall of Communism. It is in this sense that the countries in Eastern Europe have been rebuilding their boats in the open sea, to use Otto Neurath's metaphor. They have not been able to seek refuge in a dry dock in which the new constitution could be built with entirely new timber. As we shall see below, the metaphor is also apt in another sense: the constitution-making has been entrusted to the very bodies that are to be regulated by the constitution.

The relation between the political transition to constitutional democracy and the economic transition to a market system is much more intimate and complex. Economic reform and political reform in the formerly Communist countries have two components each. On the economic side, both price reform and ownership reform are needed. On the political side, both democracy and constitutional guarantees for individual rights are strong desiderata, both in themselves and as prerequisites for economic reform. In a deliberately stark set of propositions, one might argue that the following relations obtain.

(i)   To be efficient, ownership reform presupposes price reform. To allow private entrepreneurs in an economy with administered prices would encourage arbitrage, at the expense of productive activities. Also, profit could not be used as an index of efficiency. Since bankruptcies would not necessarily reflect inefficiency, support measures would be introduced and, inevitably, extended to inefficient firms.

(ii)   Conversely, to set prices free while relying on bureaucracy-cum-bargaining for the allocation of capital and labour, would blunt the impact of market forces. Prices would not reflect the scarcity of resources but, ultimately, the distribution of political clout.

(iii)   Political democracy excludes price reforms, because they make the worst-off very badly off. Free price setting will certainly lead to inflation; if combined with ownership reforms free prices will also create bankruptcies and unemployment; in some countries there might even be starvation. If workers have political influence, through parties or trade unions, they will use it to stop or reverse the process. Even more commonly, populist and sometimes violent mass action may be used for this purpose. The argument that hardships are necessary only during the transition and will be no part of the steady-state system that finally emerges, may carry some weight, but perhaps not much, and for not very long.

(iv)   Ownership reforms are also incompatible with political democracy, because they lead to the best-off being very well off. Private ownership leads to income inequalities that are unacceptable to large segments of the population. In these societies, economic emulation easily degenerates into envy, because of the lack of non-political channels of upwards mobility. By a twist of history, the workers of Eastern Europe now brandish the egalitarian ideology as a weapon against the regime itself. In doing so, they find natural allies among the conservative bureaucratic forces who want nothing more than the failure of the reforms.

(v)   Ownership reforms demand legal stability and constitutional guarantees. To ensure that the economic agents are willing to make investments that take time before coming to fruition, property rights must be respected, and retroactive legislation — notably retroactive taxation — made impossible. The absence of a stable legal system will induce a very short time horizon in the economic agents. Foreign investments will be hard to attract unless there are credible guarantees against confiscation and nationalization.

(vi)   Credible constitutional rights presuppose democracy. This proposition might appear to be vulnerable. Constitutional monarchy, after all, worked in a fashion; why not a constitutional dictatorship? The difficulty is that the strength

FIGURE 1

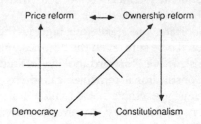

of the dictator is also his weakness: he is *unable to make himself unable* to interfere with the legal system whenever it seems expedient (Elster 1989, pp. 199–200). Constitutional monarchies were kept in line by strong intermediary bodies, whereas in modern dictatorships the society is largely atomistic. Power must be divided to ensure that the constitution will be respected.

(vii)   Conversely, democracy without constitutional constraints is ultimately impotent: it can make decisions, but not make itself stick to them. Even if individual preferences do not change, turnover among citizens and their representatives makes simple majority rule vulnerable to unstable oscillations between 51 per cent and 49 per cent. Also, preferences often do change for no good reason, in the heat of passion or under the influence of demagogy. (See Part II below).

These relationships can be summarized in a diagram. Here an arrow from x to y means that x, to be effective, requires y. A blocked arrow means that x is an obstacle to y.

If these premises are true, full scale reform is impossible. Given the direction of the causal arrows, political reform without a transition to competitive markets might appear to be possible. In the long run, however, democracy will be undermined if it cannot deliver the goods in the economic sphere. Calls for an authoritarian regime will be made, and ultimately heard.

To be sure, all of these proportions (except perhaps the first) might be questioned. Concerning proposition (ii), South Korea might be cited as a counter example. Concerning proposition (iii), we might ask whether economic and institutional mechanisms might not be capable of extending the period by encouraging and 'subsidizing patience', or trust in the future. Western credit, a well-designed safety net of social security arrangements, and the emergence of charismatic leaders offer alternative solutions to this problem. Concerning proposition (iv), Hirschman's (1973) 'tunnel effect' might seem to provide a way out. Concerning proposition (v), Taiwan has been said to provide a counter example. Concerning proposition (vi), Pinochet's Chile is sometimes cited as a counter example. Concerning proposition (vii), the danger of populist demagogy may to some extent be checked by strong 'intermediary' institutions, such as the church, trade unions, political parties and local governments. The purpose of the argument, therefore, is not to make a strong case for the impossibility of the transition, but to identify critical connections that must be broken if the dual process of transition is to succeed.

As I have tried to indicate, the stakes are high in the constitution-making process in Eastern Europe. To be sure, even the best-designed constitution cannot by itself ensure a constructive, forward-looking attitude, ethnic peace and economic prosperity. Constitutional remedies cannot by themselves eliminate destructive feelings of revenge, ethnic hatred and social envy. Some countries do not need constitutions because they govern themselves by tradition: Great Britain is an example. Other countries do not need them because they are so conflict-ridden or corrupt that a scrap of paper will not be respected by anyone. Some of the countries in Eastern Europe may fall in this category. In my opinion, however, most countries in the region can benefit from a good constitution. In some of them, it might even make a difference between failure and success. However, I am not about to make any predictions in this respect. The dismal record of the social sciences in anticipating recent events ought to induce considerable modesty. Both the fall of Communism and the eruption of ethnic violence came as surprises to the scholarly community. Hence the report is very much an analysis of what has happened, and only marginally an attempt to say what will or may happen.

II THE STUDY OF CONSTITUTION-MAKING: A GENERAL FRAMEWORK

In Eastern Europe we are witnessing a wave of constitution-making. It is by no means the first such wave. At the end of the eighteenth century, new constitutions were written in the United States, France and Poland. Other such waves have occurred in the wake of the revolutionary movement of 1848 (Tocqueville's *Recollections* contains a penetrating study of the French constitutional assembly of that year), the creation of new states after World War I, the collapse of fascist regimes after World War II (Merkl 1963), the liberation of African and Asian states from colonial rule, and the fall of the South European dictatorships in the mid-1970s (Bonime-Blanc 1987). In addition, of course, numerous countries have adopted their constitutions in a less synchronized manner. Nevertheless, the comparative study of constitution-making is virtually non-existent. Comparative constitutional law is, needless to say, an established discipline. The comparative study of ordinary law making is a central field of political science. The comparative study of revolutions has a long history. But to my knowledge there is not a single book or even article discussing the process of constitution-making in a general comparative perspective. The gap is puzzling, but it appears to be undeniable. In Part II, I shall propose some distinctions and suggest some causal mechanisms that may serve to impose a little bit of structure on this uncharted terrain.

1 Elements of the constitution
Although my main concern is with the process of constitution-making, analysis of that issue requires a brief preliminary discussion of constitutional substance.

Although the issues covered in constitutional documents vary widely, all include three main topics: individual rights, the machinery of government, and procedures for amending the constitution. I begin with the latter, because without such procedures the constitution would not differ from statutory legislation. (This is not wholly correct. In New Zealand, 'only ordinary legislative efforts are required to supplement, modify or repeal the Constitution' (Eule 1987, p. 394).) It is supposed to be a constant or slowly evolving framework for the day-to-day enactment of ordinary laws. There are two main reasons why this stability is required. If it is more difficult to pass constitutional amendments than ordinary legislation, citizens can count on the basic institutional framework remaining in place over reasonably long periods. At the very least, a change from 49 per cent to 51 per cent in favour of a given proposal will not suffice to bring it about. This certainty enables the citizens to form long-term plans, which are a condition both for economic growth and for personal security. This is a main reason why many constitutions require qualified majorities for amendments. Often, a two-thirds majority is required. It is a striking fact that under certain, reasonably weak conditions this requirement will also prevent voting cycles from arising (Caplin and Nalebuff 1988).

There is another way, with a different rationale, of making the amendment process more difficult. Instead of (or in addition to) requiring qualified majorities, one can demand that the amendment be passed by two successive Parliaments or adopt some other delaying device. If the founders fear that they or their successors might yield to impulse and passion in a crisis, they might, like Ulysses binding himself to the mast, take their precautions to reduce their opportunities for such behaviour. 'Constitutions are chains with which men bind themselves in their sane moments that they may not die by a suicidal hand in the day of their frenzy' (John Potter Stockton in debates over the Ku Klux Klan Act of 1871, as cited in Finn 1991, p. 5; Elster 1984, ch. II; Holmes 1988; Elster 1988; Suber 1990.) Or in Friedrich Hayek's phrase, constitutions reflect the idea that Peter when sober can act to bind Peter when drunk. At the Federal Convention, for instance, a ban on paper money was constitutionalized, to prevent the states from resorting to this tempting expedient.

A majority may indeed take precautions against its own tendency to act on unwise momentary impulses. It is less realistic to expect it to protect itself against its tendency to act on *standing* passions. Prejudiced founders will not regard their views as biased, but as wise. On the one hand, Cass Sunstein may well be right in observing that 'Constitutional provisions should be designed to work against precisely those aspects of a country's culture and tradition that are likely to produce most harm through that country's ordinary political processes' (Sunstein 1991, pp. 385). In societies with strong ethnic or religious conflicts, for instance, the constitution should offer strong protections to ethnic and religious minorities. On the other hand, it is precisely in the societies that most need such clauses that it may be most difficult to get them adopted. An ethnic or ideological majority in the constituent assembly may be more inclined to impose its own language or ideology than to pull its punches in the name of toleration.

The process that led up to the adoption of the 1931 Spanish constitution, for instance, was dominated by leftists and liberals who could and did write their hostile attitude towards the Catholic Church into the document (Bonime-Blanc 1987, pp. 114–15).

The problem can be overcome in three ways. First, if the founders are animated by toleration, they might refrain from using their majority power. As in the adoption of the German constitution of 1949, they might search for a high degree of consensus on the main provisions (Merkl 1963, p. 81). Second, if the majority in the constituent assembly represents a minority in the nation, as was the case in the two eighteenth-century assemblies, it can try to bind the popular majority. The late Norwegian historian Jens Arup Seip, with whom I had many discussions of these issues, often said that people never try to bind themselves: rather, politics is about binding others. Although I do not accept the claim in this stark form, it offers a salutary counterweight to more idealized or idyllicizing accounts. One may, for instance, detect an element of hypocrisy (Wood 1969, p. 562) in assertions like Madison's statement (*Records of the Federal Convention* 1966, p. 430) that 'Democratic communities may be unsteady, and be led to action by the impulse of the moment. – Like individuals they may be sensible of their own weakness, and may desire the counsels and checks of *friends* to guard them against the turbulency and violence of unruly passion' (my italics). It seems as least as plausible to say that the Senate embodied the desire of the upper class to protect itself against the lower class – not the desire of the people to protect itself against itself. However, the two views are not incompatible. On similar grounds it has been argued that 'A majority group, say the workers, who control the policy might rationally choose to have a constitution which limits their power, say, to expropriate the wealth of the capitalist class' (Kyland and Prescott 1977, p. 486). Third, if the constitution is made under foreign tutelage, as in Germany and Japan after World War II, the foreign powers can try to contain 'those aspects of a country's culture and tradition that are likely to produce most harm'. For example, the French Foreign Minister spoke out against what he saw as a dangerous centralizing tendency in the third draft of the 1949 West German constitution (Merkl 1963, p. 120). In general, nevertheless, constitutions are more likely to reflect flaws in national character than to counteract them.

Constitutions regulate the machinery of government: elections and the relation between the powers of state. Traditionally, the latter have been conceived as a trio, consisting of the executive, the legislative and the judiciary. The relations among them have been summarized in two phrases: 'separation of powers' and 'checks and balances'. The separation of powers has both a positive and a negative purpose. As with any division of labour, the allocation of different tasks to different state organs enhances efficiency. For instance, Parliament is not an efficient organ for the day-to-day conduct of war operations. Also, insulating each organ from the encroachment of others reduces the dangers of bribery, corruption and undue interference. The independence of the judiciary, for instance, is promoted by long tenure and fixed salaries of judges, as well as by random assignment of judges to cases. Checks and balances prevent any institution from usurping power, a system that has reached its highest development in the American constitution, in which the pivotal mechanisms are executive veto, judicial review, presidential appointment of Supreme Court judges and congressional power to impeach the President. Other constitutions use different devices, such as the power of the President to bypass the legislature by calling a referendum or the right of Parliament to overrule the Constitutional Court.

The traditional trio offers a very incomplete idea, however. In the two eighteenth-century assemblies, the three institutions that were supposed to control each other were the executive and the two houses of Parliament. Judicial review played only a minimal role (see Elster forthcoming (1)). In modern constitutions, the bifurcation of the legislature is less common. In its place, we often see a dual executive, in which both President and government have substantial powers, thus competing both with Parliament and with each other. Exceptionally, as in the case of Poland, more fully discussed in Part IV, we observe both a split legislature and a split executive. Adding the Constitutional Court to the cast, we get five players rather than the traditional three.

The idea of powers of state, separate from each other and mutually checking each other, can be taken further. In many countries, the independence of the Central Bank is almost as important as the independence of the judiciary. Although rarely enshrined in the constitution, the independent status of the Bank is protected by the high political costs of interference. Within the executive, the Ministry of Foreign Affairs sometimes achieves a *de facto* independence, 'above' politics, as it were. The idea in both cases is that certain matters have to be conducted in a long-term perspective that requires insulation from day-to-day politics. A similar 'quasi-constitutional' status sometimes obtains for state-owned mass media. On the BBC model, for instance, the government cannot use state television for propaganda or interfere to stifle criticism of its policies. Even private media may, in a still broader sense, be seen as part of the system of checks and balances ('the fourth power of state').

The interval between elections and the right to dissolve Parliament and call for new elections are usually matters for constitutional regulation. However, as I said, the electoral law, including rules for redistricting or changes in the number of deputies, is usually not made part of the constitution. When electoral laws or electoral districts can be changed by a simple majority in Parliament, the incumbent government has an incentive to modify them to its advantage. The argument can be made, therefore, that electoral laws have such a fundamental impact on politics that they ought to be constitutionalized. More generally, the constitution can try to deny the government all unfair means to maintain itself in power. These include discretionary control over the timing of the elections, control of electoral laws and electoral districts, registration requirement for voters, and control over the state-owned media. And even when the constitution does not contain explicit provisions to this effect, judicial review, where it exists, may regulate these issues by appealing to more general constitutional principles.

The protection of rights has been a central constitutional concern from the eighteeth-century beginnings. True, at the Federal Convention the framers decided against including a bill of rights in the constitution, but mainly because they were afraid that an enumeration of specific rights might provide a justification for governmental violation of unenumerated rights. Few years afterwards, the first nine amendments were enacted to fill the gap. At the Assemblée Constituante, too, voices were heard against adopting the *Déclaration des droits de l'homme*, but for the opposite, more ominous reason that it might give the people exaggerated ideas about their rights. These arguments were, as we know, not heeded. In virtually all later constitutions, rights have been included as a matter of course.

There is no canonical way of classifying constitutional rights. They have been distinguished as political, civil, social and economic; as pertaining to individuals or to groups; as offering protection against the state or against individuals; as legally enforceable or merely programmatic; or, by a more obscure criterion, as negative or positive. Historically, the core rights were those protecting the rule of law, liberty of conscience, freedom of expression and of association, property, and personal security. In this century rights have expanded in two main directions. On the one hand, constitutions have offered protection to members of ethnic and linguistic minorities, by allowing them the right to use and be educated in their own language and ensuring them a measure of political autonomy or at least representation. On the other hand, they have offered a guarantee of material welfare, through right-to-work provisions and related measures. As we shall see in Part III, both extensions are important in Eastern Europe.

2 The constitution-making process

The remainder of this section is concerned with constitutional process rather than substance. I shall address the following questions:

— how are the constituent assemblies called into being?
— how do they regulate their own internal procedures?
— how do individual interest, group interest or institutional interest shape the final document?
— what is the importance of extra-constitutional force in shaping the constitutional text?
— how are the constitutions ratified?

The common concern underlying these issues is that of legitimacy. First, there is a problem of *upstream legitimacy*: the document produced by a constituent assembly can only enjoy legitimacy if that assembly has come into being in a legitimate way. An assembly whose members have simply been appointed by the ruler, as was the case with the body of 66 men convened in China by Yuan Shikai in 1914 to give his rule a semblance of legality through a 'constitutional compact', does not pass this hurdle. Second, there is a problem of *process legitimacy*. If the internal decision-making procedure of the assembly is perceived as undemocratic, the document may be lacking in democratic legitimacy. Constituent assemblies for federally organized countries face the choice between 'one state, one vote' and proportional voting power. The Federal Convention in 1787 chose the former method, whereas the assembly that voted the West German constitution of 1949 used the latter. I conjecture that in our century, the principle of equality among the states would be seen as deficient in democratic legitimacy. Also, a constitution will lack legitimacy to the extent that it is perceived to be a mere bargain among interest groups rather than the outcome of rational argument about the common good. Moreover, a constitution that is visibly shaped by military force or threat of such force may suffer a lack of legitimacy. Finally, there is the issue of *downstream legitimacy*: a constitution that is ratified by popular vote will have much stronger claims to embody the popular will.

Consider first the creation of the constituent assembly. First, the assembly has to be convoked. Next, the delegates have to be elected or selected. Typically, these two decisions stem from different sources. In France in 1789, the decision to call the Estates General was made by the King, with delegates elected by and from the three orders. The Federal Convention was called into being by the Continental Congress, with delegates sent from the individual states. The assembly that wrote the West German constitution of 1948 was called into being by the occupying powers, with delegates elected by the *Länder*. Now, we may regard it as axiomatic that any creator will try to control his creature. With two creators of the constituent assembly, each will try to shape the final document. In France, defenders of the King argued that as the convener of the Estates General, he should have an absolute veto *over* the constitution and *in* the constitution. The assemblies that had selected delegates from the three orders often sent them with bound mandates on specific points. In both cases, the creature won out over the creator (Harris 1986; Egret 1950).

The victory over the convoking authority should not surprise us. Almost by definition, the old regime is part of the problem that a constituent assembly has to solve. But if the regime is flawed, why should the assembly respect its instructions? At the Federal Convention, too, the delegates decided to go beyond their mandate; to provide a wholly new constitution rather than simply a revision of the Articles of Confederation. By contrast, the decision of the French delegates to ignore the instructions from their constituencies had no parallel in Philadelphia. The delegates that came to the Federal Convention with bound mandates, such as the Delaware instructions to insist on equal representation for all the states in the Senate, did not feel free to ignore them. The American delegates did not go as far as the French in substituting process legitimacy for upstream (and downstream) legitimacy.

Consider next the internal organization of the assembly. The most urgent issues arise when the delegates come from 'natural' sub-units of the nation. The smaller of these will then tend to claim equal voting power in the assembly, whereas the larger will insist on a voting system that reflects the numerical strength of their constituencies. I have already mentioned how the Americans in 1787 and the Germans in 1948–9 adopted different solutions to the problem of territorial sub-units of different sizes. The French framers of 1789 faced a different problem: the division of the Estates General in three orders of different size (300 delegates for each of the Nobility and Clergy, 600 for the Third Estate). When the Estates first met in May, they spent six weeks debating whether they should vote by order or by head. These debates, which transformed the Estates General into a National Assembly, provide a striking illustration of the bootstrapping character of many constituent assemblies (*Procès-verbal des conférences sur la vérification des pouvoirs*, Paris 1789). In the end, the advocates of voting per head won out.

The principles of voting adopted by the assembly may survive in the document that it produces. The American case, for instance, involves three stages. In the first stage we have the convocation of the assembly by Congress. In the second stage we have the adoption of a voting procedure to be used at the convention. In the third stage we have the adoption of a voting procedure for the future Senate. *In all three stages, the principle 'one state, one vote' was followed.* It is tempting to read a causal connection into this fact. The convention adopted the principle for its own proceedings because it was used by the institution that had called it into being. And it proposed the principle for the future because the smaller states at the Convention benefited from the disproportionate strength which they derived from its use at that stage. However, the German case does not show the same continuity. Although the assembly voted along proportional lines, the representation of the *Länder* in the Bundesrat (the upper house) falls somewhere between equal and proportional representation.

Procedure can also matter in a number of other ways. In the Assemblée Constituante, it soon became clear that the radicals benefited from roll-call votes, which enabled them to note the names of those who voted against radical measures and to circulate lists of their names in Paris (Egret 1950, p. 132). (A similar phenomenon was observed in the debates of the Polish *Sejm* over the electoral laws in July 1991. The *Sejm* failed to overrule Walesa's veto because, in an excess of self-confidence, the caucus leader of the Democratic Left called for a roll-call vote. However, 'deputies preferred to be anonymous when voting against the President' (McQuaid 1991, p. 17).) For related reasons, the radicals demanded and obtained more publicity around the proceedings than the moderates wanted. Mounier, leader of the moderates, preferred committee debates, which favoured 'cool reason and experience' and detached the members from everything that could stimulate their vanity and fear of disapproval. For the patriot Bouche, committees tended to weaken the revolutionary fervour. He preferred the large assemblies open to the public, where 'souls become strong and electrified, and where names, ranks and distinctions count for nothing'. On his proposal, it was decided that the assembly would sit in plenum each morning and meet in committee in the afternoon. Soon there were only plenary sessions. At the Federal Convention, by contrast, there was no publicity. The delegates were sworn to secrecy and kept it.

The choice of open versus closed proceedings has two consequences, more fully discussed below (see also Elster forthcoming (2)). On the one hand, a public setting makes it less likely that the delegates will resort to open logrolling and horsetrading. Instead, they have to argue in terms of the common good (Macey 1986). Although many such arguments are little more than disguised self-interest, the need to pay at least lip-service to the public interest will usually have some restraining influence. On the other hand, publicity encourages the delegates to adopt rigid, inflexible positions as a precommitment device. It is also more difficult to back down from publicly stated views than from those expressed in a smaller circle. This was, in fact, Madison's main argument for keeping the Convention closed. As he said later,

> had the members committed themselves publicly at first, they would have afterwards supposed consistency required them to maintain their ground, whereas by secret discussion no man felt himself obliged to retain his opinions any longer than he was satisfied of their propriety and truth, and was open to the force of argument (*Records*, vol. III, p. 479).

However, Madison did not consider the first effect of secrecy – that of pushing the debates away from rational argument and towards self-interested bargaining. Nor did he consider that secrecy may lead to a loss of legitimacy. During the Meech Lake talks on the revision of the Canadian constitution in 1987, Prime Minister Mulroney, who had convened the Premiers of the ten provinces, deliberately kept them insulated from their advisers. 'Without advisers, there would be less posturing and grandstanding; it would be easier to get a deal. But, as a consequence, this lakeside conclave took on an aura of secretiveness that would afterwards undermine its public legitimacy' (A. Cohen 1990, p. 13). Thomas Jefferson made a similar comment about the secrecy adopted at the Federal Convention.

The role of *interest* in constituent assemblies may be considered from four perspectives. First, there is the purely personal interest of the founders in a constitution that favours them economically or otherwise. In Charles Beard's 'economic' interpretation of the American constitution, this element assumes the main explanatory burden. In more recent analyses it appears that the founders' economic interest did count for something, but that the interest of their constituents does more to explain the voting patterns at the convention (McGuire 1988). Crudely put: it mattered more whether a delegate came from a slave holding or trading state than whether he had slaves or was a trader himself. However, the correlation between interest and votes does not prove that the delegates voted solely in order to promote that interest. Even the most impartial framer had to take account of the need for the final document to be ratified in the respective states, and that a text strongly against the interest of their constituents stood no chance of being adopted. If the interests of constituencies act as constraints rather than maximands, they will leave less of an imprint on the constitution. The constituencies will tend to act as satisficers, because of the cost of going back to a new assembly and the uncertainty whether they could strike a better deal if they did. This being said, it may also be in the personal interest of delegates to promote the interest of their constituencies to the hilt, for instance if their political future depends on how well they do so.

In modern constitution-making, two other phenomena come to the forefront: the interest of political parties and of political institutions. The former interest is especially evident in the design of electoral laws, whether these are part of the constitution or not. Small parties tend to be in favour of proportional representation, preferably with a low threshold (if any), whereas large parties argue for majority voting in single-member districts. Cutting across this distinction, the power oligopolies of *all* parties have an interest in proportional representation, which allows for greater control over the candidates (Merkl 1963, pp. 87–8). A party that has a strong presidential candidate will push for a strong presidency in the constitution, whereas others will want to limit his powers. A classical case is the 1921 Polish constitution, in which the fear of Pilsudski as President inspired a strongly parliamentarian constitution; as a result, Pilsudski decided not to stand for office (Garlicki 1992, pp. 68–71). The converse case is the constitution of the Fifth French Republic, which de Gaulle essentially wrote (or had written) with himself in mind (Dwerfler 1983, ch.9).

The interest of political institutions appears most clearly when the institutions to be regulated by the constitution also take part in the constitution-making process. At the Federal Convention, for example, the states were both creators and creatures – regulators and regulated. As already mentioned, the conflict over the upper house faithfully mirrored the nature of the actors, with the small states arguing for equal and the larger for proportional representation of the states in the Senate (Rakove 1987). This conflict was largely spurious. To the argument that the large states might come to dominate the small, Madison gave a compelling answer: 'Was a Combination to be apprehended from the mere circumstance of equality of size?' (*Records*, vol. I, pp. 447–8). Yet the notion of equality provided a convenient vehicle for the self-interest of the small states (see below).

Unlike the Federal Convention, the Assemblée Constituante functioned also as an ordinary legislature. That arrangement, however, may be undesirable. A main task of a constituent assembly is to strike the proper balance of power between the legislative and the executive branches of government. To assign that task to an assembly that also serves as a legislative body would be to ask it to act as judge in its own cause. A constitution written by a legislative assembly may be expected to give large, perhaps excessive powers to the legislature. In the abstract, this problem could be solved by means similar to the ones used in legislative bodies, by checks and balances. A royal veto over the constitution might, for instance, have kept the legislative tendency to self-aggrandizement in check. The Assemblée Constituante adopted another solution, by voting its members ineligible to the first ordinary legislature. It was Robespierre in his first great speech (16 May 1791) who won the assembly for this 'self-denying ordinance' (Thomson 1988, p. 134 ff.). Although sometimes viewed by posterity as a disastrous piece of populist overkill (Furet 1988, p. 104), Robespierre's solution did correspond to a genuine problem. Similarly, if the constituent assembly is bicameral, it can hardly be expected to adopt a unicameral system. If the King or the President has a veto over the constitution, it is likely to have a bias towards the executive, or at least to be more balanced than if Parliament is the only constituent power.

I need to add a caveat to the preceding considerations. Although interest may be an important motivation in most constituent assemblies, it will not always dare to speak its name. Especially when the process is under strong scrutiny from the public, the parties will feel constrained to present their argument in terms of the common good or the public interest. Self-interest, in other words, may induce the speakers to adopt non-self-interested language (Elster forthcoming (2)). At the Federal Convention, both small and large states used the language of abstract justice and efficiency to argue their claims for, respectively, equal and proportional representation in the Senate. Similarly, small parties, when arguing for proportional voting, appeal to democratic values rather than to the interest of small parties. Conversely, large parties tend to rest their case for majority voting on the claim that it is more likely to produce a stable government. Equity in the former case, efficiency in the latter, are put forward as as impartial disguises for partiality. Similarly, when deputies argue for a strong legislative, they appeal to the need to respect and embody the popular will and not to their institutional interest. Conversely, when the executive power is involved in the constitution-making process, its representatives will argue for a strong executive on the seemingly non-self-serving grounds of stability and efficiency.

As I said, the pressure to disguise self-interest as public interest will be stronger when the process is under public scrutiny. One might wonder whether the disguise matters. Given the large pantheon of plausible-sounding impartial values, it might seem that any actor would be able to find a public-interest justification that coincides with his private interest. Three considerations tend to mitigate this conclusion. First, some private interests probably do not have *any* plausible impartial equivalent. Second, a *perfect* match between an obvious private interest and an impartial equivalent will often be perceived as too crude to be taken seriously. Third, even if an actor could find an impartial argument that might advance his interest in a given situation, he may be prevented from using it by the stand he has taken on previous occasions. These arguments suggest the idea of the *civilizing force of hypocrisy*: when discussing under public scrutiny, actors may be forced or induced to pull their punches and refrain from the most blatant expressions of self-interest. Against this positive effect of publicity, we must balance a number of negative effects: the opportunity for strategic precommitment, vanity-induced reluctance to back down, as well as the irreversibility of publicly stated positions. Here are three examples of the irreversibiltiy effect.

(i) The announcement of the radical measures taken on the night of 4 August

1789 made it impossible to go back. In a wonderful contemporary phrase: 'The people are penetrated by the benefits they have been promised: they will not let themselves be de-penetrated' (A. Mathiez 1898, p. 265, n.4).

(ii) Before the insurrection of June 1848, and apprehensive of its coming, Tocqueville felt that 'what was needed was not so much a good constitution as some constitution or other' (1986, p. 826). (The sentence is inexplicably omitted in the English translation (1990).) Acting under time pressure, he was 'much more concerned with putting a powerful leader quickly at the head of the Republic than with drafting a perfect republican constitution' (1990, p. 178). After the June days he stood by his proposal, but now for the reason that 'having announced to the nation that this ardently desired right would be granted, it was no longer possible to refuse it' (ibid.).

(iii) In the Lake Meech talks, Gil Rémillard, Quebec's Minister for Intergovernmental Affairs, 'did not want to negotiate in public. Whatever became public would become the bottom line. Quebec was accommodating in private talks but worried it would have less latitude if its proposals got out. The Parti Québécois would make them an absolute minimum, limiting the government's ability to negotiate' (Cohen 1990, p. 87).

The main way in which self-interest plays itself out is by the process of small-group *logrolling*, in the assembly as a whole if it is sufficiently small, in subcommittees, or outside the assembly. The Federal Convention was marked by a number of such bargains, the best-known being the logrolling between the trading and the slave holding states (Finkelman 1987, pp. 188–225). In the Assemblée Constituante, a famous piece of attempted logrolling took place in the last days of August 1789, when the assembly was about to debate the basic institutions of the state (Mounier 1989; Mathiez 1898, p. 266 ff.; Egret 1950, p. 139 ff.). In three meetings between Mounier on the one hand and the 'triumvirate' Barnave, Duport and Alexandre Lameth on the other, the three came up with the following proposal. They would offer Mounier both an absolute veto for the King and bicameralism, if he in return would accept (i) that the King gave up his right to dissolve the assembly, (ii) that the upper chamber would have a suspensive veto only; and (iii) that there would be periodical conventions for the revision of the constitution. Mounier refused outright. According to his own account, he did not think it right to make concessions on a matter of principle; also he may have been in doubt about the ability of the three to deliver on their promise. According to Albert Mathiez, he refused because he was so confident that the assembly was on his side that no concessions were needed.

Logrolling in the constituent assembly usually differs from that in a legislative assembly in two respects. First, there is no indefinitely continuing interaction that can force the parties to stick to their promises through fear of losing their reputation (North 1990, pp. 190–91). Second, voting on the separate issues that are being traded off against each other is not really separate and successive, because the assembly usually concludes its task by adopting the constitution as a whole. In theory the two differences should offset each other, but in practice they may not. As the assembly and its committees work their way through the issues, compromises may be reached that are hard to undo later even should one of the parties renege on their promises. Diamond 1981, summarizes the process as follows: 'complex political struggles often come down to a single issue in which all the passions, all the forces find their focus. When that single issue is settled it is as if all the passions and forces are spent. Both sides seem somehow obliged fully to accept the outcome and matters move quickly thereafter.' This emotional dynamic will be an obstacle to going back to an issue if some more or less clearly stated promise fails to be kept. One party may act on the calculation that the other will be unwilling to be seen as responsible for breaking off negotiations, or that the other has more to lose by having to start all over again. In the West German assembly of 1948, 'the Minister President of Bavaria ... persuaded the SPD to vote for [the institution of] a *Bundesrat* in exchange for a momentary advantage and concessions which were subsequently all but abandoned' (Merkl 1963, p. 69). During the debates over the Spanish constitution in 1978, the Union of the Democratic Center was accused 'of breaking a painstakingly negotiated set of compromises', leading to the withdrawal of the Socialist member on the subcommittee (Bonime-Blanc, 1987, p. 56). Tadeusz Mazowiecki (personal communication) tells about an episode in the making of the Polish 'little constitution', in which a logrolling promise was broken by one side when the proposal for which it had enlisted the support of the other side failed to be adopted, even though the other side had voted for it.

Constitutions are often written in times of crisis and turbulence. In such circumstances, armies, crowds and foreign powers can become potent influences on the work of the constituent assembly. We may distinguish between two kinds of mechanisms by which these influences play themselves out, *threats* and *warnings*. The terminology on this point is not settled. Greenawalt 1989, p. 251 ff. refers to 'warning threats', as if an utterance could be both a threat and a warning. T.C. Schelling (1980, p. 123, n.5) and R. Nozick (1969) use the distinction between warning and threat to differentiate between cases in which the actor has an incentive to carry out the announced action and those in which he does not. To tell a burglar that I will call the police unless he goes away is to warn him; to tell a girl that I will commit suicide if she does not consent to marry me is to make a threat. In the present essay, the distinction is used to contrast the outcomes that are within the control of the agent and those that are not. On the one hand, a member of the constituent assembly or some other actor may threaten to mobilize extra-constitutional forces unless a certain provision is written into the constitution. On the other hand, he may issue a warning that intervention by such forces is likely unless the provision is adopted. Explicit instances of the former strategy are rare, because of the obvious de-legitimizing effect of any resort to force. Implicit threats, disguised as warnings, are more common. In Philadelphia in 1787, delegates from both the large and the small states emitted statements that were close to threats, only to retreat and restate them as warnings when challenged. Bedford, a delegate from Delaware, suggested that if the small states did not get their way over the Senate, they might appeal to foreign powers for help. Later, he retracted by saying that he had only meant to say that the foreign powers, faced with a divided America, would find it in their interest to intervene (*Records*, vol. I, pp. 492, 531). Similar tactics were employed by delegates from the large states.

In Paris, the threats and warnings were based on the King's armies and the crowds in Paris. In the first days of July 1789 the King reinforced the presence of troops near Versailles. The implied threat to the assembly escaped nobody. In his replies to the King's challenge, Mirabeau played on the threat-warning ambiguity. In his first speech on the subject he limited himself to a warning: 'How could the people not become upset when their only remaining hope [viz. the Assembly] is in danger?' (*Archives Parlementaires. Série I: 1789–1799*, Paris 1875–1888, vol. 8, p. 209.) In his second speech he became more specific. The troops 'may forget that they are soldiers by contract, and remember that by nature they are men' (ibid., p. 213). The implied threat to help nature along by stirring fermentation among the troops is clear. We may note at this point the possibility of *self-fulfilling warnings*, which are, in this respect, intermediate between ordinary warnings and threats. By publicly telling the King that his troops were unreliable, Mirabeau may in fact have ensured the truth of that statement. Furthermore, the assembly cannot even trust itself to act responsibly: 'Passionate movements are contagious: we are only men (*nous ne sommes que des hommes*) our fear of appearing to be weak may carry us too far in the opposite direction' (op. cit., p. 213). In this argument, Mirabeau presents himself and his fellow delegates as subject to a psychic causality not within their own control. If the King provokes them, they might respond irrationally and violently. Formally, this is a mere warning. In reality, nobody could ignore that it was a threat.

Finally, I turn to the main source of downstream legitimacy: the process of ratification. Often, those who have called the constituent assembly into being want to arrogate for themselves the power to ratify the final document. The assembly frequently reacts by questioning the legitimacy of its conveners and either dispensing with any further ratification or choosing itself the procedure for ratifying the constitution. The Federal Convention took the latter course. Instead of taking the constitution to the state legislatures which had selected them, the delegates decided to have the constitution ratified by specially called conventions in the states. In that way, of course, they were much less constrained by the need to give the state legislatures a prominent place in the new system. In Germany in 1949, the procedures were modified in the opposite direction. The occupying powers had stipulated that the constitution, to be valid, had to be approved by referendum in two thirds of the *Länder*. The framers, however, managed to change the procedure so that approval by two-thirds of the state legislatures would be sufficient. In the Assemblée Constituante, by constrast, the deputies essentially decided to dispense with all ratification procedures. They viewed themselves as the incarnation of the nation, with no need for further approval.

III CONSTITUTION-MAKING IN EASTERN EUROPE: AN OVERVIEW*

In Part III and the following I shall develop some of the ideas stated above by applying them to the constitution-making processes in post-1989 Central and Eastern Europe. The present section is a broad overview both of the processes and their outcomes in the whole region, with more emphasis, perhaps, on the latter. In Part IV, on the constitutional developments in Poland, the priority is reversed, with a focus on process rather than outcomes. For purposes of comparative analysis, there are also brief references to Poland in the present section.

The constitution-making process in Central and Eastern Europe has two stages. The first was the Round Table Talks (RTT) that brought about the transition from Communism in Poland, Hungary, Bulgaria, and Czechoslovakia. Such talks also took place in the former East Germany (see U.K. Preuss; U. Thaysen 1990). Among the countries studied here, only Romania, with its totalitarian oppression and violent transition, did not have RTT. In all the talks, the agreement between the regime and the opposition included changes to the constitution – changes which were then rapidly implemented by the Communist Parliaments. The second stage is the regular constitution-making process by wholly or partially post-Communist Parliaments and, in some cases, other powers of state. Although the RTT lacked some of the normal features of a constituent assembly, they are included here *qua* constitution-making bodies based on adversarial discussion and compromise. In any case, they would have to be discussed because of their great influence on the second stage.

A brief chronological survey may be useful. In Hungary, the constitution was amended piecemeal over the autumn of 1989 and the spring of 1990. The first free elections took place in March and April 1990. Similar *ad hoc* adjustments were made in the other constitutions in the region, in the interval between the fall of Communism and the adoption of wholly new constitutions. In Romania, the downfall of Ceausescu led to the election of a constituent assembly in May 1990 and the adoption of the constitution by referendum in December 1991. In Bulgaria, the elections to the Grand National Assembly were held in June 1990, and the constitution adopted in July 1991. In Poland, partially free elections were held in June 1989. The first fully free elections were held in October 1991. In November 1992, Parliament passed the so-called 'little constitution' that regulates elections and the basic machinery of government; at the same time, the 1952 Stalinist constitution was solemnly abolished. In Czechoslovakia the first free elections took place in June 1990. The new federal legislature passed a bill of rights for the Federal Republic, but no constitution was adopted. With the breakup of the country, Slovakia adopted its new constitution in September

---

* For information about and discussion of the issues surveyed in Part III, I am indebted to Vojtech Cepl (Prague), Gyorgy Frunda (Bucharest), Lucian Mihai (Bucharest), George Poshtov (Sofia), Rumyana Kolarova (Sofia), Peter Kresak (Bratislava) and Andras Sajo (Budapest). Acknowledgements to Polish sources are given in Part IV below.

1992, with the Czech Republic following suit in December. Thus with the partial exception of Poland, the constitution-making process has come to a halt, or at least a pause, in all the countries under study. Thus now seems to be a good time to take stock.

1 The Round Table Talks

The RTT were an integral part of the events that destroyed the Communist regimes in Eastern Europe. Roughly speaking, the order in which the dominoes fell corresponds to the degree of oppression under Communism: Poland, Hungary, East Germany, Czechoslovakia, Bulgaria, Romania. In Poland, Hungary and Bulgaria, the RTT involved genuine bargaining, which was instrumental in shaping the new regime that emerged. In Czechoslovakia and especially in East Germany, they mainly amounted to a unilateral imposition of the opposition's demands on a demoralized regime.

The Polish and Hungarian RTT were roughly simultaneous (February–April and March–September 1989, respectively) and roughly independent of each other. The underlying causes were, in both cases, the disastrous economic performance of the regime, and the need to introduce a modicum of democracy in exchange for social peace and foreign aid. Yet the pace and the details of events differed. Lagging somewhat behind the Poles, the Hungarian opposition were able to learn from events in Poland. In particular, the Polish June elections, with disastrous results for the Communist candidates, had a profoundly demoralizing effect on the Communist Parties throughout the region. Hence one reason why the Hungarian opposition got a better agreement than Solidarity may have been that its bargaining power had been much enhanced by the surprising victory of Solidarity. (But there may have been other, perhaps more important reasons as well. See Bruszt and Stark 1991, p. 34 ff.) Also, the fact that the Polish RTT and elections took place without any interference or threat of interference by the Soviet Union, must have strengthened the will of the Hungarian opposition. Conversely, Poland may have suffered 'the penalty for taking the lead'. Because they were the first to achieve a compromise with the Communist regime, they were saddled with a stronger and more enduring Communist element in the post-RTT political structure.

These snowball effects became even more important in the autumn, as the revolution spread to other countries. The triggering event may have been Gorbachev's statement on 7 October, during the celebrations of the fortieth anniversary of the German Democratic Republic, that 'Whoever comes late will be punished by life itself.' Then, subsequent weeks saw ever larger rallies in the streets of Leipzig and other cities, until the regime caved in on 19 November. (For a stylized account of the dynamics of such 'intra-country snowballing', see Elster 1993, pp. 15–24. The dynamics of 'inter-country snowballing' is rather different. In Eastern Europe in 1989, the most important mechanism was probably the process of Bayesian learning by which observed non-intervention by the Soviet Union in one country changed the subjective belief that it would intervene in the next.) The RTT began on 7 December. On 17 November there were demonstrations in Prague, inspired by events in East Germany, which brought down *that* regime a week later. Here, the RTT began almost immediately, on 26 November. In Bulgaria, the opening of the Berlin wall triggered action by the Politburo to dismiss General Secretary Todor Zivkov on 9 November. His resignation set in motion a chain of events, culminating with the beginning of RTT on 3 January 1990. In the meantime, the violent fall of Communism in Romania had taken place, thus further weakening the position of the regime.

In Poland, Hungary and Bulgaria, the compromises of the RTT included an agreement on wholly or partially free elections. As further explained in Part IV, the Polish agreement was that 65 per cent of the seats for the lower house would be left uncontested for the Communists, whereas there would be free, competitive elections for the remaining 35 per cent and for all seats in the newly created Senate. In Hungary and Bulgaria, the regime and the opposition had opposed preferences on the issue of proportional versus majoritarian elections. The Communists believed they would do better with majoritarian elections, as they had the more visible candidates. Conversely, the opposition thought they would benefit more from running on a party list. In both countries, the outcome was a compromise: roughly half of the deputies would be elected by the proportional method and half by the majoritarian system. Bulgaria chose a simple system: each voter cast two votes, one for a party list and one for a single district candidate. The more complicated system adopted in Hungary is described in Hibbing and Patterson 1990. The Bulgarian elections showed that the Communists had been right in their calculations. In Hungary, however, they were saved by their opponents' insistence on proportionality. Having 75 per cent of the seats filled in single-member districts, as they had originally proposed, would have hurt them badly (Lijphart 1992, p. 215). Here, as in Poland, both the Communists and the opposition vastly underestimated the lack of electoral support for the regime.

The RTT in these three countries also included a compromise on the Presidency. In Poland, the Communists obtained a strong Presidency, on the understanding that it would be filled by their candidate. After the elections, the opposition kept its side of the bargain, helping Jaruzelski to get elected (in a joint session of the upper and lower house) with the embarrassingly small majority of one vote. In Bulgaria, the opposition obtained a weak Presidency, on the assumption that it would be filled by the Communist candidate. However, President Mladenov had to resign soon after taking power, when it turned out that during the demonstrations in Sofia on 16 December he had said, on camera, 'Let the tanks come'. He was replaced by the leading politician in the opposition, Z. Zhelev. In Hungary, it was also believed that the Communists had the most plausible presidential candidate. The Communists obtained that he be chosen in popular elections before the elections to Parliament, whereas the opposition obtained that he be given relatively few powers. However, some parties in the opposition refused to sign the agreement, and insisted on a referendum on the presidential package. By a narrow margin they obtained that the President be elected after Parliament. When a later referendum (called by the ex-Communists) for direct elections of the President failed to get the necessary quorum, the final result was the very opposite of the RTT agreement viz. a politician from the opposition elected President by Parliament.

The RTT in Czechoslovakia turned on two main issues: the formation of a coalition government and the renewal of Parliament by recall of the most offensive Communist deputies and their replacement by co-opted members of the opposition (Calda). In contrast to the other RTT, electoral laws and changes in the constitution were not discussed. Here, too, the opposition underestimated the weakness of the regime, and made several unnecessary concessions with far-reaching consequences. The most important was to give the Communists the Minister of the Interior in the new government, and hence the opportunity to take possession of the secret files. Also, the renewal of Parliament was far from complete, leaving the Communists with substantial power to obstruct the efforts to adopt a new constitution. However, the main obstacle to constitution-making in Czechoslovakia turned out to be the conflict between the two republics. Veto, brinkmanship and escalation by the Slovaks eventually led to the break-up of the country.

The transition in Czechoslovakia illustrates the consequences of a common feature of all the RTT countries, viz. the fact that the transition took place in full legality. As I observed in the Introduction, the post-Communist constitutions were (with the exception of Romania) created in strict conformity with the Communist constitutions – despite the fact that the latter had not been respected by anyone while Communism was in place. In Czechoslovakia, the 1968 Constitution had introduced, for the first time in the history of the country, a federal structure with separate assemblies (National Councils) for the Czech and Slovak lands and with far-reaching powers for the Republics in the Federal Assembly. The amendment rested a dead letter and the National Councils were not even convened. In the post-Communist constitutional debates, however, the strong Slovak autonomy became a major obstacle to constitutional reform. An amendment to the constitution required a 3/5 majority both in the proportionally elected lower house (200 seats) and in each of the two equal-sized Czech and Slovak sections of the upper house (150 seats). Thus, 31 Slovak deputies in the upper house could block any change.

Arendt Lijphart argues that the political dynamics in Eastern Europe can be explained by a generalization of the 'Rokkan hypothesis'. Rokkan had argued that countries in the transition to democracy will adopt a system of proportional representation

> through a convergence of pressures from below and from above. The rising working class wanted to lower the threshold of representation in order to gain access to the legislatures, and the most threatened of the old-established parties demanded PR to protect their position against the new waves of mobilized voters created by universal suffrage (Rokkan, cited in Lijphart 1992, p. 108).

Extending this reasoning, Lijphart suggests that three of the arrangements from the RTT were intended to guarantee a political presence for the Communist *nomenklatura* as well as for the new opposition. First, as we have seen, there were compromises over the electoral system. Second, because the Communists feared that they would be in a minority in Parliament, they demanded and got the Presidency for their candidate. Third, the bicameral system can be engineered so that the old regime will do well in elections to one house and the new forces in elections to the other. These arguments work quite well for Hungary, Poland and Bulgaria. In Czechoslovakia, however, there was no attempt to create an institutional compromise, only the inherently unstable compromise of the coalition government.

Romania did not have RTT between the regime and the opposition that could set the agenda for the constitution-making process. Instead, the inheritors of the Communist Party, the National Salvation Front, unilaterally laid down the procedures for the election of the constituent assembly. Some debates took place, however, between the Front and the emerging opposition, notably with regard to the timing of the elections (here, as in Bulgaria, the ex-Communist forces wanted early elections so as to take advantage of the lack of organization of the opposition), and the access to television during the electoral campaign. Together with Poland, Romania was the only country that chose to have a bicameral constituent assembly. However, whereas that fact was profoundly important in Poland, it had little significance in Romania – except for ensuring that the Parliament written into the constitution by the assembly would also be bicameral (Hylland).

2 Causal forces in the constitution-making process

The new constitutions in Eastern Europe are the product of the framework created by the RTT (or, in Romania, by the National Salvation Front) and the subsequent elections, together with a number of forces that I shall now go on to discuss.

(i) There is no reason to doubt that many framers have tried hard, and in good faith, to create constitutions that will serve the public interest and protect individual rights. Even though, for the reasons given in Part II, arguments based on private interest will also present themselves in this form, it would be excessively cynical to assume that all impartial arguments are hypocritical. In Part IV below, for instance, I give examples of clearly non-self-interested reasoning in the Polish debates over electoral laws. More generally, if *all* use of rational argument was strategic, there would be nothing to gain from disguising one's interest as being in the public weal. In this sense, strategic uses of argument are parasitic upon non-strategic uses (Elster forthcoming (2)).

(ii) The personal interest of legislators has not, to my knowledge, been a major factor. One possible exception, concerning the presumption in the Romanian constitution that money has been legally acquired, was mentioned in the Introduction. The main case in which such interest has played a major role was in the creation of a Senate in the Czech constitution. It seems that the major function of this body was to provide jobs for the Czech deputies in the dissolved Federal Assembly.

(iii) The interest of the political parties and groupings have played a major role throughout, restricted mainly by the need to offer public-regarding justifications. It has not simply been a question of constitutional logrolling, as at the Federal Convention. Because the constituent assemblies have also served as ordinary legislatures, a party could offer its support for a constitutional provision in exchange for support on an ordinary statute. For obvious reasons, direct evidence of such tractations is hard to come by.

(iv) The interests of institutions have also been a major force. Most obviously and importantly, the fact that Parliament has also served as constituent assembly has ensured a strong role for Parliament in many of the constitutions, notably in Hungary and Bulgaria. Also, as mentioned above, bicameral constituent assemblies tend to create bicameral constitutions. Finally, if the President can exercise constitutional initiative or veto over the constitution, there is more likely to be a strong Presidency.

(v) Extra-parliamentary threats and pressure have been relatively unimportant. To my knowledge, street demonstrations or threats of intervention by police forces or the military have not played any role. These forces mattered during the RTT, but not during the constitution-making process proper. One major exception concerns the Slovak threat of secession that was repeatedly branded during the constitutional talks in 1991. Formally, as we would expect, the Slovaks merely emitted a warning that unless their demands were granted, popular pressure for secession would become irresistible. As a trade union negotiator might say, 'I will not be able to control my members if you reject our demands', forgetting to mention that he was instrumental in creating high expectations among the members in the first place. Another exception is the role of international bodies, which have ensured better protection of human rights than would otherwise have been the case. As many countries desire affiliation with the European Community, pressure exercised by the Council of Europe has been quite effective. The deletion of a provision in the first draft of the Romanian constitution that prohibited ethnically based parties can probably be traced to this influence.

(vi) A different kind of foreign influence was that exercised by experts from abroad. The American Bar Association has organized a number of conferences to offer technical advice on how to write constitutions. A number of individuals and groups have also worked in this capacity (see Stein 1992 and Rapaczynski 1991). Even if well-meant and sound, such advice could obstruct rather than facilitate the constitution-making process. It is interesting in this connection to note that the constituent committee of the Spanish assembly in 1977 deliberately chose not to create an advisory group of experts (Pérez-Llorca 1988, p. 272). It is widely agreed that the document they produced is deficient from a technical point of view, with a number of verbose and ambiguous clauses (Bonime-Blanc 1987; Rubio Llorente 1988, pp. 259, 263). Had lawyers been more involved, the document would probably have been straightened out. It is not obvious, however, that this would have been a good thing. Sometimes, ambiguity and vagueness are essential for reaching agreement, as anyone who has taken part in collective wage bargaining knows. It may be better to dump a problem on the future, or more specifically on the Constitutional Court, than to try to resolve it immediately.

(vii) Still another source of foreign influence stems from the use of other constitutions as models. However, the countries in the region rarely look to each other, and mainly to the West. An illustration of this ignorance (or arrogance?) is that a leading constitution-making actor in one of the Central European countries did not know whether a neighbouring country had adopted a unicameral or a bicameral Parliament. While the Constitution of the United States has been marginal, several West European constitutions have exercised a strong influence. The device of the constructive vote of no confidence (Parliament cannot vote down government unless it simultaneously names a new Prime Minister), invented by C.J. Friedrich for the German constitution of 1949, has been adopted in Hungary and in Poland. The German idea of a strong Constitutional Court has also had a widespread if more diffuse impact (Schwartz 1992). The French model of semi-presidentialism bears some relation to, and may have been a source of inspiration for, the Romanian and Polish constitutions. The constitution of the Fifth French Republic also contains a frequently used provision (art.49.3) that assures the government some independence *vis-à-vis* Parliament, by enabling the government to propose a bill that automatically becomes law unless the Parliament passes a vote of no confidence within 24 hours (Burdeau, Hamon and Troper 1991, pp. 635–36). The provision may be seen as an alternative to the constructive vote of no confidence. A similar device for 'legislation by government' is found (but rarely used so far) in the Romanian constitution (art.113). Constitution-makers in both Bulgaria and Romania also claim to be influenced by the Belgian constitution of 1923, perhaps mainly by its impact on the pre-Communist constitutions in these countries.

(viii) More generally, in the process of making new constitutions many countries turn to their pre-Communist past. All the countries under study had more or less democratic constitutions for much of the period between the two wars. With the exception of Hungary, all of these continue to exercise some influence today. (Kálmán Kulcsar (1990), Hungarian Minister of Justice during the transition from Communism, nevertheless finds a long constitutional tradition in Hungarian history.) More accurately, they belong to the repertoire of arguments that can be used, sincerely or not, in favour of a given proposal. It seems that sometimes the pre-Communist constitution is invoked in defence of an idea that has no good substantive justification; sometimes it serves as a convenient focal point among a plethora of possible arrangements; and sometimes it is harnessed to a genuine need to assert the continuity of the nation's life and the parenthetical character of the Communist regime. In Poland and Romania, for instance, arguments for having a Senate regularly cite the presence of that institution in, respectively, the 1921 and 1923 constitutions. However, the pre-Communist past can also serve as a negative model, as providing examples of what is to be avoided rather than imitated. The 1921 Constitution in Poland is often cited to illustrate the dangers of an assembly that is so afraid of a strong President that it creates a fragmented and powerless Parliament which, in turn, invites an authoritarian *coup d'état* by the very person whom it feared.

> There is a certain paradox in the positions both the Sejm and the President have taken on the election law. By supporting a version that favoured small parties, notes [Senate] Speaker Stelmachowski, the Sejm was energetically 'sawing off its own branch', since a weak Sejm and weak governments were the prime ingredient in the recipe for Pilsudski's authoritarian coup in 1926. By provoking a conflict with the Sejm, on the other hand, Walesa was ostensibly seeking to strengthen its future (McQuaid '1991 election law', p. 26).

(ix) The influence of the Communist constitutions is similarly ambiguous. Sometimes, we observe the general phenomenon that constitution-makers seek to minimize the most dangerous effects of the previous regime. (They tend, perhaps, to see the sins of the fathers and the virtues of the grandfathers.) As Merkl (1963) noted

> 'Like the framers of the United States Constitution, the Council distrusted the masses and their sudden passions, Zinn [an SPD delegate] looked at the Weimar era in the same light in which the fifty-five men at Philadelphia regarded the years following the War of Independence: as a period of anarchy during which the governmental institutions had fallen too much under the sway of popular whim and fancy (p. 81.).

The general arbitrariness that prevailed under Communist rule may be part of the explanation for the central role allotted to the Constitutional Courts in the new constitutions. But we can also observe a tendency to carry over questionable elements from the Communist constitutions. Under all the Stalinist constitutions of Central and Eastern Europe, Parliament was the final arbiter in issues of the constitutionality of laws. In Poland, this arrangement still lingers on, allowing Parliament to overrule decisions by the Constitutional Court. More surprisingly, in the brand new Romanian constitution Parliament also reserved for itself the right to overrule the Constitutional Court by a two-thirds majority. Also, the pervasive presence of social and economic rights – often strikingly absurdly formulated – in most of the new constitutions is a direct heritage from Communism.

Now, a list of causal factors such as the above does not by itself produce a causal theory. In fact, I do not think we will ever be able to formulate a law-like theory of constitution-making, whether general or limited to certain space-time parameters. Rather, we must use the elements enumerated above as raw material for the specification of *mechanisms* – frequently occurring patterns of causal interaction (Elster 1993). Thus even if we cannot identify the exact mix of arguing and bargaining, we can describe main patterns of constitutional bargaining. The distinction between threats and warnings certainly does not amount to a theory, but we can use it to tell a more plausible story than if the two phenomena are conflated with each other (Sutton 1986).

3 The new constitutions

In this section, I survey the new constitutions in Central and Eastern Europe with regard to three aspects mentioned in Part II: amendment procedures, the machinery of government, and human rights.

If stringent amendment requirements are a test of constitutionalism, the new East European constitutions fare badly. They usually require qualified majorities, but rarely any form of cooling-down delay procedure. In Slovakia, only a three-fifths majority is needed, making this constitution one of the most easily amendable in the world. In the Czech Republic, amendments require a three-fifths majority in both houses of Parliament. In Poland and Hungary, the constitution can be changed by a two-thirds majority in Parliament. The Hungarian constitution provides some additional protection by specifying that statutory legislation in a number of specific domains (e.g. electoral laws) also requires a two-thirds majority. In Romania, there must either be a two-thirds majority in each chamber or a three-quarters majority in a joint session of the two chambers, followed by approval in a referendum. (The constitution says nothing about the quorum or majority required in the referendum.) In addition, Parliament can amend the constitution by a backdoor procedure, viz. by overruling decisions by the Constitutional Court. In Bulgaria, the procedure is more complicated: a simplified description follows. 'A minor' constitutional change can be adopted by Parliament in one of two ways: by three quarters of the deputies voting for it in three ballots on three different days, or by two-thirds voting in favour on two occasions with an interval of no less than two and no more than five months. Fundamental changes have to be approved by a two-thirds majority of a special constituent assembly, elections to which will take place if two-thirds of the deputies call for them. The most important 'fundamental' changes are those which 'resolve on any changes in the form of state structure or form of government', or which call for a change in article 57.1 of the constitution asserting that 'The fundamental civil rights shall be irrevocable'. A similar provision exists in the Romanian constitution (art.148.2). One may ask whether those provisions themselves are unamendable. The answer must be positive, 'because an incomplete entrenchment clause that is not self-entrenched is virtually pointless' (Suber 1990, p. 101). Finally, most constitutions contain provisions that ban amendments of the constitution during martial law or a state of emergency. This is perhaps the only way in which they reflect the idea that constitutions must be able to resist temporary fits of passion.

The machinery of government in the six countries does not lend itself easily to brief summary. Only Poland, as I said, combines a dual legislative with a dual executive: a lower house; an upper house that is both endowed with real powers and substantially different from the lower house; a government; and a president endowed with more than ceremonial powers. The emergence and evolution of this system is further discussed in Part IV below. Romania also has a bicameral system, in which the upper house is essentially similar to the lower house. Although it may serve the function of slowing down legislation which George Washington attributed to the American Senate, that end could have been achieved without creating a second chamber. (When Thomas Jefferson asked George Washington why the Convention had established a Senate, Washington replied by asking, 'Why do you pour your coffee into your saucer?' 'To cool it', Jefferson replied. 'Even so', Washington said, 'We pour legislation into the Senatorial saucer to cool it.') The Czechoslovak constitution, because of its federal structure, was bicameral. For essentially trivial reasons, as mentioned above, this is also the case in the new Czech constitution.

The extent to which the constitutions set up a dual executive remains somewhat unclear. Generally speaking, the strength of the presidency *vis-à-vis* government and Parliament would seem to depend on two factors. First, a President chosen in direct popular elections has more legitimacy, and thus more clout, than one chosen indirectly, by Parliament. Second, and more obviously, the more powers attributed to the President in the constitution, the stronger the presidency. Specifically, the strength of the Presidency depends on the ability of the President to

— conduct national defence and foreign policy
— call a state of emergency or introduce martial law
— call a referendum
— exercise legislative initiative
— exercise legislative veto
— appoint the government
— remove the government
— appoint and remove individual ministers
— dissolve Parliament
— appoint state officials without the countersignature of government

Using these criteria, a reading of the constitutions suggests the following two-by-two table:

Table 1   Constitutional comparisons

	President chosen in direct elections	President elected by Parliament
Strong powers of the presidency	Poland Romania	Slovakia
Weak powers of the presidency	Bulgaria (?)	The Czech Republic Hungary (?)

The question marks must be taken seriously. In fact, perhaps all entries in the cells with the exception of Poland should have been supplied with this modifier. In many of the constitutions, the wording is so vague that it is hard to say what the powers of the Presidency are. In Hungary, for instance, the ongoing power struggle between President Gonz and Prime Minister Antall over the appointment powers of the President turns only in part on the articles spelling out these powers, and more centrally on the general provision (art.29.1) which asserts that the President 'safeguards the democratic operation of the State organization'. It was by virtue of this clause that the President refused to appoint the government's candidates for posts in the state-owned Hungarian Television and Radio. The issue was referred to the Constitutional Court, which essentially refused to take a stand, thus perpetuating the deadlock and the uncertainty.

Also, some of the constitutions are poorly drafted and internally inconsistent. In one respect, for instance, the Slovakian Presidency is very weak. The President can be dismissed by Parliament by a three-fifths majority on political grounds, without any formal impeachment procedure. At the same time, he is the supreme commander of the armed forces, appoints and promotes top military officers without the countersignature of a minister, has the right to chair sessions of the cabinet, enjoys legislative initiative and the right to call a referendum. Obviously, strength and weakness are not simple dichotomous categories, but located on a continuum, which may even be multidimensional.

In spite of these conceptual difficulties, I think it is fair to say that Central and Eastern Europe is somewhat anomalous with respect to the usual way of thinking about the Presidency. In the table given above, the upper right hand and the lower left-hand cells are usually supposed to be empty (Linz 1990; Lijphart 1992). To choose a mainly ceremonial President by popular election or to endow a President chosen by the assembly with strong executive powers is to go against the grain of constitutional thinking. The latter, Slovakian procedure is especially strange, as it obliges Parliament to elect or approve two executives with real powers.

I conclude the section with a survey of rights, and the protection of enforcement of rights, in the East and Central European constitutions. I shall consider two rights-protecting devices: constitutionalism and judicial review (Elster forthcoming (3)).

Constitutionalism. For our purposes there are two relevant questions to be asked. What rights are included in the constitution? How well does the constitution protect them? Concerning the first question, limitations of space prevent me from offering a full answer. Instead, I shall simply point to some anomalies or other salient features, limiting myself to the countries that have completed the constitution-making process.

Although all countries have constitutional provisions guaranteeing the rights of ethnic minorities, the force of this protection differs widely. The Bulgarian constitution offers by far the weakest protection. For one thing, it contains a ban on political parties formed along 'ethnic, racial or religious lines' (art. 11.4). For another, the Bulgarian constitution is special in that it offers to ethnic minorities only the right to study their own language (art. 36.2), and not the right to study (all subjects) *in* their own language. It has a general ban on reverse discrimination, on grounds of race, nationality, ethnic self-identity, sex, origin, religion, education, opinion, political affiliation, personal or social status, property status (art. 6.2). The Romanian constitution contains a limited ban in art. 6.2, which requires the protection of national minorities to 'conform to the principles of equality and non-discrimination in relation to the other Romanian citizens'. Presumably this excludes affirmative action for the purpose, say, of promoting the situation of Gypsies. The Slovakian constitution contains both a general ban on reverse discrimination (art. 12) and a specific ban on affirmative action in favour of ethnic minorities (art. 34.3). In Hungary and Romania, the political rights of the minorities are protected by clauses ensuring their representation in Parliament. (One might wonder, though, if this does not contradict art. 6.2 of the Romanian constitution and indeed the more general principle of political equality.)

Social and economic rights have a strong presence in the new constitutions. They range from the potentially useful through the empty and absurd to the positively harmful. In fact, empty and absurd provisions are also harmful. By introducing rights that are obviously unenforceable, there is a risk of devaluing the other rights in the constitution. The right to free health care and to social assistance, including unemployment benefits, may well be useful under the turbulent economic conditions of the region. Other provisions hover between the meaningless and the ridiculous. For instance, the Hungarian provision that 'People living within the territory of the Republic of Hungary have the right to the highest possible level of physical health' (art. 70.1) would, if taken literally, imply that the whole national product should be devoted to health care. The frequently proclaimed right to a clean environment falls in the same category. A potentially more serious problem is offered by rights that *are* enforceable, but which would, if enforced, interfere seriously with the transition to a market economy. Thus art. 70.B.1 of the Hungarian constitution says that 'Everyone who works has the right to emolument that corresponds to the amount and quality of the work performed'. This is an obvious legacy of the 'principle of Socialist distribution': to each according to his contribution. It leaves little room for the operation of market forces.

The protection of rights is undermined by the fact that the relevant constitutional clauses are often circumscribed by clauses that render their import somewhat uncertain. On the one hand, there are many references to further regulation by statute (Cutler and Schwartz 1991, p. 536). For instance, art. 30.2 of the Bulgarian constitution says that 'No one shall be detained or subjected to inspection, search or any other infringement of his personal inviolability, except on the conditions and in a manner established by a law.' Similarly, art. 30.8 of the Romanian constitution says that 'Indictable offenses of the press shall be established by law.' Although the Hungarian constitution contains similar clauses, their sting is drawn by art. 8.2 which asserts that statutes 'shall not limit the essential content of fundamental rights', leaving Parliament free to expand the scope of rights but not to shrink them. E. Klingsberg (1992) concludes that this clause was intended not only to protect rights from being limited by statute, but 'to entrench fundamental rights in the Constitution beyond the reach of the amendment process'. On the other hand, many rights are limited by public or even private interests. To take a typical example, art. 37.2 of the Bulgarian constitution says that 'The freedom of conscience and religion shall not be practiced to the detriment of national security, public order, public health and morals.' To see the potentially illiberal implications of this clause, the following characterization of Communist Bulgarian practices may be useful:

> there are ... public campaigns directed at two religious practices which, though phrased in terms of their public health implications, could easily be, seen as connecting the campaign against Turkish names with an anti-Islam campaign. The government has directly called for an end to the Ramadam feast and ritual circumcision, calling the former 'A Means of Crippling the Individual', while describing the latter as 'Criminal interference with Children's Health' (McIntyre 1988, p. 73.)

Whereas many constitutions assert that rights can be limited by the rights of others, art. 57.2 of the Bulgarian constitution asserts that they shall not be exercised to the detriment of the 'legitimate interests' of others. To have rights limited by the public interest is no doubt inevitable. However, the trump-like character of rights disappears entirely if they can also be overridden by private interests.

Judicial review. All countries in the region practice *ex ante* or *ex post* reviews of legislation by constitutional courts (Schwartz 1992). The Hungarian court has been by far the most active one. In the last few years it has emerged as a major political force (Klingsberg 1992). In fact it has been characterized as the most powerful constitutional court in the world. Two sets of decisions that have been especially important concern legal reactions to acts committed under the Communist regime. In three cases the court was asked to assess the constitutionality of laws regarding restitution of nationalized land to its pre-Communist owners. (Constitutional Court Decisions No.21/1990, No.16/1991 and No.28/1991; Klingsberg 1992; Paczolay 1992.) The court decided that the only reason for discriminating between former landowners and owners of other confiscated property or, more crucially, between former owners and 'non-former owners', would be a forward-looking one. If such discrimination would facilitate the transition to a market economy or otherwise have good social results, it was allowable; if not, not. In particular, the pattern of former property holdings was irrelevant. In a recent decision (Constitutional Court Decision No.11/1992) the court struck down as unconstitutional a law extending the statute of limitations for crimes committed during the old regime that, 'for political reasons', had not been prosecuted. In the first set of decisions, the court let utilitarian considerations take precedence over backward-looking considerations of abstract justice, on the grounds that the latter did not give rise to any subjective rights to restitution. In the more recent decision, the basic premise of the court was the principle of legal certainty, which was violated both by the element of retroactivity inherent in the law and by the vagueness of the phrase 'for political reasons'.

The Bulgarian Constitutional Court has emerged as a (weak) defender of minority rights against the illiberal provisions in the constitution. On the basis of art. 11.4 and art. 44.2 of the constitution, deputies of the former Communist Party asked that the Movement for Rights and Freedom – the *de facto* party for the Turkish and Moslem minorities – be declared unconstitutional. Although six out of twelve judges found in favour of the petition and only five were against (one was sick), the petition was rejected on the basis of art. 151.1 in the constitution which requires 'a majority of more than half of all justices' for a binding decision. (Decision rendered on 22 April 1992.) The reasoning of the five judges was too tenuous and fragile, however, to provide a very solid guarantee. We should note, for instance, that the party that was created to serve the interests of the Bulgarian Gypsies has been declared unconstitutional (Troxel 1992; Troebst forthcoming).

IV   CONSTITUTION-MAKING IN POLAND: A CASE STUDY*

Poland is unique among the East European countries in having a long constitutional tradition. Although it is difficult to indicate specific events or provisions that owe their explanation to that history, the frequent reference to the past in Polish constitutional debates justifies a brief summary of the pre-1989 history. Next, I discuss the dynamics and the achievements of the RTT. I then consider the fruitless constitutional efforts by the 'contractual' *Sejm* (lower house of Parliament) that was elected by the compromise arrangement in the RTT. Finally, I survey the debates and deals that led up to the adoption of the 'little constitution' in November 1992, and the current efforts to prepare a 'big constitution.

1   Elements of Polish constitutional history

Poland's constitutional history (Biskupski and Pula 1990) before 1989 can be divided into five stages.

First, there is the tradition of the 'gentry democracy' that goes back to the fourteenth and fifteenth centuries. The decree that consolidated this tradition, 'Nihil Novi', was promulgated in 1505. In this hodge-podge document, the most important provision is the provision stipulating that 'nothing new' was henceforward to be enacted without the concurrence of the three estates in the *Sejm* – the King, the Senators and the representatives of the lower gentry. All decisions had to be made unanimously: it was required not only that all estates had to agree, but that each individual member had to give his consent (the *liberum veto*). To this unique feature of early Polish constitutionalism we must add another: the tradition that the monarchy was elective (by unanimity) rather than hereditary. It is no wonder that the chaotic and anarchic proceedings of the assembly became proverbial, whatever the original intentions may have been

* This section owes a great deal to the tireless efforts of Wiktor Osiatynski to orient me in the complexities of constitutional politics in Poland. I also rely on interviews with Jerzy Ciemniewski, Lech Falandyz, Leszek Lech Garlicki, Bronislaw Geremek, Jerzy Jaskiernia, Lena Kolarska, Jan Majchrowski, Tadeusz Mazowiecki, Adam Michnik, Andrzej Rzeplinski, Piotr Winczorek and Janina Zakrzewska.

In theory, and originally in practice, the principle of unanimity had not been intended to block all change, merely to allow further discussion until a compromise was reached. As such it was a highly democratic principle. The problems emerged because of the procedural limitations imposed upon the *Sejm*; there simply was not enough time available to accommodate government business alongside the mass of private and local concerns ... Increasingly, however, and especially in the light of constant royal attempts to widen monarchical authority, the principle of unanimity was used in a negative sense (Frost 1990, p. 48).

It is tempting, but probably invalid, to see a survival of the anarchy in some of the current parliamentary practices. A deeper continuity lies in the fact that the Polish intelligentsia, which even today dominates much of political life, descends from the gentry and has inherited many of its attitudes, notably a marked paternalistic tendency (Leslie 1980, p. 144).

Second, there is the constitution of 3 May 1791 – the oldest democratic constitution in Europe – that was adopted in a desperate attempt to reverse the slide into anarchy. By substituting majority rule for unanimity and introducing a constitutional, hereditary monarchy, it was intended to improve efficacy rather than democracy (Stone 1990, p. 65). However, the change came too late. In 1792 the 3 May government was overthrown by Russian military forces, setting in motion a process of partition that destroyed Poland as an independent state for 125 years. Although short-lived, the 3 May 1791 constitution remains a live force in recent debates. In the contractual *Sejm*, for instance, one reason for the accelerated work on a new constitution was a desire to have it adopted on the bi-centennial of the 3 May 1791 constitution. As a curiosum, one may note that at a meeting of the Central Committee of the Polish Communist Party on 18 January 1989, Prime Minister Rakowski proposed the date of 3 May 1991 for the eventual legalization of Solidarity (*Radio Free Europe Research* 20 January 1989.)

Third, there is the constitution of 1921. After the accession to independence in 1918, an initial step was taken in the adoption of a 'little constitution' in 1919, a brief document spelling out the division of powers between the *Sejm*, the government and the Chief of State. This step inaugurated a tradition: similar 'mini-constitutions' were passed in 1947 and then again in 1992. The little constitution was then superseded by the full-blown constitution of March 1921. Although the constitution gave strong powers to the legislative, the proportional system of elections also ensured that this branch would be too weak and fragmented to use those powers for a constructive purpose. As mentioned in Part II above, the attempt to prevent the emergence of a strong executive led to the very opposite result, as the obvious inability of the *Sejm* to govern effectively paved the way for Pilsudski's coup of May 1926. Over the next decade, the country was nominally ruled by the March 1921 constitution, supplemented by the August 1926 amendments that strengthened the power of the executive. In reality, Pilsudski, although he mainly remained behind the scenes, had the final say in all matters. To cite Norman Davis, 'The arbitrary acts of the [Pilsudski] regime were no more edifying than the political squabbles which preceded them. The May Coup, in the words of one bold spirit, must be likened to "an attack by bandits on a lunatic asylum" ' (Davis 1982, p. 425).

Fourth, the constitution of April 1935 codified the strong executive. In the words of Leszek Garlicki, it 'was centered around one institution, the President, and was written for one man, Jozef Pilsudski . . . It was an irony of history that Pilsudski died on 13 May 1935, ten days before the new constitution became the supreme law of the land' (Garlicki 1992, p. 73). Except for this twist, the document is of scant interest today.

Finally, the constitution of 1952, modeled on the 1936 Soviet constitution, reintroduced the form of parliamentary supremacy while simultaneously robbing it of all content. The Soviet concept of the unity of state power is incompatible with any notion of separation of powers among different organs of state. All power is concentrated in Parliament, including the power to offer binding interpretations of the constitution. In reality, of course, all power was vested in the Communist Party, and Parliament was as much a sham as the other parts of the constitutional machinery. Towards the end of Communist rule, however, the *Sejm* adopted amendments to the constitution that introduced two elements of the rule of law in an otherwise arbitrary system, the Office of the Ombudsman and the Constitutional Court (Majchrowski and Winczorek 1992, pp. 14–28).

2 The Polish Round Table Talks

The following relies mainly on W. Osiatynski, ('The roundtable negotiations in Poland', Working paper #1 from the Center for the Study of Constitutionalism in Eastern Europe, University of Chicago Law School), articles in *Radio Free Europe Research*, January–April 1989, and interviews with participants in the RTT.

The RTT, which opened formally on 6 February 1989 after several months of jockeying for position, began as a simple bargain between the Communist Party and Solidarity. Confronting a desperate economic situation, the regime needed the support of the opposition. On the one hand, social peace and consensus were needed to implement harsh but necessary economic reforms. At the very least, the opposition had to abstain from calling for continued strikes, and preferably to call for an abstention from strikes. On the other hand, the regime needed political legitimacy, both as an element of the social consensus and as a condition for foreign aid. If the opposition called for an abstention in the forthcoming elections, as it had threatened to do, this condition would be destroyed. In return, the opposition asked for a legalization of Solidarity. Initially, this demand was put forward as a prerequisite for holding talks at all, the main topic of the latter being the package of economic reforms. When the government refused, Walesa agreed to let the recognition of Solidarity be an item for bargaining together with the economic reforms. Consequently, the RTT included separate sub-tables on 'Union pluralism' and 'Social and economic policy and systemic reforms'. In addition, a sub-table on 'Political reforms' was set up to negotiate the conditions under which Solidarity could participate in the elections. This sub-table, which turned out to be the most important, was headed by Bronislaw Geremek on Solidarity's side.

In addition to union pluralism, Solidarity demanded political pluralism and free elections. The Communist Party, on its side, did not want to give up its control over Parliament. Early on, the idea was launched to reserve a number of 'safe' seats for the Communists and to have free, competitive elections for the remaining. On 26 January, an establishment intellectual (Arthur Bodnar) was quoted as suggesting that 55 per cent of the sets was enough for the Communist Party and its coalition partners to retain a 'leading role' (*Radio Free Europe Research* 6 February 1989). Although the government would have preferred to yield some safe seats to the opposition, it eventually made a concession on the principle of competitive elections for some of the seats. The proportion of safe seats, first set at 60 per cent, was raised to 65 per cent when the government negotiators claimed to need an additional 5 per cent for 'our Catholics'. With 65 per cent of the seats, the government would have control over ordinary legislation and over the formation of government.

In exchange for conceding free elections for some of the seats, the government negotiators demanded the introduction of the Office of the President to replace the Council of State, a sort of collective presidency created by the 1952 constitution. The President would be vested with large powers, and be elected by the *Sejm* together with various other bodies that could be counted on to vote with the Communists. In this way, any democratic procedures initiated by the new *Sejm* could be thwarted, if necessary. At this time (early March), the focus of the negotiations had shifted from the official and highly publicized RTT to smaller, more informal meetings at the luxury resort Magdalenka. Among the top leaders present were Walesa and Geremek from Solidarity and two ministers, Czeslav Kiszczak and Aleksander Kwasniewski from the government.

The following description of the events set in motion by the proposal of the government negotiators is taken from Wiktor Osiatynski:

Geremek's answer was that they could agree to see democracy raped once, but not two or more times. This silent deadlock was interrupted by Kwasniewski's extemporaneous thought: 'How about electing the president by the *Sejm* and the Senate, which, in turn, would be elected freely.' 'This is worth thinking about', said Geremek. The opposition did not care about the Senate, but was attracted by the idea of free elections in general. The party went along, seeing in Kwasniewski's proposal a road to electing their own candidate with some measure of legitimacy. Thus, through mutual self-interest, a compromise was reached and there occurred one of the most significant decisions of the Round Table, i.e. free elections to the Senate (p. 43).

It remained to fix the role of the Senate in the machinery of government. Whereas the government negotiators had successfully bargained for a large proportion of safe seats in the lower house, they fought a losing battle to reduce the powers of the upper house. First, they wanted it to serve as a merely advisory body. Next, when they did grant the Senate the right to veto legislation passed by the *Sejm*, they wanted the *Sejm* to be able to override the veto by a majority of 11/20, a quaint proportion that was taken from (and justified by) the March 1921 constitution. The Solidarity negotiators, however, insisted on and obtained that a two-thirds majority would be needed to override a veto by the Senate. (According to some participants, there was also an intermediate proposal of a 3/5 majority.) Agreement on this point was reached only fifteen minutes before the agreement was to be signed, an instance of the 'deadline effect' that has often been observed in negotiations (Roth 1987, pp. 36–38).

To see the significance of these controversies we need to look at some numbers. The *Sejm* had 460 members. The new Senate would have 100 members. The guarantee of 65 per cent of the seats in the *Sejm* wound ensure the party at least 299 votes in the *Sejm*, more than half of the seats of the joint session of the *Sejm* and the Senate that was to elect the President by an absolute majority. If the *Sejm* could override a veto of the Senate by 11/20 or even 3/5 of the votes, their 299 seats would be more than enough. To muster a two-thirds majority, they would need 307 votes, 8 more than what they would be certain to have. (Hence the two bargaining issues – the proportion of safe seats and the majority needed to override a Senate veto – were obviously connected. The government's victory over the first issue was empty, given its defeat over the second.) The same two-thirds majority would be needed for revisions of the constitution. Virtually nobody seems to have doubted that they would indeed obtain the eight additional votes. The following comment by the well-informed Louisa Winton, writing on 20 March, is representative:

> In the final days of the talks, the Solidarity side won an expansion of the margin required in the *Sejm* to override a Senate veto to two-thirds from the three-fifths the government had originally proposed. As the communist party and its allies have assured themselves of 65 per cent of the seats in the *Sejm*, this provision would require the authorities to win over a modest number of deputies from outside the official camp in order to override a veto. *This is likely to be more important in principle than in practice*, as the authorities have indicated that they intend to run candidates for the 35 per cent of *Sejm* seats to be filled through competitive elections (*Radio Free Europe Research* 7 April 1989, italics added.)

It came as a surprise to all, and as a shock to the Communists, when Solidarity swept the elections, winning all contested seats in the *Sejm* and all but one seat in the Senate. Soon thereafter the rats left the sinking ship, in the form of a massive defection of two small parties (the Peasant Party and the Democratic Party) that had been allied with the Communists in the old *Sejm*. Together with the 161 seats obtained by Solidarity, they formed the parliamentary majority for the first non-Communist government, appointed in September 1989 and headed by Tadeusz Mazowiecki.

In spite of the massive defeat of the Communists, General Jaruzelski, their candidate for the Presidency, was duly elected in accordance with the RTT agreement. He chose, however, to abstain from using his extensive powers. (During the December 1989 round of constitutional amendments, his only demands were for a mention of social justice and for some words about about the army. Both were satisfied.) The powers became more important with the election of Walesa to the Presidency in December 1990. It then became clear that the powers were not only extensive, but vaguely defined. According to one commentator, they had been 'left deliberately vague on the assumption, current early in 1989, that a Communist President would use whatever prerogatives he saw fit, since he could rely on the backing of the army, security forces and his Soviet sponsors' (Sabbat-Swidlicka 1992, p. 26). According to another, it was the other way around: 'Opposition negotiators have since admitted also to having deliberately designed the 'presidential clauses' of the round-table agreement to be as confusing as possible, with an eye to reduce Jaruzelski's room for maneuver' (Krol cited in Winton 1992, p. 19). According to a centrally placed participant in the RTT, however, the powers of the presidency have a different origin. Stanislaw Ciosek (Politburo Member, one of the two main party negotiators, and currently Polish ambassador to Russia) is reported to have said that 'The Politburo will never accept anything short of a strong Presidency, designed for Jaruzelski. But without a President it will not be possible to destroy the Party.'

The RTT also made two decisions about the Senate that turned out to have important consequences. The first concerned the mode of election of the senators. 'While Solidarity preferred proportional elections, the government suggested "an American model", i.e. two senators from each of 49 *voivodships* in Poland (three from the biggest cities, 100 in all). The government's rationale was the hope that industry-based Solidarity might lose in smaller, predominantly rural *voivodships*' (Osiatynski, p. 34). While that hope was frustrated, the Senate did acquire a definite rural bias. The second decision concerns a failure to translate a provision in the RTT agreement into the constitutional amendments adopted by the *Sejm* on 7 April. According to the deal that was struck, the Senate was to participate 'on the same basis as the *Sejm*' in the amendments and adoption of the Constitution (ibid, p. 46). However, the 7 April amendments left unchanged the clause in the constitution that amendments require a two-thirds majority in the *Sejm*. Below I conjecture that the fate of the 'little constitution' might have been different had the participation of the Senate in the amending power been fully recognized. At the time, however, nobody expected these details of the constitutional machinery to matter.

The Polish RTT can be used to highlight the influence of threats and warnings in constitutional bargaining. Threats are vulnerable to problems of credibility: even if the threatener is able to do what he threatens to do, his threat may not carry much weight if it will manifestly be against his interest to execute it. Although there are ways to get around this problem (Dixit and Nalebuff 1991, p. 161–84; Schelling 1960), the risk of having one's bluff called is often a powerful deterrent against making the threat in the first place. Could the Solidarity leaders credibly threaten to call for mass strikes if their demands were not satisfied? Could the government negotiators credibly threaten to call for Soviet intervention unless Solidarity backed off?

As a foreign observer, and a relatively ignorant one, I do not know the answer to these questions. However, it seems to me that they may not be very relevant, because the parties were in a position to use warnings rather than threats.

Typically, threats are made when each of the two bargaining parties is a unitary actor, whereas warnings are more likely to be made when the actors are internally divided, so that the negotiators can say, with some (always uncertain) credibility that 'I cannot control my members' or 'I cannot control my left' (or right, as the case may be). It can also be shown that a party will obtain a bargaining advantage if it can credibly claim, e.g. by virtue of geographical distance or its internal by-laws, that it needs some time before it can respond to the opponent's offer (Barth 1990). Here again, weakness is strength. The RTT distribution of forces was very much of the latter kind, with softliners in the two camps negotiating with each other and using hardliners in their own camp as bargaining chips (Przeworski 1992, ch.2). In the case of Solidarity, the inability of the leaders to control the impatient, young elements among the workers was a reality rather than an appearance created for bargaining purposes, at least sufficiently so to make the warning credible. Similarly, Janusez Reykowski, the government co-chairman of the Political Reforms sub-table, recalls that

> his most serious argument was a warning rather than a threat. This argument, which emphasized the commonality of interests, was as follows: 'If we do not come to an agreement, then all we who negotiate at the Round Table will be the losers. Others will come, they will try to use force to solve Poland's problems. It is not important if they win or lose, for in both cases Poland will lose and we, the Round Table negotiators, will lose. It does not concern only us, on this side of the table, for you will be wiped out by the more radical forces, too' (Osiatynski, p. 40).

3 Constitution-making efforts in the contractual *Sejm*

The following draws on Majchrowski and Winczorek 1992; Rapaczynski 1991; Morawska 1992; and Kallas 1992.

The *Sejm* elected in June 1989, and in session until the elections of October 1991, had a dubious democratic pedigree. It contained a large contingent of ex-Communists, who had not been chosen in free elections but nominated by the Party. For this reason many members of Solidarity, notably Mazowiecki during his period as Prime Minister, were opposed to the idea of having the new constitution adopted by this body. Geremek, on the other hand, argued that the adoption of a new constitution was a vital practical matter, because of the lack of clarity in the relations among the main organs of the state. Also, he thought, the circumstances were uniquely propitious. Up to the summer of 1990, the Communists were still so demoralized, and Solidarity still so unified, that a new constitution could easily have been passed. The occasion was missed, however. At Geremek's request, a draft was prepared by two independent drafters, one of whom served in the Mazowiecki government. He felt obliged to pass it on to the Prime Minister, who shelved it.

In December 1989, both the *Sejm* and the Senate appointed committees to draft a new constitution. The *Sejm* draft might have stood a chance of being adopted, had it not been for the election of Walesa to the Presidency in December 1990. Walesa was chosen in direct elections, following a constitutional amendment supported by the 'Warsaw' group of intellectuals who believed it would favour their candidate for President (Mazowiecki). According to Rapaczynski 1991, p. 605, note 22, the real preferences of the Warsaw group was for indirect elections. Because they miscalculated the popular support for Mazowiecki, they would have been better off had they stuck to this principle. According to Geremek, constitutions can be adopted in one of two ways: by consensus or by surprise (Interview with Geremek 21 January 1993.) By late 1990 and early 1991, the chance for consensus was gone, but surprise might still have worked. However, because of the opposition of Walesa to the *Sejm* draft, the process lost its momentum. That opposition was due both to the lack of legitimacy of the contractual *Sejm* and to the fact that the draft prepared by the constitutional committee of the Senate gave much wider powers to the President. In fact, Walesa at this time claimed that the contractual *Sejm* was dominated by 'an alliance between the compromised ex-Communists and the "leftist" intellectuals in the government' (Rapaczynski, p. 604). His chief of staff at the time, Jaroslaw Kaczynski, was probably a main influence on Walesa in this respect. Later, Kaczynski quit the office of chief of staff and became the influential leader of the Center Alliance. He and his followers now claim that Walesa himself, or at least his new staff, is also tainted by a Communist past. To capture Kaczynski's attitude, one might say that he is anti-anti-anti-Communist rather than simply anti-Communist, being more contemptuous of those who want to forget the crimes committed by the Communists than of those who committed them. The final drafts of the *Sejm* and the Senate were presented in, respectively, August and October 1991. According to some observers, the only reason why the drafters managed to reach agreement was that they knew that their drafts had no chance of being adopted.

Andrzej Rapaczynski, who served as expert advisor to the subcommittee on institutions of the constitutional committee of the *Sejm*, has offered some glimpses of the proceedings of that body. Perhaps the most interesting observations concern the debates on the electoral laws, which were delegated to this committee. Although some deputies called for the constitutionalization of electoral laws,

> the move to include the basic choice of an electoral system in the constitution lost most of its support. Among the common arguments against it was the unconvincing (and factually inaccurate) claim that few countries have such constitutional provisions. The more convincing argument was that the Round Table Parliament, containing the Communist epigones committed to proportional representation, would oppose any constitutional provision mandating a majoritarian system. And since most people who took the idea seriously favored some form of the majoritarian system, attempts to include such a provision were discontinued (p. 622).

Rapaczynski also provides an antidote to the view that the position of a party on the choice of electoral system is always and everywhere a function only of its electoral interests and prospects. He claims that many groups supported proportional representation, 'despite a potential party interest to the contrary', because they had 'a certain vision of democracy or, more precisely, of the idea of representation' (ibid, p. 617). In this vision, proportionality is needed to ensure that Parliament is a microcosm of society, a faithful reflection of all social forces. The values of governability and stability are not perceived as similarly important. In the current debates over the new electoral law, the liberal (or libertarian) party UPR has taken a similarly counter-interested stance, by favouring a majoritarian system by which it would be certain to do badly. They would seem to favour efficiency over self-interest, whereas the groups referred to by Rapaczynski let democratic values take precedence over self-interest.

4 The little constitution and beyond

The following draws on Winton 1992; Morawska 1992 and on interviews with participants in the making of the little constitution.

On 17 November 1992, President Walesa ratified the 'small constitution' barely one hour after the Constitutional Tribunal had ruled that the new parliamentary rules according to which it had been passed were constitutional. This act was the conclusion to one of two tracks of constitution-making undertaken by the Parliament elected in October 1991. The other track may eventually lead to the adoption of a 'big constitution', which will supersede the little one.

As mentioned earlier, the idea of adopting a small, almost minimal constitution has several precedents in Polish history. This time, the initiative was taken by President Walesa. In November 1991, he asked his legal staff to prepare a brief document that would bring some order and regularity to the confused relations between the Parliament, the government and the President. The draft, prepared in about four hours, replaced the parliamentary supremacy enshrined in art. 20 of the RTT constitution ('The Sejm of the Republic of Poland shall be the supreme organ of the Republic of Poland') with the supremacy of the Presidency. Two main issues were resolved in the draft. First, the dual authority over foreign affairs and security matters was removed. Under the RTT constitution, the President and the Defence Minister both had (ill-distinguished) powers in this domain. The Presidential draft resolves any ambiguity by asserting in article 9.1 that the Council of National Security has competence in all matters related to defence and security, and in article 9.2 that the President is Chairman of the Council of National Security.

Second, and more important, the draft clarified the mode of appointment of the Prime Minister. On this matter, the RTT constitution says only that the PM is appointed and recalled by the President, whereas the Sejm appoints and dismisses individual ministers as well as the Council of Ministers as a whole. (At one point, Mazowiecki had to tell one of his ministers, whom the Sejm refused to dismiss, to take an extended holiday.) Indirectly, it also implies that the presidential nominee needs the approval of the Sejm. The system contains a number of flaws and ambiguities, which became evident in the protracted struggle between Walesa and Parliament over the appointment of Jan Olszewski as Prime Minister after the elections in October 1991. Although it was clear that Olszewski had the support of a majority in the new Sejm, the President dragged his feet over the appointment, while simultaneously preparing a draft for the little constitution that gave the President strong powers in the formation of the government (see below). It is possible that the presentation of his draft for the little constitution was intended as a quid pro quo – I'll appoint your candidate for Prime Minister if you'll approve my constitution. If that was the case, the deal was not consummated. It is more likely that the draft was simply intended as an opening bid – an extremely Presidency-centred proposal that could be bargained into the eventual adoption of a semi-presidential system.

Walesa's draft for the little constitution was sent to the *Sejm*, only to be withdrawn when the commission discarded the points he most cherished. The idea of a little constitution was not dead, however. In April, the Democratic Union (the party of the 'Warsaw intellectuals' faction of the former Solidarity) submitted a draft of the little constitution to the *Sejm*. The extraordinary constitutional committee set up to examine the draft was chaired by Mazowiecki, who was also the head of the Democratic Union. The reason why the Democratic Union draft was nevertheless modified on a number of points was that the three drafters were not present to defend it: two of them had entered the government and the third was in hospital.

The two main compromises that were made relate to the mode of formation of the government and the role of the Senate. Another compromise was the inclusion of proportional elections as a specific clause in the constitution. This provision, which was granted as a concession to the Peasant's Party in exchange for its approval of the document as a whole, is compatible with the use of thresholds to prevent party proliferation and fragmentation. Before I proceed to the details, I need to explain two key terms in the debates. A *simple majority* for a proposal means that there are more positive votes than negative, the number of abstentions being irrelevant. An *absolute majority* means that more than half of the votes cast are for the proposal, with the abstentions being effectively counted with the negative votes. Given the frequent abstentions in the *Sejm*, caused by the presence of many small parties, these two majority requirements can differ considerably. In the little constitution, and even more so in the draft of the Democratic Union, the relations between the *Sejm* and the other organs of state are based on the principle of an absolute majority, thus lending the document a coherence which it lacked before.

In the presidential draft, the key articles relating to the appointment and dismissal of the government were the following:

Art. 1. The President appoints the Prime Minister and, on his motion, the other members of the cabinet.

Art. 2.1. The Prime Minister presents the programme of the government and asks for a vote of confidence. The *Sejm* adopts the vote of confidence with a simple majority, in the presence of half of the deputies.

Art. 2.2. If the cabinet does not get a vote of confidence, the Prime Minister offers his resignation to the President, who accepts it.

Art. 2.3. If the *Sejm* makes no decision in the matter of the vote of confidence within 30 days, it is assumed that the cabinet has received the vote of confidence.

Art. 3.1. The *Sejm* can vote a lack of confidence in the government with an absolute majority, in the presence of half of the deputies. (In the first version of the draft, this article also allowed the President to oppose a veto to the vote of no confidence, in which case the vote of confidence had to be adopted with a 2/3 majority. When the proposal containing this provision was published, the President himself struck it out, saying 'This goes too far'.)

The draft of the Democratic Union was somewhat less 'presidential'. Here, a four-step procedure was envisaged. First, the President proposes a candidate for the post of Prime Minister, who must be approved by an absolute majority of the *Sejm*. If his candidate fails to pass this hurdle, the *Sejm* can appoint its own candidate, if it can muster an absolute majority for him. In case the *Sejm* fails to do so within a specified period, it is the President's turn to propose again, but this time only a simple majority is needed for the *Sejm*'s approval. If that majority is not forthcoming, Parliament shall be dissolved.

Jaroslaw Kaczynski, leader of the Center Alliance (a centre-right split-off from Solidarity) and member of the extraordinary commission of the *Sejm* to examine the little constitution, had a consistently anti-presidential attitude. In principle, he was for a strong Presidency – as long as it was not occupied by Walesa, towards whom he had developed violently hostile feelings after they broke their alliance in late 1991. In the constitution-making process, therefore, he pushed for a predominant role for the *Sejm* in the formation of the government. The ex-Communist Party SLD was close to his position, but more willing to compromise. In fact, the SLD deputy Jerzy Jaskiernia was the engineer of the proposal that was finally adopted. In a procedure that is probably un-rivaled in its complexity, the formation of the government now involves five steps. After the first three steps in the Democratic Union draft, a fourth step is added in which Parliament can choose a candidate for Prime Minister by simple majority. This step makes it more likely (compared to the draft of the Democratic Union) that the government will be formed through parlia-mentary initiative.

In the RTT constitution, the *Sejm* needed a two-thirds majority to overrule a veto by the Senate. In its own by-laws, the *Sejm* also adopted the principle that a simple majority was needed to accept the amendments for ordinary legislation and a two-thirds majority for constitutional laws. This meant that an amended bill that received less than 50 per cent (67 per cent for constitutional laws) but more than 33 per cent of the votes in the *Sejm* was killed – neither the amended nor the unamended version was passed.

To overcome this problem, two solutions were attempted. In July 1992, the *Sejm* changed its by-laws so that an amended bill was automatically passed unless there was a two-thirds majority against the amendments in the *Sejm*. This solution eliminated the indeterminacy that was inherent in the earlier system, but at the cost of giving decisive legislative power to the Senate. Half of the Senate, together with one-third of the *Sejm*, could now decide the fate of any law, including changes in the constitution. The second solution was that adopted by the small constitution. Here, amendments by the Senate are accepted unless they are rejected by an absolute majority in the *Sejm*. To get the small constitution, including this provision, passed, the *Sejm* first amended its by-laws again. On 16 October, the deputies reintroduced the original procedure for ordinary statutes, but decided that in the case of constitutional amendments there would only be a vote on whether to adopt the *Sejm*'s amendment. If the amendment failed to get two-thirds of the votes, it was rejected, whereas before there had to be two-thirds against if for rejection. Next, the *Sejm* went ahead and voted down the Senate amendments to the little constitution.

Perhaps surprisingly, the new rules do not necessarily weaken the Senate. The recent debates on the regulation of television and abortion can be used to illustrate the ambiguity. On both issues, the Senate tends to be more conservative, because of the rural overrepresentation; hence its propensity to add restrictive amendments to the *Sejm*'s bills. Concerning television, the Senate added the requirement that TV has to respect 'Christian values' and '*raison d'état*'. Under the little constitution, the *Sejm* needs an absolute majority to stop the amendment, against the two-thirds majority that would have been needed under the RTT constitution. The power of the *Sejm* to kill the whole bill by simple majority would have been irrelevant, given the obvious need for some kind of bill to regulate television. The Senate, then, is definitely weaker than under the old system. Consider, however, abortion. The *Sejm* has voted a law that is only slightly more restrictive than the existing legislation. If the Senate had introduced more stringent clauses, the *Sejm* would have needed an absolute majority to block the amendments, whereas before a simple majority could kill the whole bill, and would in fact do so *if it preferred the existing law to the amended bill*. In such cases, the Senate has stronger powers under the little constitution.

In the words of one constitutional judge, the *Sejm* changing its by-laws for the mere purpose of being able to override the Senate amendments to the constitution was 'not a very elegant' procedure. However, when a number of deputies brought the case before the Constitutional Court, it was found to be wholly constitutional. The decision was made on the basis of article 106 of the constitution, which asserts that changes in the constitution need only a two-thirds majority in the *Sejm*, with no mention of the Senate. The outcome might have been different if the provision in the RTT agreement that the Senate should participate 'on the same basis as the Sejm' in the revision of the constitution had been incorporated in the 7 April amendments.

There is one provision in the little constitution that definitely limits the power of the Senate, viz. art.17.3 to the effect that 'Any amendment by the Senate, imposing a burden upon the State Budget, shall be required to indicate a source of finance thereof'. In the draft presented by the Democratic Union, similar provisions applied to individual deputies and committees in the *Sejm*. However, during the work in the extraordinary commission of the *Sejm*, these were eliminated, and only the restrictions aimed at the Senate were retained. The deputies wanted for themselves the right to behave irresponsibly which they denied the Senators. (This episode is a textbook example of the idea already mentioned: people never try to bind themselves: rather, politics is about binding others.) When a Senate amendment proposed to eliminate the offending article, the *Sejm* predictably voted it down. A centrally placed participant claims, however, that the Senate would have succeeded if it had proposed instead to reintroduce the budgetary restrictions on the *Sejm* that were part of the Democratic Union's draft.

I conclude with a few words about the second constitution-making track of Parliament. In April 1992, the *Sejm* passed a constitutional bill that regulated the procedure to be used for the adoption of a new constitution (*East European Constitutional Review* 1992). The draft will be elaborated by a joint constitutional committee of the *Sejm* and the Senate, with 46 members from the former body and 10 from the latter. In addition, the President, the government and the Constitutional Court will have non-voting representatives on the committee. To be adopted, the constitution will need a two-thirds majority in a joint session of both houses of Parliament and then popular approval in a referendum. After amendments by the Senate, which the *Sejm* then rejected on formal grounds, the bill was passed in July 1992, more or less simultaneously with the final hammering-out of the details and compromises in the little constitution. This somewhat schizophrenic behaviour does not, however, seem to have worried anyone.

It is far from clear that a 'big constitution' will ever be passed. There are two main gaps that need to be filled: a bill of rights and the organization of the judiciary. In November 1992, President Walesa submitted a bill of rights to Parliament, which is now being considered in the joint constitutional committee. If it is passed, as seems quite likely, it will be as a separate body of legislation and not as part of the big constitution. Concerning the judiciary, the main defect in the existing constitution is the ability of Parliament to overrule decisions of the Constitutional Court. Although most legal scholars are strongly against this provision, it may be more difficult to get the consent of Parliament to its abolition.

It is hard to predict what changes the big constitution might bring in the machinery of government. Although nobody really seems to think there is a need for a Senate, the fact that the Senate will vote on the new constitution makes it virtually certain that it will remain in existence. The situation is somewhat analogous to the influence of the small states at the Federal Convention when the representation of the states in the Senate was discussed. Although the small states did not by themselves have a majority for equal representation, they could obtain a majority by logrolling. Similarly, the Polish Senate will almost certainly be able to muster 87 *Sejm* deputies to vote against the abolition of the Senate, in exchange for support of their favourite proposals. Hence, one observes a curious process of backward reasoning, from the conclusion to suitable premises. Some claim that the Senate is needed as the 'guardian of the laws', although it is hard to see why the Presidential veto and the Constitutional Court do not suffice in this regard. Others claim that the Senate is needed to refine legislation or to delay and slow down the legislative process, although these ends could certainly have been realized without a second chamber. Still others refer to the tradition for a Senate in Polish history, or to the presence of a Senate in the assemblies of all large European countries, without even trying to explain why these facts provide an *argument* for having an upper house.

With regard to the Presidency, there are some indications that we may observe a replay of the adoption of the small constitution: a strongly presidential draft as an opening bid by the President, in the expectation that a semi-presidential compromise will be worked out further down the line. An alternative to this 'split-the-difference' model of constitutional bargaining could be a moderate opening bid by the President, coupled with a stated expression of unwillingness to make concessions and compromises. The President's bill of rights was offered somewhat in this spirit. Although its adoption seems to be favoured by the general surprise it caused, consistently with Geremek's hypothesis cited above, it may be difficult to play the card of surprise more than once.

5 Conclusion

In brief conclusion, I suggest that the main force behind the Polish process of constitution-making has been *institutional self-interest*. All the main actors — the Presidency, the *Sejm* and the Senate — have been concerned with preserving and expanding their powers with respect to legislation and the formation of the government. In the Assemblée Constituante, Clermont-Tonnerre observed that the 'three-headed hydra' — king, first chamber and second chamber — which the constitution should create could not itself have created a constitution (*Archives Parlementaires*, vol.8, p. 574.) The constituent assembly had to be a single body. Now, the experience from Bulgaria suggests that if that body serves as an ordinary legislature, it may write excessively great powers for itself into the constitution. To ensure a proper system of checks and balances in the *constitution*, one might in fact wish for an element of checks and balances in the constitution-making *process*. However, there is no reason to believe that the bargaining power of the constitution-making bodies will correspond to their normatively desirable influence in the machinery of government. The role of the Senate offers the best illustration of this point. Its impact *on* the constitution is arguably much greater than its normatively desirable role *in* the constitution.

The second most important force has been the perceived *electoral interests* of the political parties and groupings. The RTT agreement owed much to this factor. Party interest also shaped the electoral laws, which in turn have been an important influence on the political geography of Parliament and hence on the constitution-making process.

Third in order of importance I would rank the *continued presence of former Communists* and the dynamics created by their survival. Although one might have thought that the ex-Communists would end up as 'constitution-wreckers', somewhat analogously to the diehard fraction of the aristocracy in the Assemblée Constituante, this does not seem to have been the case. In fact, they have probably mattered less for what they have done than for what they have caused others to do. Political life in all post-Communist societies has become highly polarized over the way to treat collaborators with and agents of the former regime. Enmities and alliances formed on this basis may carry over to the constitution-making arena. The best example is Kaczynski's opposition to Walesa that was translated into an opposition to a strong Presidency.

Finally, there has been a not inconsiderable amount of sheer *sound and fury*: bad timing, miscalculation of electoral prospects, unintended side effects of hastily written provisions, and the clash of personalities. Except for the unforeseen consequences of the creation of a Senate in the RTT, such *accidents de parcours* do not seem to have had a decisive influence. Most of the time, the actors seem to have known what they were doing and to have gotten what they thought they were getting.

REFERENCES

Barth, E. 1990. 'Strategic delays in wage bargaining'. Working Paper. Oslo: Institute for Social Research.

Biskupski, M.B. and J.S. Pula (eds.) 1990. *Polish democratic thought from the Renaissance to the Great Emigration: essays and documents*. New York: Columbia University Press.

Bogdan, H. 1990. *Histoire des pays de l'Est*. Paris: Perrin.

Bonime-Blanc, A. 1987. *Spain's transition to democracy; the politics of constitution-making*. Boulder and London: Westview Press.

Bruszt, L. and D. Stark. 1991. 'Remaking the political field in Hungary'. Working Paper. Cornell University.

Burdeau, G., F. Hamon and M. Troper. 1991. *Droit constitutionnel*. 22nd. ed, Paris: Librairie Générale de Droit et de Jurisprudence.

Calda, M. 'The Round Table Talks in Czechoslovakia'. Working Paper #6 from the Center for the Study of Constitutionalism in Eastern Europe, University of Chicago Law School.

Caplin, A. and B. Nalebuff. 1988. 'On 64 per cent majority rule'. *Econometrica* 56, 787–814.

Cohen, A. 1990. *A deal undone: the making and breaking of the Meech Lake Accord*. Vancouver/Toronto: Douglas and McIntyre.

Cutler, L. and H. Schwartz. 1991. 'Constitutional reform in Czechoslovakia'. *University of Chicago Law Review* 58, 511–53.

Davis, N. 1982. *God's playground: A history of Poland*, vol. II. Oxford: Oxford University Press.

Diamond, M. 1981. *The founding of the democratic republic*. Itasca, Ill.: F.E. Peacock.

Dixit, A. and B. Nalebuff. 1991. 'Making strategies credible' in R. Zeckhauser (ed.) *Strategy and choice*. Cambridge, Mass.: MIT Press.

Dwerfler, L. 1983. *President and Parliament: a short history of the French presidency*. Boca Raton: University Presses of Florida.

East European Constitutional Review. 1992. Vol. 1, no. 1, pp. 9–11 and vol. 1, no. 2, pp. 12–13. University of Chicago Law School.

Egret, J. 1950. *La révolution des notables*. Paris: Armand Colin.

Elster, J. 1984. *Ulyssess and the Sirens*. (rev. edn.) Cambridge: Cambridge University Press.

—. 1989. *Solomonic judgments*. Cambridge: Cambridge University Press.

—. 1991. 'Constitutionalism in Eastern Europe: an introduction', *University of Chicago Law Review* 58, 447–82.

—. 1993. *Political psychology*. Cambridge: Cambridge University Press.

—. (forthcoming (1)). 'Limits to majority rule: alternatives to judicial review in the revolutionary epoch' in E. Smith (ed.) *Constitutional justice under old constitutions*.

—. (forthcoming (2)). 'Strategic uses of argument' in K. Arrow *et al.* (eds.) *Barriers to conflict resolution*. New York: W.M. Norton.

—. (forthcoming (3)). 'Majority rule and individual rights' in S. Shute (ed.) *On human rights*. New York: Basic Books.

Elster, J. and R. Slagstad (eds.) 1988. *Constitutionalism and democracy*. Cambridge: Cambridge University Press.

Eule, J.N. 1987. 'Temporal limits on the legislative mandate', *American Bar Foundation Research Journal* 379–459.

Finkelman, P. 1987. 'Slavery and the Constitutional Convention: making a covenant with death' in R. Beeman, S. Botein and E.C. Carter II (eds.), *Beyond Confederation: origins of the constitution and American national identity*. Chapel Hill: University of North Carolina Press.

Finn, J.E. 1991. *Constitutions in crisis*. New York: Oxford University Press.

Frost, R.I. 1990. ' "Liberty without license?" The failure of Polish democratic thought in the seventeenth century' pp. 29–54 in M.B. Biskupski and J.S. Pula (eds.) *Polish democratic thought from the Renaissance to the Great Emigration: essays and documents*. New York: Columbia University Press.

Furet, F. 1988. *la révolution 1770–1870*. Paris: Hachette.

Garlicki, L. 1992. 'The development of the presidency in Poland', pp. 65–113 in K.W. Thompson (ed.) *Poland in a world of change: constitutions, presidents and politics*. Lanham: University Press of America.

Greenawalt, K. 1989. *Speech, crime and the uses of language*. New York: Oxford University Press.

Harris, R.D. 1986. *Necker and the Revolution of 1789*. Lanham: University Press of America.

Hibbing, J.R. and S. Patterson. 1990. 'A democratic legislature in the making: the historic Hungarian elections of 1990', *Yearbook of the Hungarian Political Science Association*.

Hirschman, A. 1973. 'The changing tolerance for income inequality in the course of economic development', *Quarterly Journal of Economics* 87, 544–65.

Holmes, S. 1988. 'Precommitment and the paradox of democracy', pp. 195–240 in J. Elster and R. Slagstad (eds.) *Constitutionalism and democracy*. Cambridge: Cambridge University Press.

Hylland, A. 'The Romanian electoral law of 1990'. Working Paper, Norwegian School of Management.

Kallas, M. (ed.). 1992. *Projekty Konstytucyjne 1989–1991*. Warsaw: Sejm Publishing Office. (Table of Contents in English).

Klingsberg, E. 1992. 'Judicial review and Hungary's transition from Communism to democracy', *Brigham Young University Law Review* 41, 41–144.

Krol, M. 1992. Interviewed in *Tygodnik Powszechnv*, 10 May, in L. Winton 'Poland's "little constitution" clarifies Walesa's powers', *RFE/RL Research Report*, vol. 1, no. 35, pp. 19–26.

Kydland, F. and E. Prescott. 1977. 'Rules rather than discretion', *Journal of Political Economy* 85, 473–92.

Leslie, R.F. (ed.). 1980. *A history of Poland since 1863*. Cambridge: Cambridge University Press.

Lijphart, A. 1992. 'Democratization and constitutional choices in Czechoslovakia, Hungary and Poland, 1989–91', *Journal of Theoretical Politics* 4, 207–24.

—. (ed.). 1992. *Parliamentary versus presidential government*. Oxford: Oxford University Press.

Linz, J. 1990. 'The perils of presidentialism', *Journal of Democracy* 1, 51–69.

Macey, J. 1986. 'Promoting public-regarding legislation through statutory interpretation: an interest-group model', *Columbia Law Review* 86, 223–68.

Majchrowski, J. and P. Winczorek. 1992. 'La Pologne dans le processus des changements constitutionnels (1989–1991)', *Notes et Documents pour une Recherche Personnaliste*.

Mathiez, A. 1898. 'Etude critique sur les journées des 5 & 6 octobre 1789, Part I, *Revue Historique* 67, 241–81.

McGuire, R.A. 1988. 'Constitution-making: a rational choice model of the Federal Convention of 1787', *American Journal of Political Science* 32, 483–522.

McIntyre, R.J. 1988. *Bulgaria: politics, economics and society*. London: Pinter.

McQuaid, D. 1991. 'The "war" over the election law', *Report on Eastern Europe*, vol. 2, no. 31, (2 Aug.), pp. 11–18.

Merkl, P. 1963. *The origin of the West German Republic*. New York: Oxford University Press.

Morawska, E. 1992. 'The constitutional commission of the Diet', Report to the Center for the Study of Constitutionalism in Eastern Europe, University of Chicago Law School.

Mounier, J.J. 1989. 'Expose de ma conduite dans l'Assemblee Nationale', in F. Furet and R. Halévi (eds.) *Orateurs de la Révolution Francaise, I: les constituants*. Paris: Gallimard.

North, D. 1990. 'Institutions, transaction costs and exchange', pp. 182–94 in J.E. Alt and K. Shepsle, *Perspectives on political economy*. Cambridge: Cambridge University Press.

Nozick, R. 1969. 'Coercion' in S. Morgenbesser, P. Suppes and M. White (eds.) *Philosophy, science and method*. New York: Macmillan.

Osiatynski, W. 'The Round Table negotiations in Poland'. Working Paper #1 from the Center for the Study of Constitutionalism in Eastern Europe, University of Chicago Law School.

Paczolay, P. 1992. 'Judicial review of the compensation law in Hungary', *Michigan Journal of International Law*, 13, 806–31.

Perez-Llorca, J.P. 1988. 'Commentary' pp. 266–75 in R.A. Goldwin and A. Kaufman (eds.) *Constitution makers on constitution-making*. Washington DC: American Enterprise Institute.

Preuss, U.K. 'The (central) Round Table in the former German Democratic Republic'. Working Paper #4 from The Center for the Study of Constitutionalism in Eastern Europe, University of Chicago Law School.

Przeworski, A. 1992. *Democracy and the market*. Cambridge: Cambridge University Press.

Rakove, J.W. 1987. 'The great compromise: ideas, interests and the politics of constitution making', *William and Mary Quarterly* 44, 424–57.

Rapaczynski, A. 1991. 'Constitutional politics in Poland', *University of Chicago Law Review* 58, 595–632.

Records of the Federal Convention. 1966. New Haven: Yale University Press.

Roth, A. 1987. 'Bargaining phenomena and bargaining theory', pp. 14–24 in A. Roth (ed.) *Laboratory experimentation in economics*. Cambridge: Cambridge University Press.

Rubio Llorente, F. 1988. 'Writing the constitution of Spain', pp. 239–65 in R.A. Goldwin and A. Kaufman (eds.) *Constitution makers on constitution making*. Washington DC: American Enterprise Institute.

Sabbat-Swidlicka, A. 1992. 'Poland', *RFE/RL Research Report*, vol. 1, no. 27 (special issue on the rule of law in Eastern Europe) (3 July), 25–33.

Schelling, T.C. 1960. *The strategy of conflict*. Cambridge, Mass.: Harvard University Press.

Schwartz, H. 1992. 'The new East European constitutional courts', *Michigan Journal of International Law* 13, 741–85.

Stein, E. 1992. 'Post-Communist constitution-making' (unpublished manuscript, University of Michigan Law School).

Stone, D.Z. 1990. 'Democratic thought in eighteenth-century Poland', pp. 55–72 in M.B. Biskupski and J.S. Pula (eds.) *Polish democratic thought from the Renaissance to the Great Emigration: essays and documents*. New York: Columbia University Press.

Suber, P. 1990. *The paradox of self-amendment*. New York: Peter Lang.

Sunstein, C. 1991. 'Constitutionalism, prosperity, democracy', *Constitutional Political Economy* 2, 371–94.

Sutton, J. 1986. 'Non-cooperative bargaining theory; an introduction', *Review of Economic Studies* 53, 709–24.

Thaysen, U. 1990. *Der runde Tisch*. Wiesbaden: Westdeutscher Verlag.

Thomson, J.M. 1988. *Robespierre*. Oxford: Blackwell.

Tocqueville, A. de 1986. *Souvenirs*. Paris: Laffont.

—. 1990. *Recollections: the French Revolution of 1848*. New Brunswick: Transaction Books.

Troebst, S. (forthcoming) 'Nationalismus als Demokratierungshemnis in Bulgarien (Oktober 1989–Oktober 1991)' in H. Sundhausen (ed.) *Sudosteuropa – Krisen, Reformen, Konflikte*. Berlin-Wiesbaden: In Kommission bei Otto Harrassowitz.

Troxel, L. 1992. 'Bulgaria's Gypsies: numerically strong, politically weak', *RFE/RL Research Report*, vol. 1, no. 10 (6 March).

Winton, L.1992. 'Poland's "little constitution" clarifies Walesa's powers', *RFE/RL Research Report*, vol. 1, no. 35, pp. 19–26.

Wood, G. 1969. *The creation of the American Republic*. New York: Norton.

FROM TRANSFORMATION TO MODERNIZATION: ADMINISTRATIVE CHANGE IN CENTRAL AND EASTERN EUROPE

JOACHIM JENS HESSE

I INTRODUCTION

Administrative change in the post-Communist or rather post-Socialist countries of Central and Eastern Europe on which the present volume concentrates – Poland, the Czech and Slovak Republics, and Hungary – has reached a stage which allows for an initial stock-taking of developments since the demise of Communist rule at the end of the 1980s. The renewal and partial re-building of public administration in these countries have arrived at a critical juncture which is characterized by a gradual shift in emphasis from administrative transformation, which provided the dominant reform pattern during the first phase of post-socialism, to administrative modernization, which is likely to shape developments over the coming years. There are two main strands in this process of re-orientation. First, the explicit rejection of the administrative heritage of the socialist past is declining in importance, whilst functional considerations are steadily gaining in weight. Second, grand reform designs are progressively losing their attractiveness, and the need for improved implementation and continuous administrative development is increasingly recognized by policy makers.

Socialist state administration differed fundamentally from the classical, 'bourgeois' models. What became known as 'democratic centralism' provided in many respects a mirror image to the organizational principles of modern western public administration. Basic distinguishing features of socialist administration included extreme centralization, with pervasive hierarchical controls over the lower levels of administration; this implied, for example, the absence of an independent sphere of local government. Centralization was coupled with concentration, i.e. the fusion of executive and legislative powers in the highest

Joachim Jens Hesse is Ford-Monnet Professor of European Institutions and Comparative Government in the University of Oxford and Director of the Centre for European Studies at Nuffield College, Oxford.

organs of the state, which were, in turn, controlled by the decision-making bodies of the ruling Communist/Socialist Party. Party control extended over all levels and branches of state administration, and the Party and state apparatuses were closely intertwined. The will of the Party was superior to the rule of law; consequently, the principle of legality played only a secondary role in administration. Accordingly, effective external controls over the legality of public administration hardly existed. Concerning administrative personnel, allegiance to the ruling party was the decisive criterion for career development.

Of course, these basic principles of socialist administration were applied with different emphases and in different forms in the countries of Central and Eastern Europe, but they had a decisive influence on the public sector in all countries under consideration here. Consequently, whilst the dismantling of 'democratic centralism' did not follow an identical course, the negation of this legacy provided the chief impetus for reform. Thus, instead of centralization and hierarchical controls, decentralization and the autonomy of lower administrative levels turned into new ideals of administrative development. In particular, local government was to be freed from the double subordination of central and party control, and an independent sphere of local self-government created. This implied a separation between state and local administration, i.e. an end to a unified administration. Executive and legislative powers were to be strictly separated, and the control of the ruling party over both to be broken. Lawfulness rather than political imperatives was to guide administrative action, and the control of legality was to be strengthened. A politically neutral career public service would take the place of the old *cadre* system.

Transformation as rejection of the old administrative model, change *via negationis*, until recently provided the dominant paradigm of administrative reform and its chief impetus. Of course, this does not mean that performance aspects were ignored; but reforms were, on the whole, less guided by a detailed assessment of organizational needs and requirements than the desire to mark a complete and irreversible break with the past. This is not to argue that these intentions were achieved. As will be shown below, only certain levels and branches of administration have undergone more far-reaching transformation and the implementation of reform initiatives has often lagged behind the original intentions. More recently, there are signs that functional considerations, focusing on administrative performance deficits, are beginning to eclipse the concern with the administrative past. Increasingly, the discussion is revolving around the functional challenges to the partially reformed administrations of Central and Eastern Europe, whilst less and less attention is being focused on exorcizing the ghosts of the last decades. There are several explanations for this: at least a partial break with the past is undeniable, so that reform energies can now be directed towards the future; a total and complete break is no longer considered either possible or desirable; and, perhaps most importantly, there has been a growing realization that administrative reform requires positive and detailed conceptions which the schematic juxtaposition of 'democratic centralism' versus 'classical European administration' is too broad to provide.

The second element of re-orientation in the reform process is very closely related to this point. As functional considerations come to the fore, implementation issues and the stabilization and institutionalization of administrative reform are receiving growing attention. Grand reform designs are certainly viewed with increasing suspicion; instead, policy makers are beginning to underline the need to secure what has already been achieved, to complete the reform process, and to pursue selective corrections where initial transformation processes resulted in dysfunctional arrangements. As the idea of complete and immediate change is discarded, there are more and more calls for a segmented and phased approach to administrative reform. At the same time, disappointment with the results of the first wave of reform initiatives is heightening the awareness of the need for implementation and monitoring capacities. The understanding of administrative reform as a one-off act is beginning to be superseded by a conception which stresses the continuous character of administrative adjustment. In this connection, the influence of the results of the past decades of Western research on administrative reform is clearly visible. It is, then, only logical that the merits of stabilizing and institutionalizing reform capacities are increasingly being acknowledged in Central and Eastern Europe.

The need to move from a first phase of transformation to continuous, institutionalized modernization was initially stressed in the academic discourse. However, the contributions in this volume show clearly how these ideas have also begun to inform practical policy making. Against this background, the following conclusion, firstly, seeks to summarize the main tendencies in administrative development in Poland, the former Czechoslovakia and Hungary during the transformation period. This will be done by examining relevant changes in the environment of public administration, its structural organization, processes and techniques, and administrative personnel. Despite significant differences in the reform experiences of the countries mentioned, a comparative analysis also reveals a perhaps surprising extent of commonalities, a fact which has thus far not been sufficiently recognized. This stock-taking is followed by a detailed consideration of the challenges to administrative reform as it moves from transformation to modernization. As regards the substance of the modernization initiatives currently under discussion in Central and Eastern Europe, the shortcomings of the first reform phase are playing, of course, a decisive role. Thus, local government, territorial administration, intergovernmental relations, interadministrative co-ordination, and personnel policies are amongst the top priorities of the currently evolving second-stage reform agenda. In procedural terms, the next phase in administrative development is indeed likely to be characterized by the gradual crystallization of an alternative to the hitherto dominant transformation paradigm in the form of continuous administrative modernization. There are, furthermore, growing signs that an administrative policy is beginning to develop whose attributes include an emphasis on implementation, segmentation and sequencing, and the stabilization and institutionalization of reform capacities.

II ADMINISTRATIVE TRANSFORMATION IN CENTRAL AND EASTERN EUROPE: A REVIEW

1 The political and economic context of administrative reform

The dynamics of administrative reform in the post-Communist countries of Central and Eastern Europe cannot be fully understood in terms of adaptation and adjustment to a changing environment. Nonetheless, political-institutional and economic reform, on the one hand, and administrative development, on the other, are, of course, interdependent. Thus, political and economic reconstruction fundamentally affects the definition of the systemic role of public administration. In other words, democratization, pluralization, de-étatisation, marketization, privatization and liberalization are connected with strong pressures for administrative adaptation, which extend to tasks, structures and procedures as well as to aspects of personnel policy. At the same time, public administration is a key agent of political and economic reform, the success of which depends crucially on governance capacities.

Concentrating on contextual developments and their impact on public administration, it should, first, be remembered that the initial period of political and economic transition was, unsurprisingly, characterized by a great deal of instability, volatility and changeability in contextual conditions. As a result, the formulation and implementation of realistic adaptation strategies proved extraordinarily difficult, if not impossible. Administrative reform was, accordingly, less guided by an assessment of the new administrative requirements associated with political and economic change than the intention to overcome the administrative legacy of socialism. Put differently, administrative transformation provided the prevailing reform pattern because the turbulence of political and economic developments impeded a performance-oriented analysis of tasks, structures, procedures and personnel.

There are, however, signs of an increasing consolidation in contextual conditions. In the political sphere, the process of institutionalizing a framework of democratic governance has been more or less concluded, and the main outlines of the future political order have become increasingly evident. The unpredictability and uncertainty of political life which characterized the transition years is gradually declining, as more settled patterns of political behaviour evolve. As regards economic reconstruction, it is, of course, still far from being completed; the transition from socialist planning to market-based economies through privatization, liberalization and marketization has proved a much more complex and long drawn-out process than many had originally predicted. Moreover, the disruptive effects of this reconstruction process, in terms of falling production, rising inflation, mushrooming unemployment or declining living standards, are much more severe than the proponents of reform were initially ready to admit. However, whilst economic policy faces mounting problems, the basic structural foundations of the different national economies also begin to emerge more clearly. Generic declarations in favour of creating market-based economies are increasingly replaced by more differentiated policies. This concerns, for example, the role of publicly owned enterprises; the mix between small, medium-sized and large firms and corporations; or the sectoral composition of the economy. Here, a comparative analysis reveals significant policy differences between Poland, Hungary and the Czech and Slovak Republics, even though they share a basic commitment to the idea of a market economy. At the same time as the guiding objectives of economic reconstruction become more specific and, accordingly, policies more distinct, the creation of the legal institutions of a market economy is progressing.

For administrative development, the stabilization of important variables of political and economic reform implies an increased degree of dependability and predictability. As the context of public administration begins to settle, political expectations and functional demands in the medium and long-term become more apparent. Consequently, there is a more realistic chance for positive purposive reform, which goes beyond the rejection of the administrative inheritance of 'democratic centralism'.

Before pursuing this thought in more detail, it does, however, seem sensible to take a closer look at the experience of administrative transformation in Poland, Hungary, and Czechoslovakia up to the end of 1992. In doing so, the following discussion concentrates on organizational patterns of the central, intermediate and local levels of government and public administration (including constitutional preconditions), administrative procedures and techniques, as well as personnel policy.

2 Organizational patterns

a) Constitutional preconditions

The first observation to note about post-socialist constitutionalization processes in Poland, Hungary and the former Czechoslovakia is that they took a very different course from the one originally envisaged. In all three countries, there was, after the downfall of the Communist regimes, a broad political consensus that new constitutions should be worked out and adopted as quickly as possible. In Poland and Hungary, this meant replacing the socialist constitutions of 1952 and 1949 respectively; in Czechoslovakia, the aim was a radical revision of the federal constitution, followed by the adoption of constitutions in the Czech and Slovak Republics.

However, a complete break with the socialist constitutional past has thus far only proved possible in the former CSFR. Here, federalization issues dominated the constitutional debate from the outset. Although after November 1989, the federal constitution was extensively amended, including the adoption of a Charter of Fundamental Rights and Freedoms, there was never any doubt that a comprehensive constitutional settlement was only possible if the dominant Czech and Slovak political forces could reach agreement on the future shape of the Federation, i.e. the relations between the Republics and the central government. When, after the federal and republican elections of June 1992, the eventual dissolution of the Federation became almost a certainty, the constitutional debate quickly shifted to the two Republics. The 1968 Act on the Federation, through which Czechoslovakia was legally transformed from a unitary into a federal state, has provided for republican constitutions; however, it is indicative of the weak political position of the Republics under Communist centralism that such constitutions were never adopted. In Slovakia, a republican constitution was approved by the National Council on 1 September 1992 and came into force on 1 October. With this act, Slovakia effectively became an independent state. In the Czech Republic, the constitutionalization process had not been completed by the time the country officially became an independent and sovereign state on 1 January 1993. Stumbling blocks included the controversial adoption of a bill of rights; the role of the President; the question of whether Parliament would consist of one chamber only or be bicameral; and the Republic's future territorial organization. Although the political disagreements on these issues delayed the adoption of a Czech constitution, it was never seriously doubted that national independence would soon be followed by a constitutional settlement.

In contrast to the Czech and Slovak Republics, in Poland and Hungary a final settlement in the form of a new constitution has thus far proved elusive. Instead, there have been numerous amendments to the constitutions inherited from the socialist regimes, which have fundamentally altered constitutional law and created a legal framework for pluralist, democratic government and market-based economies. It might be argued that the failure of the main political forces to agree on a new constitutional document introduces a critical element of unsettledness and instability into the reform process. However, there are indications that the delay in adopting new constitutions is as much a reflection of a gradual calming down of the constitutional debate as the result of fundamental political disagreements. In Poland, with President Walesa's signing of the 'Little Constitution' (Constitutional Act on the Relations between Legislative and Executive Branches of the Republic of Poland and on Local Self-government) on 17 November 1992, the relations between the President, government and Parliament were redefined. With the 'Little Constitution,' months of bitter political conflict, which repeatedly resulted in institutional deadlock, came to an end. This is not to say that a swift conclusion of the work of the Constitutional Committee of the National Assembly can now be expected. But from the perspective of administrative reform, the clarification of the highly contentious inter-institutional relations represented a considerable gain in contextual stability.

In Hungary, too, the process of constitutional reform has taken a different course from the one initially envisaged. The present Hungarian constitution is the result of compromises reached in the course of 1989 between the then ruling Hungarian Socialist Workers Party and the opposition forces. The main aim of the radical constitutional amendment adopted by Parliament in October 1989 was to create legal bases for a state founded on the rule of law, a competitive multi-party system, parliamentary democracy and a market-oriented economy. Although clearly committed to democratic ideals and economic liberalization, certain constitutional provisions betray the compromise nature of the 1989 amendments. Thus, Hungary is constituted as an independent, democratic state in which 'the values of civil democracy and democratic socialism prevail in equal measure' and public and private ownership enjoy 'equal rights and protection'.

At the time of the adoption of the amendment, it was commonly accepted that the new constitutional order would merely have a transitory character and that a completely new constitution should be adopted after the first free parliamentary elections. Whilst a number of additional amendments have been passed since October 1989, the aim of a new constitution has proved increasingly elusive, and the constitutional debate has become notably less intense. There are several reasons for this: the new government has found that it can pursue its political aims within the limits of the amended constitution; there is, therefore, no urgent case for a new document; agreement for a new constitution would have to be found with the opposition, but the latter expects to be in a considerably stronger position after the next general elections due in 1994, and is not interested in reaching major compromises now. With neither side pressing for an early constitutional settlement, the decisive impetus for constitutional reform is lacking. In short, the main political actors have learned to live with the amended constitution, and the adoption of a new document is more likely to resemble a 'tidying up' exercise than amount to a radical departure from the newly established constitutional conventions and practices.

b) Central government: a case of limited adjustment
In contrast to the intermediate and local levels of public administration, reorganization at the centre of government remained – until the end of 1992 – by and large restricted to structural adjustments that were immediately connected with democratization and economic liberalization. For the main part, these adjustments focused on two areas: internal security and economic administration.

It might come as a surprise that the extensive array of government departments and national offices, which form the core of the central machinery of government, has not been subject to a comprehensive reform since 1989. That is not to say that no significant changes have taken place; nor does it mean that the need for a wholesale re-examination of the central institutions of governance has remained unacknowledged. However, political instability since the autumn of 1989 and uncertainty about the future role of central administration and its relationships with subcentral levels of government have thus far prevented far-reaching reforms. In Poland, for example, and compared to adaptive processes during the last years of Communist rule, macro-institutional changes under a number of different governments have been limited indeed. The more notable included the separation of powerful ministries or the merger of less important ones. The creation of a Ministry of Ownership Changes (or Privatization) and the establishment of an Anti-Monopolies Office should be mentioned also. Especially in economic administration, further changes, although not yet formally approved, seem likely, the main idea being to bring together almost all competences for economic policy making into one central government department, modelled on the German Ministry of Economics. Under these plans, the current Ministries of Industry and Commerce, Foreign Economic Relations and Ownership Changes would be merged; this new ministry would also take over the remaining responsibilities of the Central Planning Office.

Next to the field of economic administration, it has indeed been the politically highly sensitive area of internal security where the most dramatic changes as a result of the transition to democratic government have taken place. Since the internal security apparatuses were highly centralized in the Ministries of the Interior, a comprehensively militarized institution, reorganization attempts concentrated on this department. Whereas some sections were abolished, new sections (for the protection of the constitution, the protection of the economy and studies and analysis) were added. The organization of the Interior Ministry remained – nonetheless – heavily geared towards internal security and intelligence work. In Poland, it was only at later stages of the reform process that comprehensive legislation concerning the police, the secret service and the organization of the Interior Ministry was adopted, aiming at the demilitarization and depoliticization of the ministry and the security apparatuses it controlled. The ministry itself has been drastically scaled down, and the various security and intelligence offices have been reorganized and moved outside the main bodies of the ministries (giving them something approaching agency status), whilst remaining within the political responsibility of the Minister of the Interior. The ministry itself is now predominantly staffed with civilians, and, as a result of the drastic pruning of the internal security services, the total number of employees has more than halved.

Mention should also be made of further reform proposals concerning the Interior Ministry which, if adopted, could have a major impact on the further development of the public sector. It looks, for example, as if the plan to transform the Polish Interior Ministry into a Ministry of Public Administration, which had been voted down by Parliament in 1991, is to be revived. The idea behind these proposals is to create a complete civilian public administration ministry, which would take over the responsibilities for the public service from the Office of the Council of Ministers. In this way, a focus for the development of public administration as a whole (including regional and local administrations) could be created, which might be of value in supporting the development of a horizontally and vertically integrated administrative system.

In general, there is a broad agreement amongst policy makers that a comprehensive restructuring of departmental competences at the central level will only be possible once the future tasks of central administration have been defined more clearly. In other words, decisions are required on the scope of the future powers and responsibilities of the national administration as opposed to regional/provincial and local governance.

In the Czechoslovakian case, conflicting views about the actual allocation of competences rendered the reform of central government even more complex – due to a duplication of activities, when both federal and republican authorities claimed responsibility, or due to inaction, when either side denied its obligations or chose to ignore them. A co-ordinated approach to administrative change was made particularly difficult by the extraordinary flurry of legislative activity at the federal and republican levels since late 1989. In 1990 and 1991, a total of more than 1,100 laws, amendments and secondary legal acts (bye-laws, directives, etc.) were adopted, and it is estimated that 90 per cent of these were aimed principally at public administration, affecting its tasks, structures and procedures. Change has therefore been unusually partial and unsystematic, without reference to a broader reform design.

Hungary followed more or less the pattern described before. Apart from a reorganization of the internal security services, which – owing to the more liberal climate compared to Czechoslovakia, for example – has been modest, the emphasis is on economic administration in the widest sense. On top of streamlining ministerial organization, a new Ministry of Industry and Trade has been established by merging two previously existing departments. The reorganization in ministerial economic administration has not, however, been as far reaching as in some other Central and Eastern European countries, largely because the industrial branch ministries typical of socialist central administrations had already been abolished in Hungary in the early 1980s. Apart from the further abolition of institutions closely identified with the planned economy, such as the National Planning Office and the Office of Price Controls, new offices have been created, reflecting a new regulatory framework and new administrative tasks. They include the Office of Economic Competition, the task of which is to implement anti-monopoly legislation and, importantly, the State Property Agency (SPA), which plays a central role in Hungarian privatization policy. Unlike in some other Central and Eastern European countries, no ministry for privatization has been created. Instead, a minister without portfolio, who takes special responsibility for privatization policy, has been appointed. This mirrors the pattern found in some other policy areas, where the main administrative responsibilities are allocated to a central non-ministerial institution.

Turning from the main outlines of the central administrative institutions to their internal organization, the main emphasis has thus far been on streamlining and on limited, more or less *ad hoc* adjustments rather than a fundamental revision of structures and procedures. However, two important innovations, both with potentially far-reaching consequences were adopted (in Hungary) or are underway (in Poland) in the organization of the top leadership level in government ministries. The first concerns the establishment of a separate personal staff working directly for the minister. At the moment, there seems to be a great deal of variation in the size of this staff between the individual ministries and also in the roles they play. Whilst in some ministries this personal staff seems to adopt the role of a French-type *cabinet*, with a potentially important role in policy making, in others it appears to have a much more mundane function, providing essential back-up services for the minister, without being involved in policy making. Should the *cabinet* model become more widely accepted, this would obviously have important implications for the internal division of labour in the ministries, reducing the policy-making role of line departments.

The second important innovation at the top leadership level concerns the attempt to separate the (temporary) political leadership from a (permanent) administrative leadership. Here, the basic idea has been to introduce a greater degree of stability and continuity by creating two clearly distinguished spheres of leadership in the ministries and to shield civil servants from direct ministerial interference. Under this model, the top political sphere would consist of the minister and a political (parliamentary) secretary, with both positions being explicitly political appointments, whereas the top administrative level is represented by an administrative (chief) secretary, who is, in principle, appointed on a permanent basis and acts as the head of the ministry's employees.

Whilst this division between political and administrative leadership might appear functional and follows similar models in many Western democracies, its practical application raises questions as to whether it can really achieve its aims. To start with, ministers are free in appointing administrative secretaries who by no means have to be career civil servants, that is they do not necessarily have to rise through the ranks. There is little doubt that administrative secretaries are political appointments, with party-political considerations playing an important role. As civil servants, administrative secretaries cannot normally be removed from the service; but the minister can at any time remove them from the particular position they hold, without having to give reasons for such a decision. In other words, employment is permanent, but the position of administrative secretary is not. The political nature of their employment and the fact that they rely on the minister's good will obviously greatly limit their capacity to act as a barrier to attempts at ministerial interference. It also means that continuity is by no means guaranteed. Eventually, at least in some ministries in Hungary, there seems to exist no clear-cut division of labour between the political and the administrative secretaries. With the position of the latter clearly politicized, it would indeed be difficult to delimit precisely their respective spheres of competence.

Whilst until now the institutional changes in central administration have been comparatively limited, recent reform initiatives could eventually result in much more comprehensive modernization. The central project here has been launched by the Hungarian government in spring 1992 with the adoption of a 'government resolution on the modernization of public administration', plans to which Imre Verebélyi refers in this publication. This resolution spells out the basis for a comprehensive programme involving a detailed analysis of practically all tiers and branches of public administration. The aim is to examine tasks, structures, procedures and personnel, with a view to developing proposals for improvement. In the context of this initiative, the critical review of central administration is amongst the key concerns.

As part of the resolution, all government departments and national offices have been required to produce a detailed plan specifying the areas where they see a need for organizational change and containing proposals for improvement by the end of 1992. On the basis of these individual plans, a general plan is to be worked out which defines the directions and principles of the government's modernization policy. The comprehensiveness of this approach goes far beyond the limited adjustments that have thus far taken place. It is also worth noting that the government resolution explicitly addresses the issue of how to ensure that modernization projects, once adopted, are actually implemented. Here, it seems crucial that the Ministry of the Interior and the Prime Minister's Office are jointly responsible for continually assessing and reporting on the progress of implementation.

But, however skillfully prepared and however carefully monitored, the ultimate success of any modernization programme depends crucially on the ability of reformers to overcome intra-organizational resistance to change. Here, administrative reform analysts appear to agree almost unanimously that coercive strategies, relying on the exercise of power to push through reforms, are unlikely to produce the desired results. Instead, they stress the need to adopt an essentially persuasive approach, aimed at mobilizing those belonging to the organization to be reformed. In other words, 'without winning over the potentially reformed, i.e. those who will be expected to adopt, assimilate and routinise the reforms, only perfunctory implementation occurs at best' (G.E. Caiden). At the moment, it is certainly too early to tell whether Hungarian and Polish administrative reformers will succeed in the task of gaining the active support of those who have to make the reforms work. But given the potential scale of the modernization project, there can be no doubt about the magnitude of the challenge.

Although it will be several years before the success of the modernization process can be judged, the high degree of importance which is attached to administrative organization is encouraging. Perhaps to a greater extent than in some other post-socialist countries, the vital role of the state and public administration in social transformation has been recognized. It would appear that reformers have made a good deal of progress in overcoming understandable, but damaging anti-state attitudes by stressing the positive contributions of a modernized public administration to a functioning market economy. Another positive feature of the current discussion is that the need for an inclusive approach to administrative reform is explicitly acknowledged. In concrete terms, this means, for example, that tasks, structures, procedures and personnel are not considered in isolation. It also implies that horizontal and, in particular, vertical linkages and interdependencies between different levels of public administration are taken into account and the likely implications of reform at one level of the multi-layered administrative system are addressed at an early stage in the deliberations. The described process of dismantling the administrative infra-structure of the planned economy and of building up, in its place, an institutional framework for effective regulation and economic promotion that should help to administer privatization and restitution, is indeed a positive sign. The attempts to depoliticize public administration by a separation between the political leader-ship and the administrative sphere no doubt go, though only partially successful, in the right direction.

c) The intermediate level: uncertainty and confusion
Turning to the intermediate level of government, one is again able to detect

a number of common characteristics in Poland, the Czech and Slovak Republics and Hungary. This refers first of all to the uncertainty about the future of the intermediate level and intergovernmental arrangements at large. Whilst the previous district offices were abolished almost everywhere, since they served as organs of state government, the future of the regional level is wide open. Whereas in Poland the role of the *voivods* and *voivodship* offices underwent major changes, important issues were left untackled. There seems to be a broad consensus on the need for further structural reform, although without indication of what kind of regional government unit would be the most appropriate. The comprehensive regionalization of political authority, as proposed by the former Bielecki government, would have represented a radical departure from Poland's unitary state tradition. It should not come as a surprise, therefore, that the ambitious reform did not materialize and is unlikely to be revived in the foreseeable future.

In its central features, the present structure of regional or provincial governance in Poland dates back to the mid-1970s. Reforms in 1973 aimed at strengthening the economic development functions of local governments were followed, in 1975, by the abolition of districts and an increase in the number of provinces (or *voivodships*) from 22 to 49. The *voivodship* offices formed units of central field administration, but specialist territorial divisions and field services multiplied. It was here, in particular, that the former district level maintained an important role for the internal administrative organization, despite its formal abolition. In law, the *vovoidships* were, at the same time, organs of state and local government. To assist and guide the *voivodships* in the latter function, there existed provincial people's councils. However, under the dual control of the state executive and the party bureaucracy, they could develop little independent initiative.

With the new law on the territorial organs of state administration of 1990, the role of the *voivods* and the *voivodship* offices underwent major changes. Under the new regulations, the *voivod* is responsible for the tasks previously assigned to the people's councils and some of the territorial organs of state administration. *Voivods* are the representatives of the government in the provinces; they are appointed by the Council of Ministers, and have to follow governmental guide-lines. The *voivodship* offices serve as the main organs of central general field administration, although the new law does allow for the continued existence of special territorial offices that come under the direct control of central government. As regards the internal organization of the *voivodship* offices, the *voivod*'s discretion under the new regulations is considerable. Whereas previously the internal structure was determined by central government, thus ensuring organizational uniformity, decisions on administrative organization are now the responsibility of the head of the *voivodship* administration, a fact which encourages organizational diversity.

Importantly, the 1990 law on territorial administration also introduced so called *rejon* offices, which serve as territorial subdivisions of the *voivodship* administration. The heads of the *rejon* offices are appointed by the *voivod* and come under the *voivod*'s supervisory control. As yet, *rejons* do not constitute a separate tier of state administration, with tasks and responsibilities of their own. They may, however, serve as 'nuclei' for future district administrations, should they be reintroduced.

With the law on territorial administration, direct popular representation at the *voivodship* level, in the form of the people's councils, was abolished. The Local Government Act of March 1990 does, however, provide for *voivodship* assemblies, composed of delegates from all local councils in the respective areas. For the most part, their activities remain within the realm of local government. Thus, they are charged with monitoring the performance of local government institutions, the dissemination of information on communal activities, the mediation in disputes between local governments, or the convening of extra-ordinary sessions of communal councils. This is complemented by a number of functions directly related to the *voivodship* administration.

The strengthening of the position of the *voivod*, the concentration of administrative responsibilities and the *voivod*'s supervisory powers could have been expected to help to overcome the problem of co-ordinating state govern-ment action at the intermediate levels. But although the 1990 reforms would seem to have gone some way towards addressing the need for more co-ordinated administrative action, important issues were left untackled. This refers pre-dominantly to the still underdeveloped horizontal ties at the regional level, mirroring, to a certain extent, the lack of adequate departmental co-ordination at the level of the central administration.

Returning to likely future developments, it is first worth noting that there is a broad consensus on the need for further structural change, as the current territorial organization of state administration is widely seen as ineffective. In the accompanying reform discussion, two closely related issues dominate and also, to a certain extent, divide the proponents of reform. The first concerns the future of the *voivods*, who seem unlikely to survive in their current shape and form. Though there is widespread support for a reduction in the number of *voivodships*, it is yet unclear not only by how much their number should be reduced, but, more importantly, what their future constitutional and administra-tive role should be. The emphasis here is on the question of how functions of decentralized state administration might be joined with local government tasks.

The potential reintroduction of a general district level constitutes a second principal issue in the debate in territorial administrative organization in Poland. There is a politically influential current of opinion which argues that a change at the *voivodship* level must be accompanied by the simultaneous establishment of a new administrative tier, consisting of districts (*powiaty*). What all current proposals essentially amount to is the return to the situation as it existed before the 1970s' reforms, although, of course, district councils and administrations would function under radically changed political conditions. Few opponents of current plans question the desirability of creating an intermediate level of administration between enlarged *voivodships* and municipal governments.

Rather, the principal objections have to do with the timing of the proposed reforms and the ways in which the reconstitution of the districts is likely to be achieved. It is argued, therefore, that the inevitable upheaval associated with the redrawing of the *voivodship* map would be compounded by the simultaneous establishment of a new layer of public administration and necessarily result in administrative chaos. In addition to functional considerations, critics of a simultaneous *voivodship* and district reform point, of course, to financial problems. Eventually, a perhaps more fundamental, but related objection concerns the manner in which the return to district authorities is to be achieved. If the districts are primarily to be dynamic institutions of local government, rather than merely the lowest tier of state administration with some limited local government functions, then, it is argued, the initiative for a higher level of local administration needs to come from the localities; in other words, reform should not be imposed from above. According to this scenario, a two-tier system of local government would emerge gradually from below, as functional communal associations gradually develop into higher level authorities.

Turning to Hungary, the intermediate level of public administration has been subject to a torrent of reforms, which have profoundly altered its tasks, its structures and its functions within the intergovernmental system. As part of these reforms, the lower level of general administration, the districts, were completely abolished; the county level underwent fundamental change, being transformed, for the time being, from a key institution for the implementation of central policies and for the supervision and control over local governments to a marginal player in the intergovernmental system. Specialized state administrations, operating through their own offices at the regional and county level, have proliferated and a genuinely new institution for inter-agency co-ordination and the supervision of local government has been created in the form of the Commissioner of the Republic.

The most important structural reform was arguably the abolition of districts, representing the culmination of a process during which the centrality of the districts in the intergovernmental system had become increasingly undermined and their number steadily reduced. The idea behind the districts' abolition and the creation of a uniform system of town-regions and large villages was to establish the foundation of what was intended to become a much more simplified and streamlined two-tier territorial administration, a hope which remained, however, unfulfilled.

One of the main criticisms levelled at the 1983/84 reforms was that they left the county level untouched. Though the reforms in 1990/91 have left the county boundaries unaffected, their position in the inter-governmental system has now altered dramatically. Whereas under the socialist system, they were the main institutions of deconcentrated state administration, the counties have now lost their supervisory role over the localities as well as their crucial function in allocating state grants. They have also been deprived of their role as the main territorial agents of central government institutions. In sum, then, the counties have lost all their main functions in the intergovernmental system. Today, their tasks are defined in terms of a service provision function; the counties are charged with providing services which either cover the entire territory of the county or services where most users live outside the jurisdiction of the local authority where the service is actually situated.

The old county administrations in many respects mirrored the central ministerial administration, with specialized county office departments structured along those of the central ministerial bureaucracy. This facilitated both direct linkages between the technical ministries and county administration and inter-sectoral co-ordination at the county level. Concerning the first aspect, it must be noted that with the reform of the counties, many central institutions were suddenly left without adequate implementation organs at the intermediate level. This included not just many of the specialized technical ministries, but also the Ministries of Finance and the Interior. In response, Hungary had witnessed a proliferation of specialized deconcentrated administrations over the last two to three years. At present, there are no less than 19 different deconcentrated state organs represented at the county level, and 14 different deconcentrated units maintain offices that are responsible for several counties. It can be argued that the increase in the number of these units constitutes in part a return to administrative normality, as the county councils discharged some responsibilities which in the majority of developed Western administrative systems would be carried out by specialized administrations. Nonetheless, it is commonly agreed that the more or less unchecked establishment of deconcentrated units has led to 'excesses', which need to be rectified.

Perhaps the main problem arising from the uncontrolled increase in deconcentrated units is that of inter-administrative control at the medium level. Although too much can be made of the co-ordinating capacity of the county offices, formal concentration did at least allow for a certain degree of integration. With the local government reforms, this capacity was lost. That horizontal co-ordination is vital is commonly accepted by policy makers in Hungary. The main institution now charged with this task is the Commissioner of the Republic, a position newly created as part of the 1990 local government reforms. As mentioned, there are eight commissioners in Hungary, one located in the capital, the other seven in major provincial cities. In legal terms, they exercise legal supervision over local governments, first degree jurisdication, perform tasks of state admin-istration and co-ordinate the activities of state administrative organs in their region.

Their administrative functions have thus far remained very limited. Although the Commissioners' offices have taken over a significant part of the staff of the old counties, their tasks had in many cases been assumed by deconcentrated offices, and it has proved exceedingly difficult to stop and reverse this process. As regards their co-ordinating capacity, there is as yet little evidence on which an assessment could be based. It seems beyond dispute, however, that at present the Commissioners are ill-equipped to achieve substantial rather than merely formal co-ordination. It is proposed, therefore, to examine the system of deconcentrated units and to strengthen the Commissioners' powers to coordinate the activities of the centrally controlled administrative units.

With the adverse effects of a fragmented intermediate level widely acknowledged, the question arises why up to now no decisive action has been taken to try to remedy the situation. Here, two basic options can be identified: either to widen the tasks of the county councils or to strengthen the administrative powers of the Commissioners' offices. Both would amount to a partial re-integration of the deconcentrated units, tackling the roots of the problems of horizontal co-ordination. Under current political conditions, however, neither solution is likely to be adopted, since they conflict with the political interests of the government and the opposition respectively. In this connection, it is important to realize that the political majorities at the central level differ profoundly from those at county and local levels. In sum, then, the intermediate level of Hungarian public administration poses serious challenges, which need to be amongst the top priorities of any modernization programme. The institutional system existing under the old regime has been uprooted, resulting in institutional fragmentation and critical shortcomings in inter-administrative co-ordination and integration. Yet, the politicized nature of intergovernmental relations makes swift reforms unlikely, since, under current circumstances, they would almost inevitably result in the decline of power for either the governing parties or the liberal opposition. As a result, major reforms will almost certainly not be implemented before the next round of parliamentary and local elections.

Turning to the Czech and Slovak Republics, the most visible changes at the intermediate level certainly consisted in the abolition of the regional administrative tier. Until 1990, there existed seven regions in the Czech Republic and three regions in the Slovak Republic (the two capitals, Prague and Bratislava, formed separate units), with special regional offices of general administration. Their key function was to act as links between the central administration and the main pillar of field administration, the districts. In other words, the emphasis was on steering and controlling lower-tier administrative institutions, rather than on administrative activity. With the changes in the political environment, the regions' supervisory functions, which had been focused on political criteria, became obsolete. At the same time, local government was divorced from state administration, taking over some functions previously exercised by the regions. As a result, the regions had at least partially become superfluous.

With the abolition of the regions, the only tier of state administration remaining in the Czech lands has been the districts, of which there are 75. The district level also exists in Slovakia (38 districts). Here, an additional level of general state administration is to be found in the form of 'sub-districts', of which there are usually two to four per district. Such sub-districts do not exist in the Czech Republic, whose system of general state administration possesses, therefore, only one level, whilst the Slovak system is two-layered. In functional terms, though, a Czech equivalent is to be seen in the system of designated or commissioned local authorities, which carry out certain delegated functions on behalf of smaller, neighbouring local authorities.

In both Republics, special administrative units at the district level have proliferated since 1990. Their number has greatly increased since then, as new special offices have been set up in areas such as school administration or environmental protection. As a result, vertical links have been strengthened, but the resultant growing fragmentation of the intermediate level makes intersectoral co-ordination increasingly difficult.

Looking towards the future, it is very likely that the intermediate level will be profoundly affected by the break-up of the federation. This is particularly the case in the Czech Republic. Here, there have long been calls for the re-establishment of some forms of regional government for the historical lands of Bohemia, Moravia and Silesia, and there is ample evidence that this topic will be high on the political agenda during the coming months. Should these regions be reconstituted, it is most probably that they will take the form of self-governing entities, i.e., they would not be part of state administration, although this does not, of course, preclude state administrative functions being delegated to them. Such a process of political decentralization would, inevitably, affect the status of the general district authorities. The question here is whether they would remain subordinated to the republican ministerial departments or become executive organs of the new regions. One might also envisage a situation in which the districts would be transformed into a higher level of local government, with their own popularly elected assemblies, whilst retaining many of their present administrative tasks through central delegation. At the moment of writing (January 1993), these questions are still open, but it appears to be predictable that the intermediate level will remain a prime focus of administrative reorganization.

In sum, then, we still witness a great deal of instability and confusion concerning the appropriate intermediate level in Central and Eastern European countries. In none of the systems under close observation here, was it possible to provide a satisfactory solution so far. Whereas the old intermediate authorities have been discredited and, accordingly, decisively weakened, the new ways promoted have led to a proliferation of specialized, deconcentrated units of state administration. What emerges is an attempt to disentangle governmental levels, although there is a growing awareness that problems of co-ordination and control might be at the forefront of the administrative reform process over the years to come. Owing to the multitude of institutions with partly overlapping competences, it should not come as a surprise that tangible performance deficits tend to worry administrative reformers. Unusual models, such as the Commissioner of the Republic in Hungary, are therefore under close scrutiny, but there seems to be significant evidence that they do not really fit into the given administrative structure. Taking all that together, intergovernmental arrangements and the intermediate level seem to have developed into a serious bottleneck of the ongoing reform process. Since they serve as the main level of implementing administrative policies, intermediate institutions undoubtedly deserve special consideration over the coming months and years.

d) The local level: towards a pragmatic approach

In discussing the attempts to rebuild local government in Central and Eastern Europe, it is important to distinguish between the changes in the normative framework, on the one hand, and the actual practice of local government and administration, on the other. Although the reform legislation mostly adopted in 1990 is not free of internal contradictions and ambiguities and is, partially, in need of clarification and specification, it did not provide solid legal bases for a separation of state administration from local government and constituted an independent sphere of self-government. The concept of a 'unified' or 'homogenous' state authority (in which local authorities act as representatives of central state government and are unequivocally subordinated to central directives and control) was rejected and replaced by a dual system, in which state and local governments act within their own spheres of influence. In view of the recentness of the reforms and the still unstable constitutional, political, economic and social environments in which they have to be implemented, it should not come as a surprise that the reality of local government partly lags behind this normative ideal; looking at the legal framework alone would, therefore, provide an incomplete and, in fact, distorted view of the state of local government. However, despite the shortcomings of local government legislation and quite evident practical problems in implementing the new legal provisions, it would appear that in both legal and political terms the most far-reaching departure in public administration from the Communist past has thus far taken place at the local level.

Looking at Poland, the local level consists, at present, of about 2,400 units, including 1,547 rural communities (*gminy*), 247 towns (*miasta*), 572 'town-communes' (*miasta-gminy*) and the union of borough communes, comprising the seven boroughs of the capital Warsaw. The basis for their current activities were laid in 1990, with the adoption of a series of legal acts which, considered in combination, amounted to a comprehensive redefinition of the role of the local level in the country's governmental and administrative structures.

Evaluating those, it should first be noted that the tasks of local authorities did not change dramatically through the reform acts. In the main, the local councils and authorities have assumed the functions of the former local 'national councils', notably in such areas as the maintenance of roads, bridges and traffic control; planning and territorial development; public utilities; waste collection, disposal and sewerage; public transport; local social services; municipal housing; education and the arts; the management of public parks, markets, cemeteries and buildings; certain health services; the enforcement of local law and order; or fire stations. In addition, local authorities now perform some functions that have been passed down from the now defunct *voivodship* councils to local councils and, more importantly, delegated tasks which they fulfil on behalf of the state. These include, *inter alia*, responsibilities in the fields of registration, civil defence and child care. At the same time, some important tasks have been moved upwards, i.e. from local administration to the state territorial administration, for example: property registration; certain aspects of environmental protection; building inspection; or car registration and the granting of licences.

The break with the Communist tradition of unified state power was then not primarily achieved through a decentralization of tasks to the local level; rather, it is the degree of autonomy and discretion which local governments now enjoy in performing public functions which distinguishes the present system. The twofold subordination of local government under the Communist Party bureaucracy and the directives of central government have been broken. The exercise of supervisory powers was shifted from the Minister of the Interior to the Chairman of the Council of Ministers (i.e. the Prime Minister), the *voivods* and, as far as financial matters are concerned, the regional offices of the Supreme Control Chamber.

Whether local authorities are, in fact, able to use their enhanced powers and discretion does, of course, depend crucially on the state of local finance. For the most part, the current regulations build here on the new system introduced in 1991. Essentially, one can at present distinguish between six categories of local income: a local share of national income tax; local taxes where only ceilings are stipulated by central government; taxes fixed by central government; fees and charges; income from local property and enterprise; and central grants (with a fiscal equalization component).

Local government and administration in Poland have, therefore, gone through major upheavals during the past two years. The territorial organization of local governance has remained largely unchanged; but there have been far reaching functional, political-administrative and financial reforms which have begun to transform the role of the local level profoundly. As in other spheres of public sector reform, however, implementation is lagging behind legislation; in other words, a revised legal framework for local governance has been established, but, in many respects, the reality of local government has still to catch up with the legal changes.

In the former Czechoslovakia, the principal legal basis for a fundamental reform of local government was laid through a federal constitutional law in 1990. It abolished the previous system of (local) national councils and recognized local authorities as the basic units of local government. This federal constitutional act served as a framework law, i.e. more detailed regulations were left to the republican legislatures. In September 1990, both National Councils adopted laws on the municipalities and laws on municipal elections defining, *inter alia*, mandatory, discretionary and delegated local powers, the role of municipal councils, boards, the mayor, the municipal offices, certain aspects of local finance, and rules governing local elections.

Focusing on the situation in the Czech Republic, decentralization, deregulation and de-étatisation have been identified as the main principles behind local government reform. This has implied the constitution of local authorities as independent legal subjects; the transfer of substantial powers from the former regions and the districts to local authorities; the establishment of a broad sphere of discretionary local powers; and the restrictions of state government control over local activities to matters of legality (in the case of mandatory and discretionary tasks). The new system of local government became fully operational with the elections to the local councils on 24 November 1990.

In Hungary, local government reform has probably been the most controversially discussed and most intensively studied element of the transition period. Through the constitutional amendments regarding local government of 1989, the Act on Local Government of 1990 and several other pieces of legislation adopted subsequently, the local level was radically transformed. The basic features followed those described above; as a result of the dissolution of the joint councils, the number of local authorities doubled from 1,542 in March 1989 to 3,089 in 1991.

Whilst local government reform legislation has, undoubtedly, greatly strengthened the role of the local government level and succeeded in establishing a sphere of genuinely autonomous government, many argue that the reforms have shown too little an appreciation of the need for effective intergovernmental co-ordination and co-operation and integrated policy making. Such criticisms appear at least partly justified. Thus, county councils have completely lost their supervisory role over municipal councils. The Commissioners of the Republic are supposed to act as the decisive link between central government and the local level, but they are essentially restricted to controlling the legality of local actions, at least in as far as local government tasks are concerned. As regards delegated tasks, the Commissioners' supervisory competences are more extensive, but, crucially they do not include financial matters. The absence of a general purpose intermediate level of state administration and the institutionally weak position of the Commissioner mean that intergovernmental relations are institutionally underdeveloped and highly sectoralized.

Problems of sectoralization are compounded by the fragmented nature of the local government map. Weak intermediate institutions mean that central bodies are increasingly expected to build up direct links with local governments, a task made more difficult by the great number of local units and, especially in the case of many very small localities, the lack of professional capacity. Conversely, local governments cannot rely on the county councils to represent their interests at the central government level, but need to find alternative channels of access. The Commissioner of the Republic seems ill-positioned for this role. As a result, the sectoralized and fragmented nature of intergovernmental relations is further perpetuated.

However, the fragmentation of the local government level does not only adversely affect intergovernmental co-ordination and co-operation, it also affects local government's own administrative capabilities. Difficulties resulting from increased tasks, inexperience with the fundamentally altered political, legal and financial framework, and a lack of central guidance are magnified by the extreme deconcentration of governmental and administrative resources at the local level. One common objection to local government reform is that it has resulted in an atomized local tier incapable of performing its new functions efficiently and effectively. There can, indeed, be little doubt that many of the very small localities, with few or no professional staff and very limited financial resources, face great difficulties in carrying out their mandatory tasks and cannot take advantage of the considerable scope for local government action which the new legal framework affords. In such circumstances local government autonomy has to remain a legal fiction.

This line of argument can be carried too far, though. Whilst the number of local governments has doubled, many small municipalities have decided to join local offices. Thus, there may be, for example, two local councils and two mayors, but only one local council office. The government provides financial incentives for such arrangements, by paying part of the salary of local notaries, i.e. professional heads of local council offices. Through such arrangements, the negative effects of fragmentation are reduced, but few doubt the necessity of at least a modest territorial reform.

Under the constitution, local government legislation requires a two-thirds majority in Parliament. In view of this fact and given the politicized nature of intergovernmental relations, further major reforms of the local government system are unlikely. Instead, the attention of administrative reformers is focused on gradual, small-scale adjustments, which would leave the major structures of the system more or less intact, but optimize the allocation of tasks and improve intergovernmental co-ordination. Thus, consideration is currently being given to the transfer of certain municipal tasks to the counties; to an increase in the supervisory powers of the Commissioners; and towards encouraging the merger of localities. For the most part, such proposals aim not so much at changes in local government itself, but to make improvements at the intermediate level, which would enable towns and villages to perform their functions more effectively. It remains to be seen what progress can be achieved in this respect, but major advances are unlikely before the next parliamentary election in 1994.

In sum, it then seems that the reformers might have placed too high hopes in local government reform. The very understandable emphasis on what one could call a bottom-up approach led to significant shortcomings: the capacities of local governments were partly overestimated; conversely, there has been a significant underestimation of the need for central steering and control; eventually, the over-emphasized principle of local autonomy led to significant problems of intergovernmental co-ordination and co-operation. As a result, there are growing calls for a partial 'reform of the reform', seeking to adopt a more pragmatic approach towards local government.

3 External controls over public administration

Moving on from organizational reforms to the factual workings of administrative authorities, most of the socialist countries did not possess an institutionally fully developed and effective system of independent external controls over administrative actions. The principle of the unity of state power and the subordination of state administration under the control of the Communist Party were incompatible with the existence of autonomous control institutions operating outside the influence of state and party. The legality of administrative action was officially viewed as an important principle of public administration, but where the imperatives of the ruling party conflicted with legal regulations, the former invariably predominated. Likewise, the efficient and effective use of administrative resources was recognized as an important aim, but an independent auditing system did not exist. Academic researchers acknowledged this lack of external controls already at an early stage, noting that the forms of institutionalized supervision are either of an expressly political nature or they function within the organizational system of public administration. As a consequence, the creation of external controls of legality and economy have been an important, though unspectacular and sometimes overlooked element in the process of administrative transformation and accompanying modernization.

Comparing Poland, Hungary and the former Czechoslovakia, one has to conclude that external controls are still very much in their infant stages in the Czech and Slovak Republics. Before November 1989, no federal or republican Constitutional Court existed; a specialized administrative judiciary was unknown as was the institution of an independent audit office; in Czechoslovakia's exceptionally repressive political climate, the creation of an institution comparable to the Polish Commissioner for Civil Rights Protection was virtually unthinkable. It is only since 1990 that the first legislative steps towards the creation of external control mechanisms have been taken, and delays in the implementation of reform legislation have meant that the controls created are only just beginning to become effective.

In the Hungarian case, the most important change has undoubtedly been the establishment of an independent Constitutional Court, which began to work at the beginning of 1990. The Court's competences are widely defined: it can examine the constitutionality of all pieces of parliamentary legislation as well as secondary legal regulations, and, in certain cases, individual decisions by governmental and administrative institutions. Importantly, the Court can exercise both different forms of *ex-post* concrete control and an abstract control of norms. The Court can annul a piece of legislation, a secondary legal act or a governmental or administrative decision, where it finds that it violates the constitution. As regards both the protection of individual citizens and the resolution of conflicts between constitutional organs and other governmental institutions, the proof of the Court's independence and effectiveness as a guardian is its readiness to take decisions regardless of whether they meet with the approval of those in power. In this respect, the Court's record over the last three years is impressive.

But although constitutional review undoubtedly represents a key element in administrative control, the majority of disputes do not involve constitutional issues. Therefore, whilst the Constitutional Court plays a central role in adjudicating inter-administrative disagreements and in protecting the individual citizen, it is the court system more generally, and in particular administrative jurisdiction, where most cases will be dealt with. In this respect, it should be noted that until 1991 individuals could challenge administrative decisions in court only in a small number of narrowly defined cases. This situation has changed fundamentally with the adoption of a law by the National Assembly in June 1991. It provides for a major extension of judicial control over administrative decisions. As far as court organization is concerned, a separate administrative court system has not (yet) been created. However, there are now separate chambers within the general civil law courts specializing in administrative matters. Given that the changes in arrangements for the judicial review of administrative decisions are still very recent, it is not yet possible to pass judgement on the effectiveness of the regulations and institutions; but it ought to be acknowledged that the basic legal and institutional prerequisites have been put in place to achieve a substantial improvement in protecting citizens' rights against unlawful or arbitrary administrative acts.

Turning from judicial administrative review to external financial–economic supervision, the system of public auditing in Hungary has been profoundly transformed through the establishment of a State Audit Office, which began its operations in January 1990. Although there is a good deal of continuity as regards the Office's staff, the institution represents a genuinely new organization. The respective legislation establishes the State Audit Office as the financial-economic control organ of Parliament, subject only to the law and the Assembly. The Office is the supreme control organ of the state.

Unlike most other Central and Eastern European countries, Poland already possesses a developed set of institutions for external administrative control. The present system consists of four main pillars: the Constitutional Court, the Administrative Court, the Commissioner for Civil Rights Protection (often referred to as ombudsman) – all of which are primarily concerned with the legality of administrative activity – and the Supreme Control Chamber (NIK), whose main functions are those of an audit office. All four institutions were in place before the political changes of 1989; although notably the courts had to function within an overall framework in which political imperatives dominated, their contribution to the development of an effective system of rule of law and the protection of citizens' rights should not be under-estimated. Despite attempts at political interference and intervention, these institutions – and most evidently the highly popular Commissioner for Civil Rights Protection – performed important 'preventive and corrective' functions and constituted more than just a facade for the untrammelled exercise of state power. As a result, there is little pressure today for structural changes in the existing system of administrative control; rather, the focus is on a gradual strengthening of control powers and on ensuring their effective use.

The legal foundations of the Polish Constitutional Court were laid through an amendment to the constitution passed in March 1982, which provided for the establishment of a Constitutional Court, and a subsequent law of April 1985, detailing its competences and procedural rules. The Court's competences were formulated in such a way that the principle of unified state power remained intact. This meant that the Court was not empowered to nullify laws adopted by the *Sejm*; rather, in cases where the Court declares a law as unconstitutional, its decision has to go before the *Sejm*, which can revoke the law, change the relevant constitutional provision, or dismiss the Court's decision (for this a two-thirds majority is required). However, the Court's decision is final in respect to all legal acts pursuant to laws adopted by the *Sejm*, including orders and instructions issued by the Council of Ministers, individual ministers and other central government institutions. A significant extension of the Constitutional Court's responsibilities resulted from the far-reaching constitutional changes of April 1989, which introduced, *inter alia*, the post of the President. Where hitherto the Constitutional Court had only been entitled to rule on existing laws, the President now has a right to seek a decision on the constitutionality of legislation adopted by the *Sejm* before signing. Moreover, the Court now has a right of universally binding legal interpretation.

In contrast to the Constitutional Court, the Polish Administrative Court represents a specialized legal institution for the solution of conflicts between administrative organs and, more importantly, citizens and public administration. In its main features, the present Administrative Court system was put in place at the beginning of the 1980s. The accompanying legislation provided for the creation of a single Administrative Court, with headquarters in Warsaw and six regional offices. The matters which could come before the Court were initially defined by positive enumeration; starting from a relatively restricted list, new subject matters were steadily added. The enumerating principle was, therefore, formally given up and replaced by a general clause. Since 1980, the number of cases to come before the Administrative Court has risen continuously; in 1990 there were more than 13,000 cases. Although the Administrative Court had, just like the Constitutional Court, to operate under political conditions in which the independence of the judiciary could, at best, only be a partial one during the first years of its existence, it is generally agreed that the Court has contributed very significantly to the protection of citizens rights and the development of a legal system based on the rule of law.

Since the beginning of 1988, the work of the Administrative Court has been complemented by the activities of the Commissioner for Civil Rights Protection. The ombudsman (or rather ombudswoman, as in the case of Ewa Letowska) is an independent organ of the state; though elected by Parliament and ultimately responsible to it, the ombudsman/woman acts autonomously. Compared to similar institutions in Western countries, the Polish Commissioner enjoys an exceptionally wide range of competences. Thus, the ombudsman has the right to examine whether the actions (or the failure to act) of organs, organizations and institutions violate civil rights and liberties or, and this is unusual, contradict 'the principles of social life' and social justice. Accordingly, the Commissioner is authorized to control not only administrative organs (including the military), but also social organizations to which public tasks have been delegated; this control is not restricted to legality, but extends to ethical and moral concerns.

To secure effective redress, a number of avenues are open to the Commissioner. He or she can appeal directly to the administrative organ or organization suspected of having violated civil rights liberties, social justice or 'the principles of social life'; turn to their superior authorities to demand action; instigate civil action or become a party to such a civil action; request the institution of proceedings under penal, disciplinary or administrative law; ask that a legal sentence be quashed; propose legal changes; and, importantly, request that the Constitutional Court decides on the constitutionality of a particular law or the compatibility of second order legal acts with laws of the first order.

All three institutions have begun their activity under politically unfavourable conditions; nonetheless, they have been able to gain widespread recognition and respect. By contrast, the Supreme Control Chamber was quite closely identified with the Communist regime and has found it difficult to adjust to the changed political circumstances. The Chamber is today in a state of adjustment, as the whole public sector is undergoing far-reaching changes, requiring new approaches in public auditing.

4 Personnel: rebuilding the public service

Any lasting progress in structural and procedural administrative reform in Central and Eastern Europe is ultimately dependent on a far-reaching transformation of the public service system. Both the legal framework inherited from the previous regimes and the actual practices in personnel policy are, for the most part, incompatible with the needs and requirements of a public service operating in a profoundly changed environment. The difficulties facing personnel policies are not just shortages in qualified staff, salary scales that offer few performance incentives, a mismatch between existing and required skills in the public service, and a general feeling of demoralization in a disoriented public service. More fundamentally, it is necessary to re-establish or re-constitute a distinct public service identity.

In most socialist countries, the legal and practical distinction between public service employment or employment in mass organizations, the party apparatus, and the dominant state-owned sector of the economy was, at best, slight. Labour relations tended to be regulated uniformly in a single Labour Code, applicable to the entire work-force, with merely a minimum of special regulations for employment in state administration. In other words, the legal framework of the public service was rudimentary. This had, of course, important practical implications: the public service, at least in its middle and lower ranks, did not tend to be perceived as a strictly separated sphere of employment and, accordingly, the movement of personnel between state administration and other bureaucratic organizations was by no means unusual.

Contrary to what is sometimes assumed, the main quantitative problem in rebuilding the public service does not lie in the reduction of the number of employees working in core state and local administrations. In Poland, for example, the number of administrative personnel totalled in 1990 approximately 150,000, which puts Poland towards the bottom of the international league table as regards the number of administrative personnel in relation to the size of the national population. Of these, roughly half worked for organs of state administration (46,000 for central organs; 34,000 for specialized territorial administrations;

and some 29,000 in the *voivodship* and *rejon* offices); the other half worked in the now legally separated local government sector. As the tasks facing public administration change, a certain share of these posts will become redundant; but more recent, though less differentiated figures show that such losses have been more than compensated for by gains in other branches of public administration. As a result, the overall number of employees in public administration rose to around 188,000 by the end of 1991, an increase of roughly 16 per cent as compared to 1990. It should be noted that this increase follows a prolonged period of contraction; between 1986 and 1990, administrative personnel was reduced by about 11 per cent.

Rather than in core public administration, or the public service proper, the real quantitative challenge is found in what used to be called the 'socialized sector' of the economy, including (in addition to organs of state and local government) social and political organizations, trade unions, and, most import- antly, public sector enterprises. The 'dismantling of bureaucratic socialism' means, then, that many of the social and political satellite organizations which used to surround the core of state and party administration have become obsolete; their abolition will inevitably be accompanied by job losses. Cut-backs in direct and indirect state subsidies for enterprises in the 'socialized sector' force the management to look for productivity increases and to address the wide- spread problem of overmanning. Similarly, commercialization and privatization can be expected to result in further job losses – at least in the short and medium term – with private owners seeking to reduce artificially high staffing levels.

What emerges, then, is a differentiated picture. Far from contracting, state and local public administration are actually expanding in terms of the number of employees. From the currently available data, it is not possible to identify which levels of public administration have been mainly responsible for the notable rise in administrative employment since the end of 1990; but it seems safe to assume that the bulk of it is made up by growth in local government employment. Expansion in core public administration stands in stark contrast, though, to the rapid decline in the socialized sector of the economy; here, jobs are shed at a very high rate indeed, which is likely to accelerate further.

By-passing the Czech and Slovak Republics, because of the very unusual consequences following the break-up of the federation, a look at the Hungarian example shows a situation comparable to that in Poland, although there has been considerable progress due to the adoption of two substantial laws on the legal status of public servants and public sector employees respectively. How- ever, whereas these laws undoubtedly represent a major advance on the previous situation, they can only represent a first step in the direction of a comprehensive legal framework for public service.

With a total of approximately only 49,000 employees in civil public admin- istration (including central, intermediate, and local levels) in 1990, it would, as in Poland, be misleading to see the core administrative apparatus in Hungary as generally overstaffed. Rather, the main quantitative issue facing the Hungarian public service is the question of what to do with those employees whose services have become redundant as part of the old administrative apparatus is dismantled. At the central level this has affected, for example, employees who worked in now defunct central national offices such as the National Planning Office, the Office of Price Control and the State Office of Church Affairs. At the intermediate level of public administration, the most drastic scaling down certainly affected the county offices, while at the local level, with its tasks increased as part of the reforms mentioned, there was little need to shed staff. In relation to employment in public administration as a whole, however, the number of those directly affected by the dissolution of administrative institutions and/or radical restructuring and cutbacks has been small. In most cases, it has been possible to transfer staff to other existing administrative institutions or to new bodies that have been created as part of the reform process.

A very different picture emerges, again, if attention is focused on those bureaucratic apparatuses that were closely connected with state administration and, even more critically, the state-owned sector of the economy. The former party bureaucracy has been completely dismantled, the social mass organizations have either ceased to exist or have been reduced to shadows of their former selves. The job losses in both cases are eclipsed, however, by the jobs lost in the public enterprise sector. Under Communist rule, Hungary's publicly owned enterprises enjoyed a greater degree of freedom and financial autonomy than state sector firms in other Central and Eastern European countries; direct political interference in the running of firms and, consequently, pressure to keep employment at artificially high levels were less marked than in other states. Nonetheless, in Hungary, too, cuts in subsidies to public enterprises and the effects of recession have combined to squeeze public enterprise employment, and growth in private sector employment has failed to keep up with these job losses. As a result, since 1990 unemployment has been growing extremely fast.

But focusing on public administration, it is, then, in all three countries more qualitative issues rather than the need for dramatic cuts in employment that pose the most serious challenges to personnel policy. There are a number of issues demanding urgent and sustained attention. They arise in virtually all main areas of personnel policy, including personnel recruitment, personnel utilization, personnel motivation, staff representation and participation, and personnel training and qualifications.

As regards personnel recruitment, the attraction and selection of staff to state and local administrations are, at present, open to much criticism. There are no concerted efforts to attract qualified candidates to a career in the public service. As a result, personnel selection is largely supply-led. The process is less about finding the right candidate for a particular post (which is typically not clearly defined), than about finding the most suitable jobs for those willing to work in the public service, despite comparatively low pay and social prestige. To simplify, the public service does not hire the staff it needs, but the staff it can get. Selection is further hampered by favouritism (often based on party-political allegiance) and nepotism. Although formal entrance requirements for the public service exist, they are often ignored in practice.

The lack of job descriptions and requirement profiles also hampers functional personnel utilization policies. The latter are still hardly developed. The allocation of staff, promotion, and staff transfer or secondment owes, at the moment, more to chance than to a systematic evaluation of needs and requirements. Government departments and other central organs act largely independently of each other, as there is no institutional focus for considering the needs of state administration as a whole. A career public service still needs to be created, and only then is it possible to develop transparent promotion criteria. Staff transfer between central organs rarely takes place, and there is no systematic interchange between central organs and their territorial administrations. Secondments are still largely unknown.

Inadequate personnel utilization compounds the task of motivation. Here both material and immaterial incentives are, at present, insufficient to secure an adequate degree of commitment amongst the majority of public employees. As regards material factors, low wages in the public as opposed to the private sector, play a key role. Rises in public sector pay fail to keep up with inflation, with the consequent fall in public employees' living standards. As a result, many of the most enterprising administrators leave the public service, thereby further compounding performance problems. Other material incentives, such as regulations on pensions, hours of work, or annual leave do not provide advantages over the private sector that are substantial enough to compensate for the short-fall in basic remuneration; nor does a higher degree of job security in the public service act as a strong inducement, at least not as far as highly qualified staff with employment opportunities in the private sector are concerned. Regarding non-material incentives, the uncertainty both about the future role of the public sector as a whole and individual branches and tiers of public administration make it almost impossible to specify any kind of organizational 'mission' which might guide and mobilize public sector employees. Disorientation and confusion about the future of the public sector translate into a motivational crisis amongst staff.

The last major qualitative issue to be mentioned here concerns the representation and participation of administrative staff in decision making on matters affecting their interests and working conditions. In legal terms, officially recognized trade unions tended to possess extensive rights of consultation, co-decision making and collective bargaining in the Communist states of Central and Eastern Europe. In practice, however, their activities were closely controlled by the state and the party apparatus, and the possibility of a fundamental conflict of interests was negated. Although there is, of course, no single model for the institutionalization of employee representation and participation in market-oriented democratic systems, the basic aims and methods of participation should be taken into account. Conflict resolution and collective negotiation and bargaining are clearly only one element of those; the protection of employees' individual rights and the structured channelling of their views andconcerns into decision making on organizational development are of equal significance.

Comparing the Central and Eastern European countries, Hungary seems to be in a slightly more favourable position than some of its neighbours. The study of public administration was less marginalized here and allowed for the development of a small but internationally oriented community of administrative scientists. Arguably, this has been one of the main reasons why the implications of political and economic reforms for the structures and procedures of governance were recognized earlier than in some other countries and why the pivotal role of a reconstituted public service was swiftly acknowledged. Of course, identification of a problem is not equal to its solution; nonetheless, the availability of national expertise and its early integration into the reform effort have yielded some positive results. But personnel policy and management has to respond to a multitude of interlinked challenges. It needs to do so under conditions of resource scarcity and a still turbulent political, legal and economic environment. In view of these circumstances, the adoption of a completely revised Labour Code and laws on the legal status of public servants and public employees in spring 1992 represents an undeniable achievement. However, the legal framework now in place requires completion and modification and, above all, forceful implementation if it is to make a significant contribution to solving the problems facing personnel policy and management. Moreover, the functionality of some of the new regulations is questionable. On the other hand, an encouraging start has been made, and in its main directions, the new legal framework which has been adopted would seem to provide a solid foundation for the further development of personnel policy and management.

III FROM TRANSFORMATION TO MODERNIZATION

To conclude, it is, first of all, worthwhile recalling that the dynamics of administrative transformation are indeed intimately linked to changes in the legal, political, social and economic environments in which public institutions operate. Although public administration is both the object of reform and, almost invariably, its chief agent, the reform process is – as commented upon in the introduction – an interactive one.

Looking, therefore, at the different environments of public administration again, the break with the Communist past has thus far been most obvious in the political-institutional framework. Since autumn 1989, a largely competitive multi-party system has evolved, and a number of elections have been held for the presidency, the chambers of national Parliament, and regional and local government. As a result, there has been a far-reaching change of personnel in the major positions of executive leadership. However, whilst the old order has been broken, the new political framework is, despite the mentioned positive signs, still in the process of evolving. The party system, for example, remains often extremely fragmented. The formation of a government enjoying a workable parliamentary majority, or at least tacit support, has sometimes proved exceptionally difficult. Perhaps even more importantly, the popularly elected presidents, on the one hand, and the national assemblies, on the other, appear occasionally in fundamental disagreement about their respective roles, resulting in a situation of political deadlock and potential paralysis of the policy-making system.

In the context of the present situation, three observations are particularly noteworthy about changes in the political framework. First, the past three years have been characterized by a high turnover of political leadership. There have, in the case of Poland, for example, been five different Prime Ministers, with little continuity in government personnel and a rapid succession of ministers in key portfolios. This instability in government and executive leadership has been accompanied for some time by a lack of clear policy orientation. The second point worth emphasizing is directly related to this. Even where clear-cut government policies had time to develop, support in Parliament was often difficult to obtain. In the event of a ruling coalition, not commanding a reliable majority, for example, the withholding of parliamentary approval for key government proposals is almost commonplace. Third, the power struggle between presidents, governments and Parliaments is partly unresolved. Attempts to strengthen presidential powers *vis-à-vis* governments and Parliaments have repeatedly led to long and agonizing political confrontations.

The picture that emerges, then, is still one of transition and volatility: the old political framework has irrevocably broken down, but the new framework has yet to be consolidated. In particular, key aspects of the triangular relationship between president, government and Parliament remains contentious. It is unlikely that this will change until their respective powers and privileges are authoritatively redefined in new constitutional agreements. However, a decisive breakthrough in the constitutional debate has not yet been achieved. Contrary to the high hopes in 1989, when many expected a swift new constitutional settlement, the preparation and adoption of completely new constitutions have not yet progressed significantly. As time has passed, the process of constitutionalization has, perhaps inevitably, become more and more subject to the same political pressures affecting other areas of reform. No longer is there a common spirit of opposition against a hostile regime which could hold the contending forces together.

It cannot be denied that the failure to resolve fundamental constitutional questions introduced a critical element of fluidity into the reform process at large. However, it should also be recognized that, as Jon Elster has pointed out, 'for countries undergoing rapid social and economic change, commitment to standing rules may not be desirable. The future of many Eastern European countries may prove to be a succession of emergencies, in which constitutional self-binding might be disastrous'. It would, therefore, make more sense to talk of an open rather than an unstable constitutional situation at the present time. Yet, as Elster also notes, the potentially tragic element is that the future without a constitution to regulate expectations and behaviour might be equally bleak.

Moving on to economic transformation, it is worth noting that even under Communist rule, the economies were peppered with some elements of a market-based system. Yet this does not imply that for the introduction of a market economy an evolutionary approach could have been sufficient. Rejecting gradualism and a piecemeal approach, most governments embarked, therefore, often under the guidance of the IMF, on a radical economic reform programme whose key elements included stabilization, liberalization, the creation of market institutions and privatization. With modifications, these programmes still provide the basis for ongoing reform policies. Although much academic interest has focused on the privatization element in the economic transformation process, it is important to realize the multidimensional character of systematic change. It includes macroeconomic stabilization and control, price and market reforms, private sector development and, importantly, indeed a redefinition of the role of the state. So there can be no simple yardstick, such as the number of privatized firms, by which the overall progress of economic transformation can be assessed.

Another aspect is worth mentioning in discussing economic transformation. Compared with changes in the political framework and constitutional provisions, it is still difficult to gain a precise idea of where the reform process actually stands. As a result, there is a temptation to overestimate the real economic change that has already taken place. More critically, whilst it is comparatively easy to ascertain what reform measures have been formally adopted and legislated for, the state of implementation is difficult to judge. Increasingly, informed observers are suggesting that economic transformation might take much longer than many had initially expected. World Bank and OECD reports, therefore, emphasized in the meantime a partial fall in output in some of the countries mentioned, the fact that the prospects of catching up with developed market economies are now discussed in terms of decades rather than years, and the potential political implications of rising unemployment, combined with the failure to generate a visible improvement in overall economic conditions. Indeed, should current growth scenarios not offer more than the prospect of the present recession giving way to 'a recovery *sometime* during the 1990s', the legitimacy of the present political leadership and, perhaps, the democratization process as a whole, will be put to a severe test for several years to come.

The last 'environmental' category refers to processes of societal dislocation. Whilst economic change is on its way, some of its negative repercussions have become increasingly obvious and visible. These include not only rising unemployment, a fall in living standards and increasing absolute poverty, but also the emergence of new types of broader-scale and longer-lasting social disparities. At the same time, the quite comprehensive social safety and benefit provisions which used to take care of basic life necessities are under threat. The squeeze on public resources has led to attempts at cutting back social expenditure; social benefits in the public sector are disappearing as many enterprises are transferred to private ownership; other provisions are considered incompatible with a market economy. In short, there is a danger that the social safety network will disintegrate at the moment when it is most needed. However, it is not just economic circumstances which are changing: almost no sphere of life is unaffected by the societal transformation process. As a consequence, individuals are faced with the task of adjusting to an environment which is changing rapidly and fundamentally. Similarly, the social environment of public administration is characterized by signs of dislocation and disorientation at the individual level and many established norms and values are being challenged. Moreover, profound qualitative change in the triangular relationship between the state, society and individuals is certainly not concluded yet. What we may witness in the future is the re-emergence of a civil society, associated with processes of de-étatisation, the de-politicization of social and private life, and the redefinition and expansion of the private against the social and political.

What kind of further pressure for adjustment results from those developments? Two points need emphasizing at the outset. First, it is obvious that the contextual conditions under which the public sector operates are subject to a degree of change which has made large-scale administrative adjustments inevitable. Although bureaucratic organizations are, of course, capable of absorbing considerable external 'shocks' without having to resort to fundamental institutional reforms, the unprecedented character of the Central and East European transformation processes calls into question some of the most basic principles on which the administrative apparatus has been built. The public sector is, therefore, under tremendous pressure to adapt. Secondly, however, adjustment is still made exceptionally difficult by the continuing volatility of the contextual conditions. The elements of the framework in which the public sector operates are frequently subject to abrupt changes whose direction is often unpredictable. Consequently, it is difficult to formulate a realistic administrative policy. The latter requires dependable information about the environment, so that effective implementation strategies can be formulated. Where such information is lacking, adequate adjustment policies are, of course, difficult to devise. Given these conditions, political priorities and preferences can alter very quickly – dependable information about the future resources for public administration is often unavailable and any projections must be taken with great caution. Moreover, reform attempts require an increasingly high degree of horizontal and vertical co-ordination. However, firm decisions on the future allocation of powers, responsibilities and finances between the different levels of governments have partly not yet been reached. In short, administrative modernization is urgent and underway, but it can often be no more than tentative and provisional as long as crucial external parameters remain undetermined.

It follows that reformers in Central and Eastern Europe are being confronted with an unusually difficult task: reform efforts should clearly aim at introducing stability, dependability and continuity into the administrative system. Yet, at the same time, the structures and procedures established must not hamper later revisions and modifications, which are bound to be required as the environment continues to be transformed. Thus, stability needs to be combined with flexibility, dependability with openness, continuity with adaptability. Under such conditions, one needs to be careful in prescribing specific institutional arrangements. As our findings have shown, it is, however, possible and, perhaps, useful to outline the general direction which reform efforts need to take, if the public sector is to make a positive contribution to the intertwined processes of political, economic and societal change.

Putting it this way, the transition from socialist one-party rule to democratic pluralism has a number of immediate consequences for the structures and procedures of administrative activity. As regards organizational questions, the implications of a break with the principle of 'democratic centralism' deserve particular attention. 'Democratic centralism' had at least two dimensions: vertically, much emphasis was placed on a hierarchical administrative structure in which lower-tier units enjoyed limited discretion and were subject to comprehensive control by central institutions, whereas the horizontal organi-zation of state power was characterized by a lack of an effective separation of powers. There were, of course, separate legislative, executive and judicial institutions. The rule-making powers of the executive were, however, extremely extensive, so that, in effect, legislative and executive functions were merged. The institutional consequences of the renunciation of the principle of 'democratic centralism' are, therefore, far-reaching. They include not only the obvious need to separate party bureaucracy from public administration, but also to establish clear institutional boundaries between legislative and executive institutions and to combine this with new forms of democratic accountability and control; to lessen controls over sub-central administrative units and to create a sphere of local government; and to provide effective legal controls over administrative activities.

Therefore, if the implications of democratization point to the need for structural and procedural reforms, the processes of privatization and market-ization focus attention on adjustments in administrative tasks and the modes of administrative action. Public administration is losing some of its former tasks as the state is partly withdrawing from the economy by means of liberalization, deregulation and privatization. At the same time, however, there is an urgent need to create administrative capacities which can support economic transforma-tion and development. Consequently, different tasks call for different instruments of intervention. Administrative commands and restrictions, as well as require-ments to seek administrative permission for private actions, will remain important instruments of public activity. In addition, however, executive policies will need to rely increasingly on the provision of incentives and services, persuasion and public-private cooperation. This implies that the administration is likely to make increased use of instruments such as rewards, incentives, financial transfers, and information and advice.

In the longer term, the perception of public administration and its role in society will, perhaps, be most decisively reshaped by the process of de-étatisation. The partial withdrawal of the state from civil society and the acceptance of a domain of private life protected and, to a certain extent, immune from political interference implies that public administration will have to assume a much less extended and far-reaching role than under the previous regimes. This means that non-public forms of service delivery will play an increasingly central role. In this connection, one should not just think in terms of the replacement of the state by the market, although privatization and marketization at present dominate the political agenda. What might emerge in the longer term is a rigorous 'third sector' between state and market, comprising a wide variety of institutions of societal self-organization and self-administration. The redrawing of the boundaries between the state, the social and the private promises to be accompanied by a positive recognition of the potential contribution of associational self-government.

In sum, our analysis of crucial elements of the ongoing process of transforming public administration in the countries of Central and Eastern Europe has suggested that for the first three years of the transition period a negation of the legacy of 'democratic centralism' provided the chief impetus for reform. More recently, though, there are growing signs that functional considerations, focusing on administrative performance and the implementation of the various policies adopted are gaining ground. This concerns, as mentioned at the outset, the need to secure what has already been achieved, to complete the ongoing reform processes, and to pursue selective corrections where initial transformation policies resulted in disfunctional arrangements. The emphasis is, therefore, on complementing structural reforms at the central government level with processes of internal differentiation; to define the intermediate tiers of government and to take into account the demands of horizontal and vertical co-operation and co-ordination; and pragmatically to re-orient reform efforts at the local level, adapting over-ambitious reforms to the given needs and capacities. So the task is to give effect to a framework partly in place, whilst adopting corrective strategies where necessary. Whether one stresses in this context the need for a steady administrative development or asks for a deliberate 'administrative policy' is of minor importance. What seems to be more significant is the need to differentiate reform policies segmentally and sequentially, to recognize their interdependence, whilst focusing on particular tiers, branches and institutions of government at the same time. Given the enormous task of implementing the reform agenda, a certain prioritization and consequent phasing of policies is turning out to be inevitable. Different perceptions of policy makers and implementors need not automatically be judged negatively in this respect. They may rather induce 'creative tension' or a 'climate of reform' that reinforces the need for an effective collaboration between different actors and institutions. Questions of policy design are of importance here too, complemented by a recognition of growing institutional self-interests, and an acute awareness of the time and resources needed.

Though party political linkages are, of course, important in securing political will and in enforcing implementation, it might also be time to free some areas of administrative activity from the political grip. As there is a growing stabilization of administrative issues and procedures, functional imperatives are gaining in importance. On the other hand, the consequent reorientation of the reform process should not imply that most of the crucial decisions have already been taken, that legislation is in place and that it merely needs implementation. This would, no doubt, be much too simplistic a view of the present situation:

many crucial decisions concerning the public sector have still to be taken (on the future of the civil service systems, on intergovernmental arrangements, on the role of the intermediate level), so that the development of respective policies has to remain part of the political agenda, apart from concentrating on implementing previously adopted policies.

The given evidence concerning public sector reform in Central and Eastern Europe leads us, then, to conclude that administrative reform is moving on from what one could call basic transformation to modernization. Whereas the emphasis of the first three years after the revolutionary processes of 1989 had been on democratization, marketization and basic institutionalization, the countries of Central and Eastern Europe are now faced with the challenge of paying increased attention to functional requirements. In the midst of growing signs of some stabilization with respect to the basic characteristics of the public sector, and an enhanced visibility of the future outline of public administration, gloom and doom scenarios appear increasingly misplaced. Though warnings must not be ignored (especially given the state of the transformation processes in a number of neighbouring countries), Poland, the Czech and Slovak Republics and Hungary have entered a new phase in administrative change. The basic transformation period has more or less come to an end, and the reform process is moving on to a large-scale modernization of the public sector. This is accompanied by an increasing reliance on domestic expertise and self-help; the days of fleeting visits by self-styled foreign experts and what East Europeans learned to label 'academic tourism' ought to be over.

What has happened, and still does happen, within the Central and Eastern European public sector, should remain of interest, though, to analysts and practitioners of public administration in the West. Whilst there are a number of important similarities in the external and internal challenges facing public administration in Western and Eastern Europe that make for fruitful comparisons in studying administrative reactions, one ought to be aware of the fact that administrative reform in Central and Eastern Europe has not yet reached the stage where it would make sense to compare systems' characteristics directly. The intertwined processes of democratization, marketization and de-étatisation pose indeed an historically unprecedented challenge and require an empirically based understanding before prescribing solutions. Nevertheless, foreign assistance and expertise can, of course, play a significant role, too, although it should be mentioned that three years of close observation of Western assistance provokes mixed feelings. Most programmes of Western 'donors' came late, their implementation was slow (if taking place at all) and the policies were, on quite a number of occasions, curiously unfocused. 'Throwing money at problems' as a dominant attitude cannot work, and it does not work, in the Central and Eastern European administrative context. However, there is a growing awareness that this kind of assistance might be misguided. Some of the international organizations and most of the research foundations have changed their policies in collaboration with the recipient countries, now targeting them at crucial bottle-necks of the implementation process. That might indeed be the most

promising way of providing help in an efficient and unpatronizing manner, aided
by the mentioned segmental and sequential orientation towards the process of
modernizing the public sector in Central and Eastern Europe.

The final observation refers to the fact that there is undoubtedly a growing
public awareness that democratization and marketization in Central and Eastern
Europe will not work without a stable institutional and administrative underpinning. Even the representatives of the private sector have learned to develop
an interest in institutional and administrative change, asking for advice on how
to promote institutional stability and to implement administrative policies. It
appears that not only politicians have realized, in the meantime, that administrative issues are not at all peripheral but at the heart of the ongoing processes of
change, that to stabilize the political and social situation, to secure investment,
to create markets and to reach target groups it needs a solid, not only legal but
institutional and administrative basis. This could be interpreted as an encouraging
sign in the midst of a reform process that is moving slowly towards modernizing
the public sector at large, but that remains, at the same time, still characterized
by a rather unstable, fragile and in some cases even precarious environment.

NOTE:

This conclusion builds in its empirical parts upon the main findings not only of the papers of this
volume but also of a policy-oriented study on recent changes in the Polish, Czech and Slovak,
and Hungarian public sector, which was carried out at the Centre for European Studies, Nuffield
College, Oxford (J.J. Hesse and K.H. Goetz, 1992). Special thanks go to Klaus H. Goetz and Jens
Bastian for comments and suggestions on a draft of this paper.

REFERENCES

Ackerman, B. 1992. 'Von der Revolution zur Verfassung', Transit 3, 4, 46–61.
Ågh, A. 1990. 'Transition to democracy in Central Europe: a comparative view'. Centre for the
    Study of Public Policy. Glasgow: University of Strathclyde.
Arato, A. 1990. 'Revolution, civil society and democracy', Praxis International 10, 1–2, 24–38.
Atkinson, A.B. and J. Micklewright. 1992. Economic transformation in Eastern Europe and the
    distribution of income. Cambridge: CUP.
Batt. J. 1991a. East Central Europe from reform to transformation. London: Pinter Publishers.
—. 1991b. 'The end of communist rule in East Central Europe: a four-country comparison',
    Government and Opposition 26, 3, 368–90.
Beyme, von, K. 1991. 'Parteiensysteme und Wandel politischer Eliten in Osteuropa', Ge-
    werkschaftliche Monatshefte 42, 10, 621–33.
Bogdan, H. 1990. Histoire des pays d l'Est. Paris: Perrin.
Bolton, P. and G. Poland. 1992. 'Privatization policies in Central and Eastern Europe', Economic
    Policy 15, 277–303.
Bozoki, A. 1992, 'Political transition and constitutional change in Hungary', pp. 60–71 in A.
    Bozoki, A. Körösényi and G. Schöpflin (eds.), Post-communist transition: emerging pluralism in
    Hungary. London: Pinter Publishers.
Brown, J.F. 1991. Surge to freedom: the end of communist rule in Eastern Europe. Duke: Duke UP.
Bútora, M., Z. Bútorova and T. Rosová. 1991. 'The hard birth of democracy in Slovakia: the
    eighteen months following the 'Tender Revolution', The Journal of Communist Studies 7, 4,
    435–59.
Cepl, V. 1992. 'Retribution and restitution in Czechoslovakia', Archive Européennes de Sociologie
    33, 1, 202–14.

Cerny, Ph. 1990. *The changing architecture of politics. Structure, agency and the future of the state.* London: Sage.

Dabrowski, J., M. Federowicz and A. Levitas. 'Polish state enterprises and the properties of performance: stabilization, marketization, privatization', *Politics and Society* 19, 4, 403–37.

Dahrendorf, R. 1990. 'Übergänge: Politik, Wirtschaft und Freiheit', *Transit* 1, 1, 35–47.

Dallago, B., H. Brezinski and W. Andreff. 1991. *Convergence and system change. The convergence hypotheses and transition in Eastern Europe.* Aldershot: Gower.

Ekiert, G. 1991. 'Democratization in East Central Europe: a theoretical reconsideration', *British Journal of Political Sciences* 21, 2, 285–313.

Elster, J. 1990. 'When communism dissolves', *London Review of Books* 12, 2, 3–6.

—. 1991. 'Constitutionalism in Europe: an introduction', *The University of Chicago Law Review* 58, 2, 447–82.

—. (ed.) 1993. *Round table talks in Eastern Europe.* Cambridge: Cambridge UP (forthcoming).

Falandysz, L. 1992. 'From communist legality to the rule of law in Poland', pp. 27–44 in K. Thompson (ed.), *Poland in a world in change.* Lanham: UP of America.

Fehr, H. 1991. 'Solidarnosc und die Bürgerkomitees im neuen politischen Kräftefeld Polens', pp. 256–80 in R. Deppe, H. Dubiel, and U. Rödel, (eds.), *Demokratischer Umbruch in Osteuropa.* Frankfurt: Suhrkamp.

Frydman, R. and A. Rapaczynski. 1992. 'Privatization and corporate governance in Eastern Europe: can a market economy be designed?, pp. 255–85, in G. Winckler (ed.) *Central and Eastern Europe roads to growth.* Washington: International Monetary Fund.

Gomulka, S. and A. Polonsky. (eds.) *Polish paradoxes.* London: Routledge.

Grosfeld, I. and P. Hare. 1991. 'Privatization in Hungary, Poland and Czechoslovakia', pp. 129–56 in *European Economy*, special edition, no. 2, *The Path of Reform in Central and Eastern Europe.* Brussels: Commission of the European Communities.

Hankiss, E. 1990. *East European alternatives.* Oxford: Clarendon Press.

Hare, P. and T. Révész. 1992. 'Hungary's transition to the market economy: the case against a 'big bang" *Economic Policy* 14, 227–64.

Hendrych, D. 1992. *Transforming Czechoslovak public administration: a survey of reform steps taken.* Paper presented at the EC workshop on 'Administrative modernization and management in Central and Eastern Europe', held on 1/2 May 1992 at the Faculty of Law, Charles University, Prague.

Hesse, J.J. 1991. 'Administrative modernisation in Central and Eastern European countries', *Staatswissenschaften und Staatspraxis* 2, 2, 197–217.

—. 1993. *Analysing institutional change in Central and Eastern Europe.* Ms. Oxford (forthcoming).

Hesse, J.J. and A. Benz. 1990. *Die Modernisierung der Staatsorganisation. Institutionspolitik im internationalen Vergleich: USA, Grossbritannien, Frankreich, Bundesrepublik Deutschland.* Baden-Baden: Nomos.

Hesse, J.J. and K.H. Goetz. 1992. 'Public sector reform in Central and Eastern Europe: the case of Poland', *Staatswissenschaften und Staatspraxis* 3, 3, 406–51.

—. 1992. *Public sector reform in Central and Eastern Europe: the case of Czechoslovakia.* Discussion Paper No. 18. Oxford: Centre for European Studies, Nuffield College.

—. 1992. *Public sector reform in Central and Eastern Europe: the case of Hungary.* Discussion Paper No. 20. Oxford: Centre for European Studies, Nuffield College.

Heyns, B. and I. Bialecki. 1991. 'Solidarnosc: reluctant vanguard or makeshift coalition?', *American Political Science Review* 85, 2, 351–70.

Hughes, G. and P. Hare. 'Competitiveness and industrial restructuring in Czechoslovakia, Hungary and Poland', pp. 83–110 in *European Economy*, special edition, no. 2, *The path of reform in Central and Eastern Europe.* Brussels: Commission of the European Communities.

Hungarian Institute of Public Administration. 1992. *Public administration in Hungary. Collection of Studies Published by the Institute in 1992.* Budapest: Hungarian Institute of Public Administration.

Institut für Ostrecht 1992a. 'Chronik der Rechtsentwicklung in den osteuropäischen Staaten', *Recht in Ost und West* 36, 7, 208–19.

—. 1992b. 'Chronk der Rechtsentwicklung in den osteuropäischen Staaten', *Recht in Ost und West* 36, 9, 275–87.

Jeffries, I. (ed.) 1992. *Industrial reform in socialist countries. From restructuring to revolution.* Aldershot: Edward Elgar.

Kaltenbach, J. 1990. 'Die Entwicklung der kommunalen Selbstverwaltung in Ungarn', *Jahrbuch für Ostrecht* 31, 1, 77–93.

Kaminski, B. 1992. 'Poland: underpinning the transition: the shadow of the round table agreements', pp. 307–31, in Ch. T. Saunders (ed.) *Economics and politics of transition.* London: Macmillan Press.

Kitschelt, H. 1992. 'The formation of party systems in East Central Europe', *Politics and Society* 20, 1, 7–50.

Kloc, K. 1991. 'Poland's political system—change and future scenarios', pp. 11–19, in G. Blazyca and R. Rapacki (eds.) *Poland into the 1990s: economy and society in transition.* London: Pinter Publishers.

Kornai, J. 1992. *The socialist system: the political economy of communism.* Oxford: Clarendon Press.

König, K. 1992. 'The transformation of a "real socialist" administrative system into a conventional western European system', *International Review of Administrative Sciences* 58, 2, 147–62.

Kopits, G., R. Holzmann, G. Schieber and E. Sidgwick. 1990. *Social security reform in Hungary.* Washington: IMF.

Lindstrom, U. 1991. 'East European social democracy: reborn to be rejected', pp. 269–301 in L:. Karvanen and J. Sundberg (eds.) *Social democracy in transition: Northern, Southern, and Eastern Europe.* Aldershot: Dartmouth.

Lijphart, A. 1992. 'Democratization and constitutional choices in Czechoslovakia, Hungary and Poland 1989–91', *Journal of Theoretical Politics* 4, 2, 207–23.

Loewenstein, G. and J. Elster (eds.) 1992. *Choices over time.* New York: Russel Sage Foundation.

Marer, P. and S. Zecchini. 1991. *The transition to a market economy,* 1 and 2. Paris: OECD.

Matyschok, E. 1992. 'Der Entwurf einer neuen Verfassung der Republik Polen und die Verfassungsgerichtsbarkeit', *Recht in Ost und West* 36, 8, 225–33.

Maurel, M.C. 1989. 'Administrative reforms in Eastern Europe: an overview', pp. 111–23 in R. Bennett (ed.) *Territory and administration in Europe.* London: Pinter Publishers.

Meuschel, S. 1992. *Legitimation und Parteiherrschaft in der DDR.* Frankfurt: Suhrkamp.

Michnik, A. 1992. 'Die zweite Phase der Revolution in Polen', pp. 15–86 in idem. *Der lange Abschied vom Kommunismus.* Reinbeck: Rowohlt.

Müller, K. 1992. 'Modernising Eastern Europe: theoretical problems and political dilemmas', *Archives Européennes de Sociologie* 33, 1, 109–50.

Myant, M. 1992. 'Economic reform and political evolution in Eastern Europe', *The Journal of Communist Studies* 8, 1, 107–27.

OECD. 1991a. *Transformation of planned economies: property rights reform and macroeconomic stability.* Paris: OECD.

—. 1991b. *OECD economic surveys: Czech and Slovak Federal Republics.* Paris: OECD.

—. 1991c. *OECD economic surveys: Hungary.* Paris: OECD.

Offe, C. 1991. 'Capitalism by democratic design? Democratic theory facing the triple transition in East Central Europe', *Social Research* 58, 4, 865–92.

—. 1992a. 'Coming to terms with past injustices', *European Journal of Sociology* 33, 1, 197–201.

—. 1992b. 'The politics of social policy in East European transitions', paper presented at the conference: *Comparative studies of welfare state development: quantitative and qualitative dimensions.* Bremen: Zentrum für Sozialpolitik, Sept. 3–6.

Olsen, J.P. 1992. 'Rethinking and reforming the public sector', pp. 217–33 in B. Kohler-Koch, (ed.), *Staat und Demokratie in Europa.* Opladen: Westdeutscher Verlag.

—. 1992. 'Analyzing institutional dynamics', *Staatswissenschaften und Staatspraxis* 2, 2, 247–71.

Palma Di, G. 1991. 'Legitimation from the top to civil society: politico-cultural change in Eastern Europe', *World Politics* 44, 1, 49–80.

Pfersmann, O. 1992. 'La loi constitutionelle no. 91 du 27 février 1991 concernant la Cour Constitutionelle de la République fédérale tchéque et slovaque', *Revue Franqaise de Droit Constitutionelle* 9, 161–70.

Piontek, E. 1992. 'Democratic political transformation in Poland and challenges of the 1990s', pp. 113–32 in K. Thompson, (ed.), *Poland in a world in change.* Lanham: UP of America.

Preuss, U.K. 1990. *Revolution, Fortschritt und Verfassung. Zu einem neuen Verfassungsverständnis.* Berlin: Wagenbach.

Przeworski, A. 1991. *Democracy and the market.* Cambridge: CUP.

Rapaczynski, A. 1991. 'Constitutional politics in Poland: a report on the constitutional committee of the Polish Parliament', *The University of Chicago Law Review* 58, 2, 595–631.

Rice, M. 1992. 'Public administration in post-socialist Eastern Europe', *Public Administration Review* 52, 2, 116–24.

Rose, R. 1991. *Between state and market—key indicators of transition in Eastern Europe.* Glasgow: University of Strathclyde Studies in Public Policy, no. 196.

—. 1992. 'Problems of postcommunism. Toward a civil economy', *Journal of Democracy* 3, 2, 13–26.

Schöpflin, G. 1991. 'Post-communism: constructing new democracies in Central Europe', *International Affairs* 67, 2, 235–50.

Sokolewicz, W. 1992. 'The legal-constitutional bases of democratization in Poland: systemic and constitutional change', pp. 69–97 in Sanford, G. (ed.) *Democratization in Poland, 1988–90.* New York: St. Martin's Press.

Standing, G. and G. Sziráczki. (eds.) 1991. 'Labour market transitions in Eastern Europe and the USSR', *International Labour Review*, 130, 2, special issue.

Staniszkis, J. 1991. 'Dilemmata der Demokratie in Osteuropa', pp. 326–47 in R. Deppe, H. Dubiel, and U. Rödel (eds.), *Demokratischer Umbruch in Osteuropa.* Frankfurt: Suhrkamp.

Surdej, A. 1992. 'The politics of the stabilization plan in Poland', discussion paper presented at the seminar: *States, markets and inequality.* Florence: European University Institute.

Swain, N. 1992. *Hungary: the rise and fall of feasible socialism.* London: Verso.

Swianiewicz, P. 1992. 'The Polish experience of local democracy: is progress being made?', *Policy and Politics* 20, 2, 87–98.

Szakolczai, A. 1992. 'On the exercise of power in modern societies, East and West', EUI *working paper*, SPS no. 92/22. Florence: European University Institute.

Szakolczai, Å. and Å. Horváth. 1991. 'Political instructors and the decline of communism in Hungary: apparatus, nomenclatura and the issue of legacy', *British Journal of Political Sciences* 21, 4, 469–88.

Szalai, E. 1990. 'Elites and system change in Hungary', *Praxis International* 10, 1–2, 74–9.

Tanzi, V. 1991. 'Eastern Europe: the state's role in mobilising savings', IMF *Survey* 20, 11, 166–70.

Thompson, K. (ed.) 1992. *Poland in a world in change. Constitutions, presidents, and politics.* Lanham: UP of America.

Transit. 1991. 'Die Mühen der Ebene. Demokratisierung und Modernisierung in den postkommunistischen Gesellschaften'. *Transit* 2, 3.

Walicki, A. 1991. 'From Stalinism to post-communist pluralism: the case of Poland', *New Left Review* 185, 93–121.

Wasilewski, J. 1990. 'The patterns of bureaucratic elite recruitment in Poland in the 1970s and 1980s', *Soviet Studies* 42, 4, 143–57.

Wedel, J. 1992. *The unplanned society: Poland during and after Communism.* New York: Columbia UP.

White: S. 1991. *Handbook of reconstruction in Eastern Europe and the Soviet Union.* Essex: Longman Group.

World Bank. 1991. *The reform of public sector management. Lessons from experience.* Washington DC: World Bank.

—. 1992. *Hungary: reform of the social policy and expenditures.* Washington, D.C.: World Bank.

Ziemer, K. 1992. 'Polen auf der Suche nach einem neuen Ort in Europa', pp. 390–405 in M. Kreile (ed.) *Die Integration Europas*, PVS Sonderheft 23. Opladen: Westdeutscher Verlag.

Index*

*Compiled by Jean Frostick